Warman's®
Antique
Jewelry

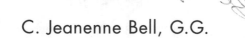

FIELD GUIDE

C. Jeanenne Bell, G.G.

© 2003 by
C. Jeanenne Bell and Krause Publications, Inc.

All rights reserved.
No portion of this publication may be reproduced or transmitted in any
form or by any means, electronic or mechanical, including photocopy,
recording, or any information storage and retrieval system, without per-
mission in writing from the publisher, except by a reviewer who may
quote brief passages in a critical review to be printed in a magazine or
newspaper, or electronically transmitted on radio or television.

Published by

krause publications
An F&W Publications Company

700 East State Street • Iola, WI 54990-0001
715-445-2214 • 888-457-2873
www.krause.com

Please call or write for our free catalog of publications.
Our toll-free number to place an order or obtain a free catalog is
800-258-0929 or please use our regular business telephone:
715-445-2214.

Library of Congress Catalog Number: 2002107617
ISBN: 0-87349-527-6

Printed in the United States of America

Contents

Introduction

Congratulations! You are holding the perfect companion to take along to garage sale, flea markets, auctions, and antique shows. Its small size assures that it will fit in a bag or pocket without adding a lot of weight. But, be assured that despite its small size and weight, it is filled with information that can empower you to know about the pieces that you already have and to be a knowledgeable buyer. Remember, knowledge is power!

This tiny book is filled with illustrations and examples of what to look for when examining jewelry. The makers' mark section will help determine who made the piece. A name listed in this section always means added value. Examples of the evolution of findings will help you to determine when a piece was made. To tie these elements together, included is a short synopsis of each time period from the Victorian era through the 1950s to show how world events influenced the styles and scale of jewelry.

Not only does this small companion enlighten you about antique, estate, and collectible fine and costume jewelry, but it also includes watches. May it bring you grand adventures and great buys! Happy hunting!

There is an innate tendency in most people to want to own, collect, or wear something unique, unusual, and beautiful. Cave men picked up beautiful stones, wrapped them in a hide cord, and wore them around their necks. Or maybe they just brought them back to their caves to place in safekeeping with their other treasures. And so it has been since the beginning of recorded history, people have been drawn to unusual things with which to adorn themselves.

Jewelry has always represented more than its tangible function of adornment. Warriors wore certain rings into battle to keep them from harm. Diamonds derived their name from the Greek word Adamas, meaning invincible or unconquerable. Bloodstones were worn into battle to ensure the warrior would not bleed to death. As late as the 1920s and '30s, amber necklaces were worn to cure a goiter in the neck. When women today learn that a mineral in the beautiful pink kunzite is used to make Valium, they are even more inclined to get a ring and bracelet containing this stone.

For centuries, much of a country's wealth was contained in its royal jewels. Remember, jewelry is portable property that can usually be sold or bartered wherever one goes.

Jewelry is and has always been worn as a symbol of status or achievement. The industrial revolution made jewelry affordable to almost everyone. This, coupled with the emergence of the "middle class," which longed to show its new status in society, assured that men projected their wealth by furnishing a proper home and adorning their wives with the finest jewelry that they could afford. Throughout the ages the military has always awarded medals as signs of achievement. Today, class rings, watches, and medals of all types are often given for the same reason.

As everyone knows, jewelry can also be a used as a love token, to convey one's sentiment. Rings are given as symbols of love and commitment. Jewelry is also a favorite gift for a loved one at any time of the year. DeBeer's famous slogan, "A diamond is forever," translates to the wearer as "our love will last forever."

Old jewelry is fascinating! The more you learn about it, the more you want to know, and the more you enjoy it. I have been actively pursuing my jewelry passion for over 30 years. It is still one of my favorite things to research, own, and wear.

Over the last 35 years, I have seen interest in and the body of information about jewelry swell in size and scope. Certain pieces have come into and out of fashion, even with old jewelry. For instance, with the softening of clothing in the last few years, modern versions of lavalieres (1890-1910) and the crossover "negligee" style necklaces (1920s) have come back into fashion.

Consequently, the originals of the time period have become even more sought after and their prices reflect this demand.

The last decade has seen a distinct rise in the amount of jewelry being worn by men. It's not unusual to see a well-dressed man wearing a watch, bracelet, at least two rings, and cuff links. For casual dress, a chain or a pendant around the neck will likely be added. This has increased interest in antique men's rings, cuff links, and vintage watches. Like women, men like to wear something unusual, distinctive, and unique. Again, this has increased the demand and consequently the prices of these pieces.

C. Jeanenne Bell

C. Jeanenne Bell, G.G., is an avid collector and retailer. She is a member of the Society of Jewelry Historians (USA), National Association of Watch and Clock Collectors, The Alumni Association of the Gemological Institute of America, and the National Association of Jewelry Appraisers. Ms. Bell also does appraisals for the PBS program, Antiques Roadshow. *She is also the author of the highly acclaimed book,* Answers to Questions About Old Jewelry, *as well as* How to Be a Jewelry Detective.

Circa Dating Clues

by C. Jeannenne Bell

Fittings and Findings

Catches

The following drawings represent the types of catches found on
antique and period jewelry.

"C" Type

*The "C" type is the earliest type of catch, but it can still be found on
some new pieces.*

ca. 1890

This type of catch was used for only a short period of time.

ca. 1895

I have found this type of catch on European pieces as early as 1896, but my research indicates they were not generally used in the United States before 1912. They continued to be popular throughout the 1920s.

This catch dates from the 1920s.

Tube or Trombone

Tube or Trombone
ca. 1890

The tube or trombone type was popular in the 1890s, but it can be found on many European pieces from the 1940s.

Hinges

There are two types of hinges found on antique and period
jewelry.

Tube Hinge

The tube hinge is the earliest type.

Ball Hinge

The ball hinge has been used from the 1890s to the present.

Earring Findings

Here are the five principal types of earring findings.

Fish Hook

The fish hook is the earliest type of ear wire.

Kidney Wires

Kidney wires have been traced as far back as the 1870s. They are still popular today.

Threaded Stud

The threaded studs are circa 1890s. They are used today, but are smaller in diameter and the nut is usually a lighter weight.

Screw Backs

Screw backs date from 1909. They are still used, but are not common on new pieces.

1930-70 Ear Clips

Clips date from 1930-70 and are still used on some new earrings.

Findings not only help in circa dating, they can also give clues about any additions or alterations to the piece. If a piece has a safety catch, we know it is either a 20th century piece or that the safety was added later. Whether or not it was a later addition can usually be ascertained by a careful examination. Look for signs of soldering. Often the new catch is attached to a small plate joined to the back of the brooch. This plate is a sure sign that the safety catch is not original.

Periods

Victorian

Queen Victoria reigned from 1837 until her death in 1901. Consequently, many pieces of jewelry can be referred to as Victorian. I have chosen to use Margaret Flower's divisions of Early Victorian 1837-1860, Mid-Victorian 1860-1885, and Late Victorian 1885-1901. I have added Edwardian 1901-1910 to the Late Victorian period. Keep in mind that there is never a clear-cut line dividing these periods, because some styles and motifs continued to be popular for a longer period of time in some areas. Styles also tend to overlap. A style that was waning in England could be at its peak of popularity in the United States.

Early Victorian: 1837-1860

Popular Motifs:

Classical Greek and Roman designs

Gothic and medieval designs

Garter jewelry

Grapes (usually formed of seed pearls)

Vines and leaves

Eyes (eye miniatures)

Hands

Knots of all types

Serpents

Hearts

Materials:

Gold (all colors except white)

Pinchbeck

Rolled gold

Gold electroplate (after 1840)

Jet

Gutta-percha

Bogwood or Bog Oak

Hair

Tortoise

Ivory

Aluminum (after 1855)

Embellishments:

Stones often cut in cabochon

Amethyst

Citrine

Coral

Garnets

Paste

Ruby

Topaz

Pique

Mosaics

Cameos (stone, shell, lava, coral)

Bloodstone

Cairngorm

Dark blue enameling

Mid-Victorian: 1860-1885

Popular Motifs:

Acorns

Amphorae

Anchor, heart, and cross
   (hope, love, and faith)

Beetles

Bells

Crosses

Etruscan motifs

Buckles

Fringes

Tassels

Monograms

Insects

Garter jewelry

Hearts

Serpents

Ram's head

Archaeological motif

Materials:

(see Early Victorian)

Bloomed Gold

Tiger Claws

Real Beetles

Amber

Embellishments:

(see Early Victorian)

All forms of enameling

Amethysts (sometimes incised with a
    flower motif)

Diamonds

Emeralds

Coral

Pearls

Sapphire

Turquoise

Cameos (done in amethyst, emerald, garnet, jasper, hematite, coral, agate, lava, and shell)

Intaglios

Lapis

Cornelian

Tourmaline

Spinel

Rock crystal

Aquamarine

Zircon (natural brown)

Demantoid garnets (after 1869)

Late Victorian and Edwardian:

1885-1910

I'm taking the liberty of combining these two periods. Officially Edward VII reigned from 1901-1910, but his influence was felt much earlier. Many Victorian motifs were reflections of his activities; e.g. racing motifs and good luck motifs. During this period, clothing was lighter and softer than it had been in almost a hundred years.

The jewelry also became lighter in scale. Dainty pieces such as the lavalier became popular.

Popular Motifs:

Clovers

Crescent and stars

"Crossover" designs

Hearts (single and double)

Birds

Flowers

Horseshoes and other good luck signs

Moon and owl

Man in the moon

Shamrocks

Sporting

Bats

Insects

Materials:

Gold (multicolored)

Platinum

Silver

Oxidized silver

Copper

Rolled gold

Celluloid

Watch cock covers

Gun metal

Embellishments:

Opals

Moonstone

Diamonds

Pearls

Peridot

Sapphires

Topaz

Amber

Glass

Jet

Turquoise

Garnets

Mother of pearl

Aquamarine

Crepe stone

Onyx

Amethyst

All forms of enameling

Art Nouveau: 1885-1917

Popular Motifs:

Female head

Serpents

Dragonflies

Interwoven, asymmetrical flowing lines

Flowers

Swans

Peacock

Bats

Materials:

Gold

Silver

Silver-plates

Gold-filled

Horn

Ivory

Tortoise

Embellishments:

Stones cut in cabochon

Opals

Moonstones

Pearls

Diamonds (usually small)

Pate de Verre

Glass

All forms of enameling

Rock crystal

Art Deco: 1920-1930s

Popular Motif:

Geometric lines

Abstract designs

Motifs denoting speed

Dramatic interplay of colors

Shimmery colors

Stylized floral motifs

Materials:

Platinum

White gold

Silver

White metal

Bakelite

Embellishments:

Emeralds

Ruby

Sapphire

Onyx

Diamonds

Rock crystal

Marcasites

Cornelian

Chrysoprase

Jade

Ivory

Retro Modern: 1932-1940s

Popular Motifs:

Stylized flowers

Cones

"Spacecraft" motif

Bows

Ovals with bows

Stylized feathers

Cornucopia

Birds

Bold Polish curves

Materials:

Yellow Gold

Green Gold

Pink Gold $\longrightarrow$ all often used in the same piece (after World War II)

Sterling Silver}
Gold-filled ⟶ all often used in the same piece (after World War II)
Gold-plated

Embellishments:

Rubies

Diamonds

Blue sapphires

Pearls

Faceted and cabochon cut stones often in the same piece

Aquamarines

Synthetic stones

What Is This Metal?

by C. Jeanenne Bell

This is one of the most important questions asked about old jewelry. The metal not only plays a major role in determining value, but it can also provide clues as to when and where a piece was made.

Almost everyone knows that a gold-plated ring is less valuable than one made of karat gold, but how can the average person tell the difference? What do the numbers and letters stamped on a piece mean? How can silver, white gold, and white metal be identified? This section will answer these questions and more.

To properly examine jewelry, a magnifying glass of some sort is needed. A jeweler's loupe is a good investment whether you are a collector or a curious owner. A 2-1/2 power loupe is adequate for examining most markings and is available at jewelry supply stores for less than $10. For examining stones, a 10 power loupe is recommended, and a good one can be purchased for less than $50. With these aids in hand, you are ready to examine the metal.

Gold

In the United States, the purity of gold is designated by karat. Pure gold is 24K, but, because of its softness, it is not suitable for making jewelry. Other metals such as copper, silver, nickel, and zinc are added to gold to strengthen it. What is added and how much is added, determine the color and karat of gold.

To make this easier to understand, let's take an imaginary ring and examine it. The color of the metal is immediately apparent. Gold comes in several colors, but let's pretend that this ring is pink gold. Inside the ring is stamped 10K. What do these things tell us? First, that the gold was mixed with copper, silver, and zinc to make yellow gold. The pink look was achieved by using a larger quantity of copper. The 10K mark assures that 41.67% of the metal is pure gold, and the other 58.33% is copper, silver, and zinc. It also indicates that the piece was made in the United States (other countries do not use 10K). A 14K stamping would mean that the ring contained 58.33% gold and 41.67% other metals. If the ring was marked 18K, it would contain 75% pure gold and 25% other metals.

In Europe, gold is stamped according to its fineness. Pure gold is 1000 fine; 18K gold is 75% or 750 fine. Consequently, an 18K ring made in Europe would be stamped 750.

Below is a chart of the most common karat markings:

US karats	Percent of gold	Fineness
24	100%	1000
22	95.83%	958
18	75%	750
15	62.50%	625
14	58.33%	583
10	41.67%	417
9	37.50%	375

The 375 at the bottom of the list is the English number for 9K. It will often be found enclosed in a rectangular box with other markings. These are known as hallmarks and are discussed under the silver heading.

Rolled Gold Plate

Always be sure to look for other letters that might be stamped next to the karat sign. A piece marked 14K R.G.P. is not 14 karat gold. The R.G.P. stands for rolled gold plate, which is made by applying a layer of gold alloy to a layer of base metal. This "sandwich" is then drawn to the thickness needed for the piece of jewelry. Rolled gold plating was very popular in the 1800s and early 1900s.

Gold Filled

Other letters that sometimes appear next to the karat number are G.F. This signifies the piece is gold filled. The name is misleading, because the piece is not filled with gold as the name implies, but is made by joining a layer of gold to a base metal as in rolled gold plating. The layer of gold used in R.G.P. is sometimes thicker than the one used in gold filled, making it more durable and more valuable. Again, the numbers tell how much gold and what karat of gold was used. A piece marked 1/20 12K assures that the alloy is 12 karat or 50% pure gold and the 1/20 of the total weight of the piece is 12K gold.

Electroplating

If the piece in question is marked 14K H.G.E., it has been gold plated. The initials stand for hard gold electroplated. It means that the piece is made of base metal that has been plated with a thin coating of gold by an electrical process.

Other Markings

In the late 1800s, many pieces were stamped "solid gold" or advertised as such. Some of these pieces were only 6K to 10K gold, and most were gold filled or rolled gold plate. A law passed in 1906 required the gold content be stamped on jewelry. Before that year, many pieces of gold jewelry were unmarked. For ways to determine whether an unmarked piece is gold, rolled gold plated, or gold filled refer to "Is It Real?"

Pinchbeck

Pinchbeck is a very old metal rarely encountered today. The name is often misapplied to gold filled or rolled gold-plated items. It is not a plate or coating, but a solid metal made by mixing copper and zinc.

The formula, discovered by Christopher Pinchbeck (1670-1732), contained no gold; yet it looked like gold and wore well. The pinchbeck formula was a guarded secret passed down in the family, but other companies developed their own versions. There were so many imitations that Christopher's grandson, Edward Pinchbeck, found it necessary to place this advertisement in the July 11, 1733 edition of the *Daily Post*:

To prevent for the future the gross imposition that is daily put upon the public by a great number of Shop-Keepers, Hawkers, and Peddlers, in and about this town. Notice is hereby given, that the ingenious Mr. Edward Pinchbeck, at the 'Musical Clock' in Fleet Street, does not dispose of one grain of his curious metal, which so nearly resembles Gold in Color, Smell, and Ductility, to any person whatsoever, nor are the Toys (jewelry and trinkets) made of the said metal, sold by any one person in England except himself; therefore gentlemen are desired to beware of imposters, who frequent Coffee Houses, and expose for Sale, Toys pretended to be made of this metal, which is a most notorious imposition, upon the public. And Gentlemen and Ladies, may be accommodated by the said Mr. Pinchbeck with the following curious Toys: viz: Swords, Hilts, Hangers, Can Heads, Whip Handles, for Hunting, Spurs, Equipages, Watch Chains, Tweezers for Men and Women, Snuff-Boxes, Coat Buttons, Shirt Buttons, Knives and Forks, Spoons, Salvers, Buckles for Ladies Breasts, Stock Buckles, Shoe Buckles, Knee Buckles, Bridle Buckles, Stock Clasps, Knee Clasps, Necklaces, Corals, and in particular Watches, plain and chased in so curious a manner as not to be distinguished by the nicest eye, from the real gold, and which are highly necessary for Gentlemen and Ladies when they travel, with several other fine pieces of workmanship of all sorts made by the best hands. He also makes Repeating and all other sorts of Clocks and Watches

*particularly Watches of a new invention, the mechanism of
which is so simple, and proportion so just, that they come
nearer to the truth than others yet made.*

The advertisement referred to necessary items for travel. Quite
often copies of favorite pieces were made to wear on "travels."
The gold ones were left safely at home. McKeever Persivial in his
Chats on Old Jewelry states, "In those days when a journey of even
a few miles out of London led through roads infested by thieves
and highway robbers, careful folk preferred not to tempt these
'gentlemen of the road' by wearing expensive ornaments unless
traveling with a good escort; so not only would a traveler with a
base metal watch and buckles lose less if robbed, but owing to the
freemasonry which existed between innkeepers and pestilence and
the highwaymen, they were actually less likely to be stopped, as it
was not worthwhile to run risks for such a poor spoil."

With the invention of the electro-gilding process in 1840, and the
legalization of 9K gold in 1854, the use of pinchbeck declined and
eventually became passe.

Pinchbeck is very collectible, but there are very few pieces available. Part of the fun of jewelry collecting are the "lucky finds."
After viewing a few pieces, pinchbeck becomes visually identifiable. Until then, take care to buy from a knowledgeable dealer.

Silver

Silver is a precious metal that has always intrigued man. Because of this fascination, regulations have been applied to its use for centuries. After silver is mined, it is refined to .999 pure. Like gold, it is too soft to be used in this pure state. Instead it is mixed with other metals for strength.

Sterling

Sterling silver is .925 fine. This mixture of pure silver and copper has long been regarded for its fine beauty. The word donates quality of the highest standard. According to Seymore B. Wyler, the word "sterling" was coined when King James brought in a group of Germans to refine silver for making coins. Since they were from the east, they became known as Easterlings. When a statute concerning silver was written in 1343, the first two letters were accidentally omitted. Hence the word sterling was first applied to silver.

A lion or leopard stamped into silver signifies sterling. In the United States, the word sterling is usually stamped into the piece. All new sterling is marked or punched to signify its credibility.

Hallmarks

Since the amount of silver involved greatly determines the cost of a piece and the average person could be easily fooled, laws were passed to ensure a standard purity. As early as 1335, English law required silversmiths to punch or stamp their mark into any pieces made in their shop. By 1477, a leopard head stamp was required as proof that a piece met the accepted silver standards. In 1479, a letter designating the year of manufacture was initiated, making silver even more identifiable. These signs or hallmarks are still used today and provide clues as to when and where a piece was made.

In this hallmark, the first character, a lion passant, signifies the piece is sterling silver. The anchor is the mint mark for Birmingham, England, and the letter date signifies that it was made in 1889-1890. Sometimes, but not always, the maker's mark is included in the hallmark. The style of the letter and the shape of the box in which they are placed are all important factors when reading a hallmark. Fortunately, there are several good books on hallmarks that include lists of date letters, mint marks, and makers. These provide invaluable aid in dating and identifying silver.

Items made of sterling get more beautiful as they are used or worn. With use, tiny scratches known as patina develop, giving the silver a warm, soft look. Only gold and platinum are more durable than silver, so do not be afraid to wear it.

Coin Silver

Quite often a piece of jewelry or a watch case will be marked coin silver or .900. This means the piece is 90% silver and 10% other metal. At one time, this was the standard content of silver coins. Thus, the name "coin silver" is synonymous with this percent-age of silver items. In fact, this was so prevalent in England that a law was passed in 1696 making the standard for silver items higher (958) in silver content than coins. This did not eliminate the problem. Shrewd silversmiths continued to melt coins and add silver to bring the content up to standard. Since the act did not solve the coin problem, and the new "Britannia" was softer and less durable, in 1720, the higher standard became optional.

Silverplate

A method of silver plating was discovered in 1742 by Thomas Boulsover. While repairing a knife blade, he accidentally fused silver to copper. This accident was the beginning of the Sheffield Plate Industry in England.

In 1840, G.R. Elkington was granted a patent on a process for electroplating silver or gold to a base metal. This process uses electricity to apply a coating of silver to an article made of base metal. Although this coating is usually very thin, pieces more than a hundred years old are sometimes found in amazingly good condition. The most popular base metals were copper and German silver.

German Silver

The term German silver is a misnomer. German silver is not silver at all, but rather a combination of nickel, copper, and zinc. A German introduced it to England in the late 1700s. Because its color resembles silver, it made a perfect base for silver-plated items, hence the name German Silver. To confuse matters even more it is also known as gunmetal or nickel silver.

When a piece is marked E.P.N.S., it is electro-plated nickel silver.

Vermeil

The French definition of vermeil (Vair-MAY) is "silver gilt." Items made of sterling silver and coated with gold were favored by French nobility during the reign of Louis XIV and throughout the 18th century. In the early 1800s, scientists discovered that the mercury used in the vermeil process was causing the jewelry workers to go blind and the process was banned. Consequently, very little vermeil was made in the 19th century.

In 1956, Tiffany's reintroduced vermeil. According to Joseph Puntell, the Tiffany factory developed a process using a plating of 18-1/2 karat gold covered with second plating of 22-1/2 karat gold. This new process provided the glowing look of the mercury process without its poisonous side effects.

Platinum

Platinum, one of the heaviest, most valuable metals known to man, was first discovered in 1557 by Julius Scaligerk, an Italian scientist. In the 1700s, Spanish explorers discovered deposits in Peru and called it "plata," their name for silver.

Platinum was used very little until the late 1880s. At that time, new developments in jeweler's equipment made it easier to work, and it became popular for mounting diamonds. By the 1920s, it was the most popular metal used in jewelry. Platinum's popularity caused white gold to become fashionable. Eighteen karat white gold was advertised as "a look-alike" for the more expensive metal. Platinum's durability made it an excellent choice for the filigree styles of the 1920s and 1930s.

During World War II, the use of platinum for jewelry was restricted by the War Production Board. The metal was needed for a catalyst in munitions' plants. Reluctantly jewelers turned to palladium, a related metal, as a substitute.

The same ore that yields platinum contains five other metals—iridium, palladium, rhodium, ruthenium, and osmiridium. They are known as the platinum group; of these, platinum, palladium and rhodium are widely used in jewelry.

Palladium

Palladium is one of the six metals in the platinum group. Even though it is harder, lighter, and less expensive than platinum, it has never been as popular.

During World War II, jewelry manufacturers turned to palladium when platinum was restricted. The public could not tell the difference, and palladium was 30% cheaper. Its weight is comparable to 14K gold. After the war full page advertisements were used to promote palladium, but it never gained full acceptance by the general public.

Rhodium

Rhodium is another of the six metals in the platinum group. Because of its hardness, it is often used as a plating. Quite often a piece will be marked "sterling silver rhodium finished" or "stainless steel rhodium finish." The abbreviated mark for rhodium is "Rh."

Is It Real?

by C. Jeanenne Bell

This question is most often asked about stones. Because the answer can mean a big difference in value, it is most important that it be correct. The person most qualified to answer this question is a graduate gemologist, a person trained to identify and evaluate stones (a Gemological Institute of America graduate).

If you are a collector or a dealer, a good working relationship with a gemologist can be invaluable. Whether you own an extensive collection or just a few pieces that have been handed down in the family, an appraisal by a gemologist with a knowledge of antique and period jewelry is needed to assure proper insurance coverage. Most gemologists charge by the job or on an hourly basis. Appraisers who base their fee on a percentage of value are not recommended.

To assure a good appraisal, look for a graduate gemologist who is a member of the National Association of Jewelry Appraisers and lists antique and period jewelry as one of his/her fields of expertise. This assures that the appraiser not only has superior knowledge in his/her area of certification, but has also completed courses on appraisal theory and ethics.

Imitation and Synthetic Stones

Genuine stones have been imitated for thousands of years. The Egyptians made glass imitations and endowed them with the same supernatural power as the genuine. Paste, a glass imitation gemstone, was widely used from the 13th through the 17th centuries. In the 18th century, Joseph Strass discovered that by adding a high percentage of lead to glass he could increase its brilliance, thus creating more beautiful imitations. By the early 19th century, a process for making synthetic rubies had been discovered. But it was almost another hundred years before they were commercially feasible for use in jewelry.

Synthetic stones are not imitations. Physically, chemically, and optically, they are the same as the natural. By the use of heat and pressure, man has been able to speed up the process that takes nature thousands of years to produce.

When rubies were first synthesized in the 1800s, they were more expensive than the natural ones. In 1910, August Verneuil came up with the idea of using a smeltering torch that could provide heat equal to half of that produced by the sun. This new process produced stones at a much lower cost. Still they were so highly regarded that jewelers of the 1920s often set them in 18K gold mountings.

Synthetic spinels came on the market in 1926, followed by synthetic emeralds in the early 1940s, and synthetic star sapphires and rubies in 1947. The process for making synthetic diamonds was perfected in 1955. Today, most of the diamonds used for industrial purposes are synthetic.

Gem quality synthetic diamonds have been possible since the 1970s, but they are more expensive than the natural ones. Stones such as cubic zirconium (C.Z.s) and YAG are synthetic stones but they are not synthetic diamonds.

Doublets and Triplets

Before relatively inexpensive synthetic stones were available, a combination stone called a "doublet" was popular. The jeweler fused a layer of one stone to another, then faceted the stone as if it were one large stone. The most popular doublet was one using garnet and glass. It was used to imitate sapphires, topaz, emeralds, amethyst, rubies, and, of course, garnets.

A piece of green or blue glass with a red garnet top is intriguing. It takes a trained eye and close inspection to detect. Consequently, pieces of jewelry set with old doublets are quite collectible. Most people are fascinated by them.

The term "triplet" is used to describe a stone that is made up of three parts. This can mean three stones (genuine top and bottom with something else in between), or it can refer to two stones put together with a colored cement that provides the "stone's" color. Because synthetic emeralds are expensive, triplets made of quartz or synthetic spinel joined by emerald green cement are often encountered.

Tests for Stones

The first test for any stone is visual. Get out your 10 power loupe and look at the stone. There are many things to notice. When examining colored stones, look for color zoning. In layman's terms this is a variance of color. Usually there is more color or more intense color in some areas of the stone. This "zoning" (especially noticeable in amethyst) is an indication of a natural stone. Synthetic stones usually have more "life" and are evenly colored.

When examining the cut of a stone, notice whether or not there are sharp, precise lines. Natural stones have to be cut to their best advantage and are not always as precise as synthetic ones. Look for signs of layers that could mean a doublet or triplet. Chips and abrasions on the surface of a clear stone are usually an indication that the stone is not a diamond.

Next, look into the stone. Natural stones often have needle-like angular inclusions. Synthetics have curved lines or curved color bandings. Any stone made by a flame fusion process such as glass or synthetics will usually have round gas or air bubbles. (See figures)

Figures #1-5 are pictures taken under magnification of "glass used as gemstones." Reprinted from the G.I.A. study course on colored stones, they are courtesy of the Gemological Institute of America. Figures 1, 2, and 3 show differently shaped gas bubbles. Figure 4 shows swirl marks and flow lines. Figure 5 shows groups of "bubbles arranged in a feather-like pattern."

Another more difficult test is one for "refraction." This is done by looking through the stone and focusing on a facet line (where two facets intersect). Slowly tilt the stone back and forth. If one looks like two or splits apart and comes back together, it is a doubly refractive stone. Peridot, topaz, tourmaline, emerald, quartz, amethyst, citrine, synthetic rutile, and zircon are all doubly refracting stones. The last two are highly refractive and can often be identified by this test alone. Diamonds, garnets, spinels, and glass do not double refract. Although this test does not give all the answers, its results are well worth the effort to become proficient.

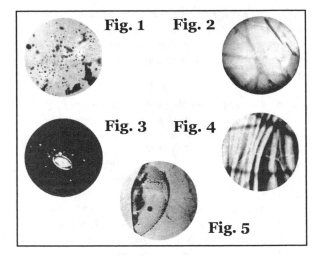

There are many other tests used by the gemologist to determine stones. Synthetics have become so sophisticated that even an expert cannot be sure without the aid of expensive equipment. Today, a trained gemologist with a well-equipped laboratory is imperative for proper stone identification.

This is not to say that the average person cannot learn to identify and enjoy stones. The best way to gain this knowledge is by becoming visually acquainted with the various stones. Take every opportunity to view and examine them. Antique shows and gem and mineral shows provide ideal opportunities to handle stones. Most dealers and participants are more than willing to share their knowledge.

Test for Diamonds

If you have a loose clear stone and want to know whether or not it is a diamond, there are some simple tests that may help in this determination.

For the first test, draw a line on a sheet of white paper. Place the stone (table down) on the line. If the stone is a diamond, the line will not be visible. Any other clear stone will allow the line to show through.

The next test is done by placing the stone on a sheet of white paper and holding a penlight under it. Be sure that the light shines up under the stone. If the stone is a C.Z., YAG, or any other clear stone, the light will outline the stone and also show through the middle. If the stone is a diamond, the outline will show through but the middle will remain dark.

Another test is the "breath test." If breathing on the stone causes it to "fog," this is an indication that the stone in question is not a diamond. All these tests should be performed for the first time using stones that are known. This provides a chance to see the accurate reactions before testing an unknown stone.

An amazingly accurate determination of whether or not a stone is a diamond can be done with a small heat probe instrument. Diamonds are the most heat conductive of stones. Using this fact, the instrument has a small pen-like probe that heats up. When this point is placed on a diamond, the heat is transmitted away from the point, and triggers a beeping sound to signify that it is a diamond. When the probe is placed on any other clear stone the heat is not conducted and no sound is heard. It's a simple, fun thing to see. Go to your local jeweler and ask him to demonstrate it.

Test for Amber

There are many tests to help determine the authenticity of amber. The Greeks were aware of its static electricity, so this was probably the first test. This version of the test was included in the February 1864 *Peterson's Magazine*:

Our article on amber and amber combs last year brought out the inquiry by whether all combs, or other articles, represented to be amber, are so, or not. We replay that very many things sold as amber are imitations. A lady who has an amber necklace, which belonged to her ancestors, sends us the following as a sure method of testing amber. "Prepare a fine bit of split straw-piece of split straw an inch long-rub the article briskly with woolen or cotton cloth a few minutes; place it immediately in contact with one end of the straw, (the straw must not lie in the hand, but on a table, or any dry substance). If the beads or combs are really amber, they will lift the end of the straw and sometimes the point of a very fine needle."

This test can be done today using bits of tissue paper. The problem is that some of today's plastics also have the same ability.

Another test is done by sticking a hot needle into an inconspicuous spot on the amber. If the piece is genuine, it will emit a pine-like odor. According to Marilyn Roos, an amber dealer, this test is not always conclusive because artificial amber made in Russia includes small bits of genuine amber. If the needle should hit any of these pieces, it would test authentic.

The only true test, according to Roos, is done with ether. She suggests putting a small amount on a cotton swab and applying it to the piece in question (in an inconspicuous place, of course). If the piece is genuine, the ether will not affect it. If it is plastic, it will become sticky and the ether will eat into it.

Gutta-percha

Gutta-percha is one of the easiest plastics to identify. It is black or brownish black in color and very lightweight. When rubbed briskly on a piece of cloth, it emits the very distinctive odor of burnt rubber.

Ivory

Unless you are an expert, identifying ivory can be very difficult. A loupe for magnified viewing is a necessity. Elephant ivory has an "engine turned" effect when viewed under magnification. Figure 1a (page 50) shows a piece magnified 15 times. Grain lines, shown in figure 2a (magnified 25x) are found in any true ivory. When ivory is touched with nitric acid, it effervesces—bone, vegetable ivory, and plastics do not.

Bone is often used to imitate ivory. Figure 4a shows a transverse section of bone magnified 25 times. A longitudinal section magnified 50 times is shown in figure 5a. As you can see, it has an entirely different look than that of ivory.

The so-called vegetable ivories are fairly easy to identify. When a few drops of sulfuric acid are applied to this type of ivory, it turns a rosy color. True ivory will not be affected by the acid. Figure 6a shows a cross-section of corozo nut magnified 25x a. longitudinal view of the vegetable ivory is seen in figure 7a. Figures 8a and 9a show the same views of the doum-palm nut. These pictures are courtesy of the Gemological Institute of America.

Jet

Bog oak, gutta-percha, onyx, and black glass are all often misidentified as jet. Brian Fall, a volunteer at the museum in Whitby, was kind enough to share his method of identifying jet. He warned me that the test should be done with care so as not to destroy the piece.

Simply rub the piece across a piece of concrete (a sidewalk?). If it leaves a brownish black mark, the piece is jet. If it does not leave a mark it is some other material.

Jet can sometimes be identified by its weight. It has an extremely lightweight feeling, much like the feel of amber. Maybe this accounts for the misnomer "Black Amber" that is often applied to jet. Jet has sharp, precisely cut lines. Mold lines are an indication of glass.

Fig. 1-a

Fig. 2-a

Fig. 3-a

Fig. 4-a

Fig. 5-a

Fig. 6-a

Fig. 7-a

Fig. 8-a

Fig. 9-a

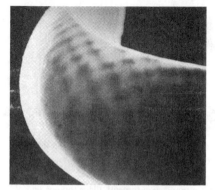

*1b. Another view of
magnified ivory
showing "engine
turned" structure.*

Pearls

An imitation pearl can usually be detected by examining the hole
through which it is strung. If it is a glass imitation covered with
essence d' orient, a thin film can usually be detected.

Another test for determining whether or not pearls are imitation
is done by rubbing them against your teeth. Imitation pearls will
feel smooth while cultured or natural pearls will feel "gritty."
With a little practice, one can become quite proficient at this. This
is an easy accurate way to tell the imitation from the cultured.

Cultured pearls are not imitation, and there is no visible difference between them and oriental pearls. Only an expert with the proper equipment (usually x-rays) is qualified to make this judgement. Since the price of cultured pearls is much lower than that of natural ones, always get an expert opinion, in writing, before making a purchase.

Other Tests

Quite a few materials can be tested by using a few items that you probably already have at home.

First get a pencil with an eraser on the end. Place the eye-end of a needle into the end of the eraser. Now all that is needed to complete this scientific testing unit is a lighted candle.

After heating the needle over the candle, place the hot point to an inconspicuous place on the piece of jewelry. The odor different materials produce can help you determine what it is.

Below is a list of several materials and their identifying odors. Always remember to stick the hot needle into an inconspicuous place:

Amber: Pine scent

Bakelite: Carbolic acid
Celluloid: Camphor
Jet: Burning coal
Tortoiseshell: Burning hair

If you are really interested in learning more about jewelry, learn to use your built-in tools. The first tool is your eyes. Notice details. Learn to recognize styles. Visually compare pieces. Expose your eyes to good examples of jewelry by visiting art galleries (notice the jewelry worn in portraits), going to antiques shows, and looking through old books.

The hands are another important tool in exploring jewelry. Learn the feel of a piece. Touch the finish. Feel the weight. The more you handle jewelry, the more adept you will become at judging it. Surprisingly enough, you may even get to the point where you can determine whether or not a piece is gold just by its feel.

The most surprising jewelry tool is your teeth. By touching a beaded necklace lightly against my teeth, I can distinguish between glass and plastic. Try it. Get used to the difference in the sound and feel of different substances against your teeth. I will admit this looks a bit strange. I have had people ask, "What in the world are you doing?"; but it does work. Again, it is something that has to be worked at, but it is well worth the effort.

Testing Gold

If a piece has no markings, there may be other clues to help
determine the metal. First, examine it closely with a loupe. Look
closely at the edges or any place that was likely to rub against
things. Many times small patches of base metal are visible at these
points. If the base metal is white and the piece is yellow gold, this
is fairly easy, but to see brass or copper base metal under yellow is
sometimes more difficult. The more accustomed your eyes
become to noting subtle differences, the easier it will become. If
there are no visible signs of wear, it is possible that the piece is
gold. It is also possible that it is not.

There is only one true test for gold, and that is done with acid.
Your jeweler can perform this test, and the charge is usually less
than $20. But if jewelry is a hobby or if you are a dealer, it would
be worthwhile to invest in a gold testing kit. A good one can be
purchased at a jewelry supply store for less than $100. This kit
will have everything you need to test gold except the most important ingredient, acid. It can be ordered through your pharmacist
or purchased pre-mixed at the jewelry supply store.

The first step in testing gold is to find an inconspicuous place on
the piece of jewelry in which to file a groove or notch. Please take
care where the notch is made. Many lovely antique pieces have

been ruined by butchers who indiscriminately filed chunks. The groove is to get past any layer of gold in a gold filled piece. Apply a small amount of nitric acid to the groove. If the piece is gold over brass, it will bubble green; if a bluish color appears, the base metal is copper. When the piece is 14K gold or better, the acid keeps its clear water color. If, after a few minutes the spot darkens, this is an indication of 10K gold.

The exact karat can be determined by using the needles that come with the kit. With these needles a mixture, called Aqua Regis (one part distilled water, one part nitric acid, and three parts hydrochloric acid) is used. Instructions are included in the test kit.

For those who do not care to invest in a gold test kit, there is a less expensive alternative. Simply purchase glass acid bottles and pre-mixed testing solution for 10, 14, 18, and 22 karat gold (less than $10 a bottle).

Nitric acid is still used to determine if the piece is gold. After the piece has tested gold, make a mark by rubbing the piece on a test stone. If the piece is 14K or better and a 14K solution is used, there will be no reaction. The mark will remain as visible as ever. Proceed by making another mark and using a higher karat solution until the mark dissolves. If an 18K solution dissolves the mark and the 14K solution does not, the piece is at least 14K. After test-

ing, always rinse the piece with a mixture of baking soda and
water to neutralize the acid.

Testing Silver

Although silver has been hallmarked and stamped for centuries,
unmarked pieces are still encountered. If there is reason to
believe a piece might be silver, examine it with a loupe. Look
carefully at wear points to see if a base metal can be detected. If
there are not indications of plating, a more extensive test is necessary.

For the serious collector or dealer, a pre-mixed silver test solution (available from jewelry supply stores for less than $10) is
highly recommended. It can be an invaluable aid in deciphering
silver content.

To test silver properly, a notch must be filed (in an inconspicuous
place) in the piece being tested. Make sure the notch is deep
enough to go through any plate or coating of silver. Apply the pre-
mixed solution to the notch and wait a few seconds for the color
reaction. If the piece is sterling, the solution will turn a dark red
color. On 800 silver it turns brown. If the piece is palladium, there
is no reaction. This simple, inexpensive test can help make you an
expert at evaluating silver content.

Misnomers

Inaccurate names are often applied to stones. They are usually used to give added importance and more sales appeal. These misnomers sometimes become so commercially accepted that the general public is unaware of what they are actually buying.

The following is a list of commonly accepted names and what they really are:

Alaskan diamond: Rock crystal

Arizona diamond: Rock crystal

Arkansas diamond: Rock crystal

Arizona ruby: Garnet

Belas ruby: Spinel

Cape ruby: Garnet

Cornish diamond: Rock crystal

Goldstone: An imitation adventurine

Herkimer diamond: Rock crystal

Siberian ruby: Tourmaline

Smokey topaz: Smokey quartz

Synthetic aquamarine: Aquamarine colored

A trade name people often wonder about is "Aurora Borealis." This name is applied to glass that has been coated with a compound to give it an iridescent look.

2b. Synthetic ruby magnified to show flux inclusions

3b. Glass "stone" magnified to show orange-peel effect and concave facets.

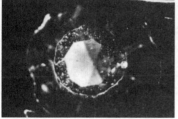

4b. Garnet and glass doublet. Magnified view shows garnet top and trapped gas bubbles under garnet cap.

Makers' Marks, Trademarks & Designers' Marks

by C. Jeanenne Bell

While some of the marks found on jewelry have been written about in the metals portion of this book, there are a number of other marks that are very important to the collector.

These are trademarks, makers' marks and designers' marks. All three can help date a piece and identify its origin, manufacturer, wholesaler, or retailer. In the United States, trademarks became popular in the mid-1800s, but there were no laws making any marks compulsory before 1906. Consequently, there are many American pieces with no markings whatsoever.

English pieces with full hallmarks inform us of the date the piece was made, its metal content, the town in which it was assayed, and its maker. Unfortunately, many pieces, especially designer ones, were never assayed. Glenais Wild of the Birmingham Museum in Birmingham, England told me this was because many times the maker's work was destroyed if for any reason the piece was slightly under specifications. This is also the reason that designers such as Lalique and Fouquet often pierced or engraved their marks.

Other markings can also be confused with trademarks. The French used an eagle's head as a gold quality mark, an owl's head in an oval for imported goods, and the head of Mercury with a number on goods to be exported. Until the late 1800s, Russia used town marks with the numbers 56, 72, and 92 indicating 14K, 18K, and 23K gold content.

Marks used to signify towns were as varied as a hand for Antwerp and a pineapple for Augsburg. Some town marks can be confused with American trademarks if one is not experienced in identifying marks. This section was added so the reader might become curious about the various marks on a piece of jewelry. Hopefully, it will kindle an interest that will cause the reader to be aware of any markings. Markings can help answer the question: "Who made this piece and where was it manufactured?"

This section of short biographical sketches is by no means complete. Some designers and makers are included because of the important part they played in the history of jewelry. Some firms are included because their inexpensive mass-produced pieces have become quite collectible.

The makers and firms are listed in alphabetical order within the Victorian time period. The art nouveau and Arts and Crafts makers and firms are also alphabetized and separated. The American companies are grouped together at the end of this section.

Victorian

Boucheron

This French firm was founded in 1858 by Frederic Boucheron (1830-1902). Over the years some of the best designers of the day were at work in the Boucheron workshops. A London branch of the company was opened on New Bond Street in 1907. Boucheron is noted today as a designer of luxury and medium-priced jewelry. Mark: BOUCHERON

John Brodgen

John Brogden was an English goldsmith and jeweler working in London from 1842 to 1885. His "archaeological" style pieces were prized for their beautiful filigree and granulation gold work. In

1867, his work earned him a medal at the Paris Exhibition. Two fine examples of his work are in the Victoria & Albert Museum in London. Mark:

Castellani

Castellani is one of the most famous names in jewelry of the 19th century. The Castellani story began in 1814, when Fortunato Pio Castellani (1793-1865) started to work in his father's jewelry workshop in Rome. He quickly acquired the status of master goldsmith and opened his own shop on the Via del Corso.

Fortunato Pio's friend, patron, and associate, Michelangelo Caetani, Duke of Sermonita (1804-1883), was instrumental in igniting Castellani's interest in archaeological jewelry. He arranged for Castellani to be present (in an advisory capacity) during the excavations of the Reguline Galassi tomb.

Castellani became fascinated with the beautiful Etruscan granulation and he was determined to find the technique used in this gold work. In Umbria, he found artists using methods similar to the

Etruscan work and persuaded them to come and work with him in Rome.

Because of the political situation in Italy, Castellani's shop was closed from 1840 to 1858. During this time, Fortunato Pio retired, leaving Casa Castellani in the hands of two of his eight sons, Alessandro (1924-1883) and Augusto (1829-1914).

These sons were extremely interested in archaeological jewelry and enthusiastically continued and expanded upon what their father had begun.

Augusto managed the business and strove to carry on his father's tradition. Later, he became the director of the Capitolini Museum in Rome.

Because of his political involvements, Alessandro was in prison from 1850 to 1858. During his exile from Rome, he continued to research and study. Setting up a workshop in Naples, he continued his experiments with granulation. In 1862, he published a pamphlet, "Antique Jewelry and its Revival" to accompany the Castellani display at the London Exhibition. This pamphlet was reprinted again in Philadelphia in 1876. Alessandro published a catalog, "Italian Jewelry as worn by the Peasants of Italy, collected by Signor Castellani," in 1868.

Both Augusto and Alessandro were collectors. Augusto's Collegione Castellani was sold to the Louvre in 1860. Alessandro's Estruscan style jewelry was acquired by the British Museum in London and by the Villa Guilea Museum in Rome. Marks:

Child and Child

This firm of silversmiths and jewelers was established in London in 1880. They were located at 35 Alfred Place, Kensington from 1891 until they discontinued business in 1916. Known for high quality enamel work, they were patronized by royalty. Mark: a stylized sunflower, the stalk flanked by the initials c & c on each side of the stem.

Peter Carl Fabrege (1846-1920)

Volumes have been written about this Russian goldsmith and jeweler. Hopefully, the reader will take the time to learn about this artist by reading some of the books that include photographs of his lavish work. Two of these are: *Carl Fabrege: Goldsmith to the Imperial Court of Russia* by Kenneth Snowman, and *Fabrege and*

His Contemporaries by Henry Hawley published by the Cleveland Museum of Art. A little booklet, *Fabrege,* available through the Victoria and Albert Museum in London contains a list of Fabrege's work masters and their marks. I highly recommend it. Mark:

ФАБЕРЖЕ

Froment-Meurice

Francois Desere Froment-Meurice was the son of France Froment, a French goldsmith who had been in business since 1774. After the death of his father, his mother married Pierre-Meurice, who was also a goldsmith. Francois Desere went to work in his stepfather's workshop and added Meurice to the Froment name. Francois Desere Froment-Meurice is said to have studied drawing and sculpture. His work shows evidence of this.

In 1839, he exhibited pieces done in the Gothic Revival style for which he is noted. He was often referred to as the "Cellini" of the 19th century. He was much admired by his contemporaries. His enameled Renaissance style pieces are truly treasures.

Emile Froment-Meurice (1837-1913) took over the family business a number of years after his father's death. He displayed jewelry at the Exposition Universelle in Paris in 1867. The pieces were executed in the styles made famous by his father. In about 1900, he began to experiment with the new art nouveau designs. Marks: Both father and sons: FROMENT MEURICE

Giuliano

Carlo Giuliano is another outstanding name in 19th century jewelry. Born in Naples, it is believed that he met Alessandro Castellani and worked in his shop there. It was probably Alessandro who instigated Giuliano's move to London. It is evident that Giuliano worked for Casa Castellani in London.

From 1867-1874, his work was sold by prestigious firms such as Robert Phillips, Hunt and Roskell, Harry Emanuel, and Hancocks. Pieces bearing his mark were sold in fitted cases imprinted with the retail firm's name. Harry Emanuel exhibited some Giuliano pieces at the L' Exposition of 1867 in Paris.

In 1874-1875, Carlo set up his own retail shop at 115 Piccadilly. Here in luxurious surroundings he sold his tiny works of art to some of Britian's most prominent families.

His sons, Carolo Joseph and Arthur Alphonse, joined him in the business and continued it after his death in 1895. The firm was relocated in 1912 at #48 Knightsbridge and was closed in 1914. Marks:

A. W. N. Pugin

Augustus Wilby Northmore Pugin (1812-52) was a multi-talented Englishman who designed silverware, scenery, ironwork, jewelry, dresses, and part of the Houses of Parliament. His writings included *Designs for Gold and Silversmiths,* 1836; *The True Principles of Pointed or Christian Architecture,* 1841; *The Glossary of Ecclesiastical Ornament and Costume,* 1844; and *Floriated Ornament* in 1849.

He was responsible for reviving the art of enameling and for making the Gothic style popular in England. His famous set of marriage jewelry was exhibited at the Mediaeval Court at the

Crystal Palace in 1851. John Hardman & Co. in Birmingham, England executed most of his designs. Mark: (AWP monogram)

Art Nouveau

Designers, Manufacturers, and Retail Firms

Edward Colonna

Edward Colonna was a German born (1862) decorative designer whose work spanned both the art nouveau and art deco periods. After finishing his architectural training in Brussels, he came to America (1882) and worked for a company founded by L.C. Tiffany. While living in Ohio, he wrote a booklet titled *Essay on Broom Corn*. The booklet of art nouveau designs was inspired by the interlaced lines formed by the stalks of corn that were used to make brooms.

In 1898, he traveled to France and designed jewelry for Maison de l' art Nouveau. The book *Modern Designs in Jewellery and Fans*, 1903, by Gabriel Mourey pictures several of his pieces. Mourey states, "His works have this great charm in my eyes, that they are neither showcase jewels or mere bejoux de parade, things intended solely for display. As a rule, they are quiet and practical."

After Bing's shop closed in 1905, Colonna returned to America. Mark: COLONNA (stamped) SANB (in a diamond, the mark for Maison de l' art Nouveau)

Wilhelm Lucas van Cranch

Wilhelm Lucas van Cranch (1861-1918) was a German painter and jeweler. His art nouveau jewelry designs are said to have an "air of decadence." He won a gold medal in Paris in 1900. Mark: WLC (in monogram)

Theodor Fahrner

Theodor Fahrner (1868-1928) was a jewelry manufacturer in Pforzheim, Germany. His mass-produced jewelry was usually done in low-carat gold or silver. He used designers from the artist's colony in Darmstadt. The book *Modern Designes in Jewellery and Fans*, 1903, pictures two pieces of jewelry executed by this firm. One of these pieces was designed by J. M. Olbrich. Mark:

Lucien Gaillard

Lucien Gaillard (born 1861) was a French silversmith, jeweler, and enameler who inherited a jewelry business in 1892 that had been founded by his grandfather in 1840. His talents as a silversmith were praised at the 1889 Paris Exposition.

A friend, Rene Lalique, is credited with persuading him to try designing jewelry. In about 1900, he opened a workshop where he experimented with materials such as horn and ivory. In 1904, he won first prize for jewelry at the Paris Salon. Mark: L. GAILLARD (engraved)

Rene Jules Lalique

The foremost designer of the art nouveau period was Rene Jules Lalique (1860-1945). At an early age, he exhibited a talent for art. At age 16, he was apprenticed to Louis Aucoc.

In 1885, he acquired a fully equipped workshop. Here he designed and made jewelry for such firms as Cartier, Boucheron, and Aucoc. Much attention was drawn to his work in the 1890s when the illustrious Sarah Bernhardt became his patron. A series of 145 pieces of jewelry, which took him 17 years to complete, is now housed at the Foundacion Gulbenkian in Lisbon. Any study of art nouveau jewelry is incomplete without a survey of his work. Mark:

R. LALIQUE
LALIQUE
R.L.

Liberty & Co.

Liberty and Company in London, England, had a most important influence on the art nouveau style. Before anyone had ever used the term art nouveau, the style was being offered by this company. In fact, the art nouveau style was known as "stile Liberty" in Italy for quite some time.

A. L. Liberty had always been intrigued by the designs of the Orient. He had been employed by Farmer and Rogers when they purchased part of the Japanese exhibit from the International Exhibition of 1862. When he opened his own shop in 1876, it was devoted exclusively to goods from India, Japan, and other parts of the Orient. The aesthetics patronized his shop, and it became a dominant force on the fashion scene.

In 1899, Liberty introduced a new line of jewelry under the name "Cymric." This jewelry was designed by a group of designers connected with the Arts and Crafts movement including Arthur Gaskin, Bernard Cuzner, and Archibald Knox. Most of these pieces were manufactured by W. H. Haseler and Son in Birmingham.

Cymric jewelry is described in a Liberty & Co. advertisement as "an original and important departure in gold and silver work. In this development there is a complete breaking away from convention in the matter of design and treatment, which is calculated to commend itself to all who appreciate the note distinguishing artistic productions in which individuality of idea and execution is the essence of the work." Liberty & Co. jewelry may bear the Haseler mark or one of the Liberty marks. Marks:

LY & CO (in a triple diamond)
CYMRIC (trademark registered with the Board of Trade in 1901)
W. H. H. (for W. H. Haseler)

Murrle, Bennett & Co.

According to Viviene Becker, this firm was strictly a wholesaler of jewelry and not a manufacturer. The firm was founded in London in 1884 by a German (Murrle) and an Englishman (Bennett).

They sold all styles of jewelry including the New Modern designs associated with the Arts and Crafts movement. Most of the pieces were made in Pforzheim, Germany. Pieces bearing the Murrle, Bennett & Co. mark are sought after by collectors. Mark:

Otto Prutscher

Otto Prutscher (1880-1961) was a pupil of Josef Hoffman in the Wiener Werkslatte. He was an architect and a jewelry designer. His designs were executed by Rozet & Fischmeister, a Viennese jewelry firm.

In the book, *Modern Designs in Jewellery and Fans*, 1903, W. Fred makes this comment on Prutscher's work: "Otto Prutscher's necklaces and rings are remarkable alike for this beauty and har-moni-ous variety of their coloring. He uses enamel to a great extent and also quite small precious stones. Very uncommon, too, is the way in which he employs metal, though only enough of it to hold the enamel in place. It would appear as if the artist had in his mind a vision of the women who are to wear his work, who are too tender and frail to carry any weight, so that the use of much metal in ornaments for them would be quite unsuitable." Mark: OP (in a square monogram)

Louis Comfort Tiffany

Louis Comfort Tiffany (1848-1933), the eldest son of C. L. Tiffany, was a painter, interior decorator, designer, glassmaker, and jeweler. In 1879, he founded Associated Artists, an interior design firm. His decorative work reflected his interest in and his love of Japanese art. In 1889, he associated himself with another expo-nent of the Oriental, Samuel Bing, owner of Maison de l' art Nouveau.

Tiffany studios started making jewelry in 1900. L. C. Tiffany became the manager of the company's jewelry workshop when his father died in 1902. Marks: Louis C. Tiffany (in italics); LCT, Tiffany & Co.

Philippe Wolfers

Philippe Wolfers (1858-1929) was a Belgian jeweler who was also trained in art and sculpturing. He designed for his family firm and enjoyed working with ivory. He designed a series of Art Nouveau jewelry and marked it with his special mark to distinguish it from the pieces done for the family firm. In the book, *Modern Designs in Jewellery and Fans*, 1903, F. Knopff gives his opinion of Wolfer's work:

M. WOLFERS seeks his inspiration in the study of the nature and the forms of his marvelous domain, and his vision of things is specially defined in his jewels. The detail therein contributes largely to the spirit of the entire work, which borrows its character from the decoration itself or from the subject of that decoration. He never allows himself to stray into the regions of fancy; at most, he permits his imagination to approach the confines of ornamental abstraction. Nevertheless, he interprets Nature, but is never dominated by it. He has too true, to exact a sense of the decorative principle to conform to the absolute reality of the things he admires and reproduces. His art, by virtue of this rule, is thus a modified translation of real forms. He has too much taste to introduce into the composition of one and the same jewel flowers or animals which have no parallel symbol or, at least, some family likeness or significance. He will associate swans with waterlilies—the flowers which frame, as it were, the life of those grand poetic birds; or he will put the owl or the bat with the poppy—the triple evocation of Night and Mystery; or the heron with an eel—symbols of distant, melancholy streams. He rightly judges that in art one must endeavor to reconcile everything, both the idea and the materials whereby one tries to make that idea live and speak.

Mark: PW (in a shield with the words 'exemplaire unique')

Arts And Crafts

Designers and Manufacturers

The Arts and Crafts movement was a reaction against the dehumanization of man by the machine. It was not a period style, but a movement that began in the late 1850s and continued until the 1920s.

Influenced by the writing of John Ruskin (1819-1900) and the philosophy of William Morris (1834-1896), its exponents believed that there should be no distinction between the designer and the craftsman, and that the best art was achieved when artists worked in partnership.

These artists formed guilds and lived and worked together. Their dreams of bringing art to the common man by executing

ordinary items in honest and handcrafted designs were never ful-
filled, because the expense involved in hand crafting the items
made them unaffordable to the very class for which they were
intended. Hollbrook Jackson in this book *The Eighteen-Nineties*,
published in 1913, has this comment about the movement:

*The outward effect of this search for excellence of quality
and utility in art was, however, not so profound as it might
have been. This is explained by the fact that the conditions
under which Morris and his group worked were so far
removed from the conditions of the average economic and
industrial life of the time as to appear impractical for general
adoption. They demonstrated, it is true, that it was possible to
produce useful articles of fine quality and good taste even in
an age of debased industry and scamped counterfeit workmanship; but their demonstration proved also that unless
something like a revolution happened among wage-earners
none but those of ample worldly means could hope to become
possessed of the results of such craftsmanship.*

Today many of these pieces are not only collectable—they are
also affordable. If you find the style of Arts and Crafts jewelry
appealing, I urge you to buy it. I feel sure that good examples are
destined to appreciate in value.

C. R. Ashbee

Charles Robert Ashbee (1863-1942) was the cornerstone of the Arts and Crafts movement. He founded the School and Guild of Handicraft in 1887-88, which served as a "training ground" for young exponents of the movement. Ashbee was an admirer of Cellini and translated and published Cellini's treatises in 1898. A copy of this fascinating work was published by Dover Publication in 1967. It gives an excellent account of how jewelry was made in the 16th century. Ashbee designed most of the jewelry executed by the Guildsmen. He exhibited at the Vienna Seccession Exhibitions number VIII, XV, XVII and XXIV, and with the Arts and Crafts Society from 1888.

Aymer Vallance, writing about British jewelry in *Modern Designs in Jewellery and Fans*, 1903, had this to day about Ashbee's work:

AMONG pioneers of the artistic jewelry movement, Mr. C. R. Ashbee holds an honorable place. He stood almost alone at the beginning, when he first made known the jewellery designed by him, and produced under his personal direction by the Guild and School of Handicraft in the East End. It was immediately apparent that here was no tentative nor half-hearted caprice, but that a genuine and earnest phase of an ancient craft had been reestablished. Every design was carefully thought out, and the work executed with not less careful and consistent technique. In fact, its high merits were far in advance of anything else in the contemporary jewellery or goldsmith's work. The patterns were based on conventionalized forms of nature, favorite among them being the car-nation, the rose and the heartsease, or on abstract forms invited by the requirements and conditions of the material—the ductility and luster of the metal itself. Most of the ornaments were of silver, the surface of which was not worked up to a brilliantly shining burnish, in the prevalent fashion of the day, but dull polished in such ways as to give the charming richness and tone of old silver work. Mr. Ashbee also adopted the use of jewels, not lavishly or ostentatiously, but just wherever a note of color would convey the most telling effect, the stones in themselves, e.g. amethysts, amber, and rough pearl, being of no particular value, save purely from the point of view of decoration. Novel and revolutionary as it were, at its first appearance, the principles underlying Mr. Ashbee's jewellery work— viz, that the value of a personal ornament consists not in the commercial value of the materials so much as in the artistic quality of its design and treatment—they became the standard which no artist thenceforward could wisely afford to ignore, and such furthermore that have even in certain quarters become appropriated by the trade in recent times.

Mark: CRA (pricked or scratched); GOH ltd (registered 1898)

Birmingham Guild of Handicraft

This firm of craft jewelers was founded in 1890. The guild became part of Gittins Craftsman Ltd. in 1910. They had a reputation for making good quality handmade jewelry. Mark: BGOH (in a square)

Bernard Cuzner

Bernard Cuznar (1877-1956) was an English silversmith and jeweler. While serving an apprenticeship as a watchmaker, he went to night school at the Redditch School of Art. Soon he gave up watchmaking in favor of silversmithing. Cuznar was strongly influenced by Robert Catterson Smith and Arthur Gaskin. Various Liberty & Co. designs have been attributed to him. In 1935, he published an illustrated book of designs titled *A Silversmith's Manual*. Cuzner was head of the metalwork department of the Birmingham School of Art from 1910 until he retired in 1942. Mark: BC

Arthur and Georgie Gaskin

Arthur Gaskin was born in Birmingham, England in 1862. In 1883, he was a student at the Birmingham School of Art. Here he met Georgie Evelyn Cave France (1868-1934). Their mutual interest in design, art, and illustrating brought them together, and on March 21, 1894, they were married. Arthur was a "born teacher" and was assistant master at the Central School from 1885 until 1903. From 1903-1924 he was headmaster and teacher at the School of Jewelers and Silversmiths.

Both Georgie and Arthur entered their work in national competitions. In 1899, they decided to learn to make jewelry. Commenting on the production of this jewelry Georgie wrote in 1929, "In the jewelry I did all the designing and he did all the enamel, and we both executed the work with our assistants."

In the March 1903 issue of *The Magazine of Art*, an article written by Aymer Vallance states:

...public demand for the jewellery is such that strenuous effort is needed by Mrs. Gaskin, who has a gift for divining the individual wants of her clients, to maintain in every case that touch of personality which contributes no little to the attractiveness of her work. I have always thought that jewellery, requiring as it does dainty taste in the designing and delicate manipulation in execution, is an industry specially suited to lady artists, and it is surprising how few comparatively appear to give it a thought. Mrs. Gaskin's achievements ought to show what can be done by anyone possessed of the above qualifications.

This same author had this to say about the Gaskins in *Modern Designs in Jewellery and Fans*, 1903:

Mr. Gaskin came to the conclusion that it was of little benefit for a draughtsman to make drawings on paper to be carried out by someone else; studio and workshop must be one, designer identical with a craftsman. It is not very many years since Mr. Gaskin, ably seconded by his wife, started with humble, nay, almost rudimentary apparatus, to make jewellery with his own hands; but the result has proved how much taste and steadfast endurance can accomplish. Their designs are so numerous and so varied—rarely is any single one repeated, except to order—that it is hardly possible to find any descriptions that apply at all. But it may be noted that, whereas a large number have been characterized by a light and graceful treatment of twisted wire, almost life filigree, the two pendants here illustrated seem to indicate rather a new departure on the part of Mr. Gaskin, with their plates of chased metal, and pendants attached by rings, a method not in any sense copied from, yet in some sort recalling the beautiful fashion with which connoisseurs are familiar in Norwegian and Swedish peasant jewelry.

Mark:

C. H. Horner

C. H. Horner is a collectable name in English jewelry. He designed his own pieces and his factory produced them from start to finish. This vast array of items included pendants, brooches, chains, and hat pins. Most pieces were done in silver and embellished with enamel. The winged scarab and insect motif were frequently used. Horner pieces are available at London Street Markets and are reasonably priced. Mark: C. H. (Chester assay)

Fred I Partridge

Fred I. Partridge was an English metal worker and jeweler who worked from about 1900 until 1908. In 1902, he went to work with C. R. Ashbee and the Guild of Handicraft. Partridge was influenced by the work of Lalique and his work reflects this interest. Partridge married May Hart, a Birmingham trained enameler, in 1906. They set up a business on Dean Street in Soho. From this location they supplied pieces for firms such as Liberty & Co. Mark: PARTRIDGE

Edgar Simpson

Edgar Simpson was an English designer who worked from about 1896 until 1910. He was one of the original designers at the Artificers Guild when it was founded in 1901. Eventually, he became their chief designer. A good example of what his contemporaries thought about his work can be gleaned from this excerpt from an article by Aymer Vallance published in *Modern Designs in Jewellery and Fans*, 1903:

MR. EDGAR SIMPSON, of Nottingham, is an artist of great gifts, as his drawings and, still more, the specimens of his actual handiwork here illustrated fully testify. Many excellent designs lose vigor and character in the process of execution from the original sketch; but Mr. Simpson, on the contrary, manages to give his designs additional charm by the exquisite finish with which he works them out in metal. Particularly happy is this artist's rendering of dolphins and other marine creatures; as in the circular pendant where the swirling motion of water is conveyed by elegant curving lines of silver, with a pearl, to represent an air bubble, issuing from the fish's mouth.

Mark: an Artificers Guild with EDWARD SPENCER DEL in a circle

Henry Wilson

Henry Wilson (1864-1934) was an English sculptor, architect, metalworker, and jeweler. He established a workshop in 1890 and joined the Art Workers Guild in 1892. He taught metalworking at the Central High School of Arts and Crafts from 1896 to about 1901. Wilson exhibited with the Arts and Crafts Society from 1889, and became its president in 1915. His book on design and techniques titled *Silver Work and Jewellery* was published in 1903.

A hair ornament attributed to Henry Wilson was sold by Phillips Blenstock House, London on July 7, 1983 for $1,958. This description was furnished by Phillips: "A good Art and Crafts gold, silver, plique-a-jour, and opal hair ornament attributed to Henry Wilson on stylistic grounds, the crescent-shaped top inset with three circular plique-a-jour plaques decorated in pink, green, and turquoise with tulips, flanked by gold florets and silver leaves, with an oval opal cabochon below and tortoise shell tines to the comb, 17 cm long." Mark: H.W. (in a monogram)

The American Arts and Crafts Revival

In Chicago, the Arts and Crafts movement was well received by those who shared its philosophy of social and cultural reforms. After a visit in the 1880s to C. R. Ashbee's Guild in London, Jane Addams became an advocate of the Arts and Crafts Movement. She was instrumental in fostering the movement in America. When Ashbee came to the United States in 1900, he lectured at the Chicago Art Institute and stayed at the Hull House, a settlement run by Jane Addams. The Chicago Arts and Crafts Society was founded there in 1897.

For more information about the Arts and Crafts revival in America I urge you to read *Chicago Metal-Smiths* by Sharon Darling, published by the Chicago Historical Society in 1977. It offers valuable insight to the movement and its exponents. Many of the designers and manufacturers listed in this book are sure to become even more collectible. The book offers excellent photographs of the makers' marks.

The Kalo Shop

Clara Black named the shop she founded in 1900 "Kalo," a Greek word meaning beautiful. At first, the shop produced leather items and woven goods but when Clara married George S. Welles, a metalworker in 1905, her interest turned to metal work and jewelry.

All the items produced by the Kalo shop were handmade. The couple set up a school and workshop known as "The Kalo Art-Craft Community" in their Chicago residence.

Jewelry bearing the Kalo stamp is much sought after by collectors. Since jewelry constituted about half of the company's total sales, pieces are still available at reasonable prices. Mark: KALO

Florence Koehler

Florence Koehler (1861-1944) was a jewelry designer and craftswoman who lived and worked in Chicago. She was one of the leaders of the Arts and Crafts revival in America and one of the founders of the Chicago Arts and Crafts Society.

Sharon S. Darling's *Chicago Metal-Smiths* lists her as Mrs. F. H. Koehler and states that she was, "…mentioned as a successful local metalworker and jewelry maker in an article by Harriet Monroe 'An Experiment in Jewelry'." (*House Beautiful*, July 1900).

Art Deco Retail Firms

The art deco period style was reflected in the jewelry made by leading jewelry firms such as Bocheron, Cartier, Chaumet, La Cloche, Mauboissin, and Van Cleef & Arpels. Some important designers of the period were George Fouquet, Gerard Sandoz, Jean Despres, and Raymond Templier.

Cartier

This firm was founded in 1847, when Louis Francois Cartier opened a small shop in Paris. In 1898, the company relocated to 13 Rue de la Paix. A London branch was opened in 1902 followed by the New York branch in 1903. Cartier is credited with making the first wristwatch in 1904. The firm executed some of the finest examples of art deco jewelry.

Marks: LFC (in a diamond-shaped shield);
          AC (with a hatchet)

Chaument & Cie

This French firm was founded in 1780 by Erienne Nitot. The company was commissioned to make the Emperor's coronation crown and sword after Nitot assisted an accident victim who turned out to be the First Consul for Napoleon Bonaparte. They also executed the wedding jewelry for Marie Louise in 1810. In 1875, they opened a showroom in London. Their art deco pieces were most sophisticated.

Georg Jensen

Georg Jensen (1866-1935) was a Danish goldsmith and silversmith who opened a shop bearing his name in 1904. He designed, made, and sold jewelry and silverware. His distinctive style is still evident in the work produced by the firm today. Mark: Jensen; GJ

La Cloche

La Cloche was both a manufacturer and retailer of art deco jewelry. Founded in Madrid in 1875, the Paris branch was opened in 1898. The firm was known for its high fashion style executed in the finest materials and embellished with colored gems and diamonds.

Van Cleef & Arpels

This French firm was founded in 1906. It is credited with creating the first "minaudiere." In 1930, this name was trademarked by them. Their main office is still in Paris, but they have branches in London and New York.

Collectible American Marks

Black, Starr & Frost Co., New York

This firm of goldsmiths and jewelers was established in New York in 1810 and known as "Marquand & Co." In 1839, the company's name was changed to "Ball, Thomkins and Black," and in 1851, it was changed to "Ball, Black & Co."

The name "Black, Starr & Frost" was with the company from 1876, until it merged with the Gorham Corporation in 1929. Their customers were prestigious and pieces from their stock were often illustrated in fashion magazines of the day. Mark:

B S & F
Black Starr
Black, Starr & Frost Ltd.

Gorham Corporation Inc., Providence, R.I.

This company, founded by Jabez Gorham in 1815, is included in this section because of some jewelry it produced in the late 19th and early 20th centuries. This jewelry was designed by a group of artists under the direction of William C. Codman and executed by a group of silversmiths selected by Edward Holbrook. The pieces were marketed under the name MARTELE and are quite collectable. They were usually made of silver, silver gilt or copper. The few pieces with stones were set with the colorless ones most popular during the art nouveau period.

Marks:

950-1000 FINE

Wm. B. Kerr & Co.

This firm of goldsmiths, silversmiths, and jewelers was founded in Newark, New Jersey in 1855 by William B. Kerr. The company mass-produced pieces in the neo-Renaissance style and the art nouveau style. The Gorham Corporation purchased the company in 1906. Today, pieces baring the Kerr trademark are prized by collectors. Marks:

(Discontinued)

Jewelry Box Antiques, Inc.,
Kansas City, Missouri

This is definitely the newest of collectible trademarks. It is the trademark of my revival jewelry lines which premiered in November 1993. I have 3 different lines, they are:

Classics: A revival of styles from the 1840s thru the 1940s. All are executed in 18K gold and platinum.

Classics Collectables: These pieces made of 14K and 18K gold feature an original antique or vintage item as a central motif or component.

Vintage 'N Vogue: A fashion line of jewelry inspired by the styles from the 1840s through the 1940s.

These lines all proudly display our trademark on authentically inspired revivals. Mark:

C. L. Tiffany

In 1853, C. L. Tiffany founded Tiffany & Co. Prior to that year he had been in partnership with J. B. Young (1837) and J. L. Ellis (1850). Pieces bearing the Tiffany name can best be dated by following the progression of moves by the company:

1853-54:	217 Broadway
1854-1870:	550 Broadway
1870:	Union St. and 15th St.
1868:	London branch opened

Tiffany & Co. exhibited at the Exposition Universelle in Paris 1867, and at the Philadelphia Centennial Exposition of 1876. In 1878 and 1889, they won gold medals in Paris.

Special marks were added to Tiffany & Co.'s usual markings for pieces made for the 1893 World's Columbian Exposition in Chicago, the 1900 Exposition Universelle in Paris, and the 1901 Pan American Exposition in Buffalo. These are shown below. Marks:

1898

1900

1901

World's Columbian
Exposition
Chicago.

Exposition
Universelle,
Paris.

Pan American
Exposition,
Buffalo.

Unger Brothers

This firm of silversmiths and jewelers has a very collectable trademark. Unger Brothers began making jewelry in 1878. Eugene and Frederick Unger opened a shop at #18 Crawford St. in

Newark, New Jersey in 1881. P.O. Dickinson, the company's chief designer, was issued a series of patents for art nouveau jewelry design in 1903. The company mass-produced these designs in silver and silver gilt from 1904 to 1910. In 1914, they discontinued the manufacturer of jewelry. Marks:

(Old Mark.)

(Old Mark.)

(1904)

Wayne Silver Co.

This firm was founded in Honesdale, Pennsylvania in 1895. They are described as making "fancy and useful articles of silver, not plated." Records indicate that they discontinued business after the turn of the century. Mark:

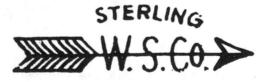

Whiting & Davis Co., Inc.

This company was founded in 1876 in Plainville, Massachusetts. In 1907, C. A. Whiting became owner; shortly after this, the first chainmail mesh machine was developed and Whiting & Davis became the world's largest manufacturer of mesh products.

Many fine examples of their early bags have survived. These are eagerly sought after by collectors, because of their beauty and durability. New bags manufactured by this company are sold in many major department stores. The company also produces a line of antique and museum reproduction jewelry. Mark:

Jewelry History

by C. Jeanenne Bell

1840-1860

The years from 1840-1860 were exciting times in which to be alive. Changes were taking place at a rapid pace. The fruits of the Industrial Revolution were bringing about new social and economic conditions.

Very little jewelry was worn during the day. Since bonnets or curls covered the ears, earrings were primarily worn only for state events. Jewelry was limited to hair ornaments, brooches, and bracelets. Of these, bracelets were by far the most popular. The arms were available to decorate so they used them to the fullest.

By the end of 1855, the neckline was worn lower. Necklaces once again came into fashion.

Cameos

When Victoria ascended to the throne, cameos were already immensely popular. Excavations had awakened interest in this old art, and Napoleon I had initiated "a Prix de Rome" in 1805 to encourage stone engraving. About that same time a public school was opened in Rome for the study of cameo engraving. It was founded by Pope Leo XII and met with much success.

The early cameos were made from stone. In the 16th century workmen turned to shell to meet the demand for more cameos at less expensive prices. Cameos were set in rings, brooches, earrings, and bracelets. The men wore them in watch fobs, rings, and pins. Stone cameos were cut from onyx, agate, sardonyx, cornelian, coral, lava, and jet. The carvers of shell cameos used the shells of the Black Helmet and the pink and white Queen's Conches which were so plentiful in the seacoast towns in Italy.

Cameos made lovely, portable souvenirs for tourists visiting the ruins of Pompeii and Hercelium. When the travelers returned home, their friends were enchanted with these small works of art. Within a short time, Italian cameo artists had shops in England, France, and America. These craftsmen carved cameos in the ancient styles or any other designs the purchaser might select.

(Jewelry Box Antiques)

*1840-1860 brooch, yellow rolled gold mounting set with
"Three Graces" shell cameo, 2-1/4" x 2-1/8".*

Price: $695

Stone cameos are generally more valuable than those made of shell. But the medium is not nearly as important as the artistry. The best way to judge a cameo is to examine it with a good magnifying glass. Graceful, smooth-flowing lines with much detail are signs of a good one. The inferior ones seem to have sharper lines, fewer details, and a harsh look. Be sure to hold the cameo to the light and examine it for possible cracks.

Many antique cameos were reset in the late seventeen and early eighteen hundreds. Some craftsmen were expert at copying antique pieces. This makes accurate dating almost impossible. However, there are usually some clues to help determine age.

If a cameo is made of lava, it is almost certainly Victorian. Other clues are the style of design (Greek, Roman, etc.), types of clothing and hair styles on the figures, and the type of mounting. If the cameo is mounted as a brooch, carefully examine the pin and hook. Safety catches are a 20th century adaptation. If the cameo has one, then it is either not older than the early 1900s or a new catch has been added.

If it is an addition, this can usually be ascertained by more careful examination. Look for signs of soldering. Often the new catch is attached to a small plate jointed to the back of the brooch. Next look closely at the pin and notice what kind of hinge it has. If the sharp point of the pin extends past the body of the brooch, it is an "oldie."

Gold, silver, pinchbeck, gold filled, cut-steel, and jet were some of the materials used for mounting cameos. The type of metal used can often give an indication of when it was made. If the mounting is pinchbeck, it was probably made between the early seventeen and the mid-eighteen hundreds.

Gold electroplating was patented in 1849 so, if the piece was plated, it was made after that date. Nine karat gold was legalized in 1854. A piece in 9K would have to be made after that date. A popular metal used for mountings in the 1880s was silver, but this does not mean that all cameos mounted in silver were made at that time. All the clues have to be examined before a judgment on age can be made.

Scenic cameos are generally more expensive than bust cameos. A very popular motif around 1860 was what is known as "Rebecca at the Well." There are many variations on this theme, but they usually include a cottage, a bridge, and a girl.

Technically, a cameo is made by cutting away the background of a material to make a design in relief, but there are some items called cameos that do not fit this description. Josiah Wedgwood's factory produced jasperware plaques in blue and white and black and white. These had the look of a cameo, but they were molded. These mass produced cameos were originally very inexpensive, but today they are quite collectible.

Chatelaines

Chatelaines were a very necessary accessory for the Victorian matron. Considered a vital part of home management, they were

(Photo courtesy William Doyle Galleries, New York 9-19-90)

Circa 1860 French chatelaine, yellow gold and silver, suspending a pair of ornamented lidded perfumes and centered by an Etui. The richly scrolled and foliated frame surrounds agate fields decorated with rose diamond and ruby nature scenes with birds and flowers.

Price: $20,000

also ornamental and prestigious. The chatelaine consisted of a large central piece that was either hooked or pinned at the waist. From this extended chains with swivel attachments for hanging a variety of household necessities such as a pair of scissors, sewing case with needles and thread, knife, vinaigrette, coin purse, pencil, note case, scent bottle, watch, and key.

Inspiration for this type of accessory may be traced to medieval times when the keeper of the keys, which were usually worn on a chain around the waist, was the person with authority. Chatelaines were in and out of fashion for several hundred years.

Chatelaines were made from gold, pinchbeck, silver, silver plate, stamped metal, and cut-steel. They are quite collectible.

Cut-Steel

England was well known for its cut-steel industry. The most noted producer was Mathew Boulton of Birmingham. He made beautiful rings and brooches, using Wedgwood cameos in cut-steel frames.

A piece of cut-steel is made by riveting rosettes fashioned from thin metal to another metal plate that has been cut in a design.

Although it is called cut-steel, the metal could be silver alloy or even tin. The glitter of cut-steel comes from light reflecting off the rosettes. Imitation cut-steel is made by stamping the rosettes from a sheet of metal. The best way to determine the authenticity of a piece is by looking at the back. If there are two pieces of metal and one is a solid plate with rivets showing, chances are that the piece is genuine.

Even though cut-steel glittered, it was not flashy, so the Victorians considered it proper for day wear. Many lovely cloak clasps, shoe buckles, brooches, and chatelaines were made of cut-steel.

Garter Jewelry

Victorian jewelers took designs from a variety of sources. One popular motif stemmed from the Royal Order of the Garter. This Order, founded by King Edward III in 1348 to strengthen military leadership, is the highest honor a British monarch can bestow. Members of the order wear a blue garter buckled on their knee. Victoria was much too modest for this tradition. Instead she chose to wear it on her arm. Thus the garter became a very fashionable jewelry motif.

Bracelets displaying this design were most plentiful. Rings were made in the form of a garter, and lockets were engraved with this motif.

Hairwork Jewelry

Victorian women wore jewelry not only as a decorative accessory but also as an outward expression of their innermost feelings. This sentimental nature fostered an increasing interest in hairwork jewelry. For years it had been popular to own a lock of a loved one's hair. This was usually kept in a special compartment in the back of a brooch, locket, ring, or even in a watch fob. In the early years of the 19th century, hair began to be used for the actual making of jewelry.

The watch chain was by far the most popular piece of hairwork jewelry. By providing her love with a chain made from her hair, a young lady was assured that she would be in his thoughts many times a day. Hair bracelets combining the hair of each child were a popular keepsake for a mother. A guard chain was always useful, and openwork crosses and earrings were quite lovely.

When the hair work was completed, it was sent to the jeweler for fittings. Beautiful clasps with compartments for photographs, closures mounted with stones, and even miniatures were used to

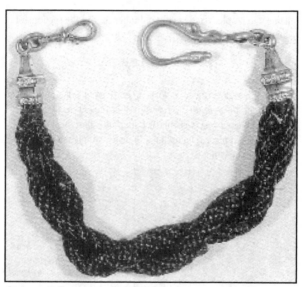

(Jeanenne Bell)

1840-1860 watch chain, gilt fittings, two pieces of hairwork inter-twined, snake and early swivel, 3/4" x 8-1/2".

Price: $175

complete bracelets. A variety of fittings were available for finishing brooches and earrings. To make long necklaces or guard chains, the jeweler used small gold tubes to join the sections of hair.

Serpent Jewelry

When Albert gave Queen Victoria an engagement ring in the form of a serpent, he generated a revival of this ancient decorative motif. The Queen was particularly fond of this design. She owned several serpent pieces, including a bracelet, which she wore at her first council meeting.

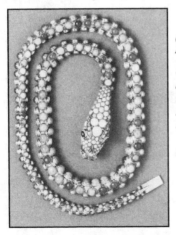

(Photo courtesy of Sotheby's, London 7-28-83)

Circa 1840 necklace, gold and turquoise serpent, head is pavé set with turquoise and rose diamonds, in fitted case, £2,090.

Price: $3,720

The snake motif, believed to be a symbol of good luck, was used throughout the Victorian period. On a stroll through London, ladies could be seen wearing serpent rings, serpents entwined around their arms, and serpents coiled on their brooches.

Popular Stones & Materials
Amethyst

The amethyst was a very fashionable stone throughout the Victorian era. Because of its ecclesiastical association, it was acceptable to wear in the latter stages of mourning. Since amethysts were plentiful, they were affordable and could be worn by all classes. In a yellow gold or pinchbeck mounting, surrounded by seed pearls, they were quite lovely.

The amethyst is a member of the quartz family of stones. It is known for its violet to red-purple hue. In fact, the name amethyst is now synonymous with the color. The finest colored and most valuable are known as Siberian amethyst. This refers to the quality of the stone and not the location from which it comes.

In olden days the amethyst was believed to possess the power to protect the wearer and bring good luck. The person born in February is fortunate to be able to claim this as their birthstone.

Bloodstone

Victorians wore and admired the bloodstone. This ancient stone, also known as heliotrope, is actually a dark green chalcedony with flecks of red. The ancients believed the red to be drops of blood; hence the name bloodstone. Many magical powers were ascribed to it including the power to stop bleeding and preserve health. Even though it is one of the birth stones for March, it is seldom used today. When a piece of jewelry contains bloodstone, it is usually old.

Coral

The Victorians had a special love for coral jewelry. Since Roman times it was believed to possess the power to ward off evil and danger. Consequently, it was a favorite christening present. A look at any family portrait of the period will show this popularity. Every baby and young child pictured will be wearing a coral necklace. These were added to as the child grew, as we do the "add a bead" and "add a pearl" necklaces today. Baby rattles with coral stems and coral teething rings were also popular.

Coral was not limited to the young. In 1845, the Prince of the Two Sicilies gave his bride, the Duchess d' Aumale, a beautiful parure of coral jewelry. This started a fashion among women of all ages that continued to the late 1860s.

Coral is the calcareous skeletons of marine animals. It is found in abundance in the Naples' area. The most prized colors are deep red and angel skin pink. Because coral is easy to work, it is used for designs that call for a profusion of flowers and leaves.

Many Victorian brooches and earrings were made using the natural or branch coral. This was a less expensive way to use the stone. Consequently, there are more of these pieces available than the highly carved ones.

Goldstone

Goldstone is quite often encountered in old jewelry. It was used for the ground of some mosaics and as a stone for cuff links or stick pins. Since it is neither gold nor a stone, it can be added to the list of misnomers in the jewelry field. Goldstone is an imitation aventurine made of glass to which copper crystals have been added. It has a gold spangled look that is quite attractive. Once seen it is very easy to recognize.

1861-1889

Thanks to the movie "Gone With the Wind," most people are familiar with the clothing and hair styles of the 1860s and 70s. It made real the beautiful dresses and manicured coiffures worn by the ladies of the period. Who could ever forget the elegant dress that Scarlett made from her green velvet draperies?

The jewelry of the 1860s and 1870s is best described as heavy, massive, and solid. Massiveness was equated with well-made and sturdy. The bigger a piece of furniture or jewelry, surely the better it must be. Colors were also visually heavy. Rich red velvets cov-

(Camille Grace)

1860s-1870s bracelet, jet strung on elastic with petra dura. 1-1/4" wide.

Price: $1,100

ered not only furniture and windows, but also "meladies" as well.
The feeling of opulence was everywhere.

The most outstanding feature of fashion was the hoop skirt,
which was introduced by the Princess Eugunie in Paris. It was not
unusual to use as many as thirty yards of material for one skirt.

Necklaces adorned every neck. "Necklaces or very thick chains
have become indispensable with a low dress, and are also worn
with high chemisettes and Swiss bodices," said the January 1864
Petersen's Magazine. "The large round jet or coral beads are preferred for demi-toilet and married ladies' often wear the thick
gold chains."

These gold chains, combined with other pieces, were the heights
of fashion.

A new way to wear chains became popular during the 1865-70
period. Instead of being worn around the neck in the traditional
way, they were suspended from over the top of the bonnet and
draped over the bust. They were known as Benoiton Chains
because a character in the play "La Famille Benoiton" wore her
necklace in this manner. These long chains were made of gold,
pearls, beads, or most any kind of material.

Jewelry was being worn at all times and in all places. The pieces were enormous, and many were in the costume jewelry category. With loved ones off to war, everyone wanted a keepsake close at hand. The locket came to be considered an important part of the total fashion picture. The ears were no longer considered unattractive. With the hair worn back, earrings became fashionable again. Combs became a very popular adornment for the hair. Not only were they utilitarian, but they could also be an asset to the overall fashion picture.

Archaeological Inspirations

Archaeological findings exerted an important influence on jewelry designs of the 1861-1889 period. The digs began in Egypt after Napoleon's conquest in 1798. The findings spurred interest in archaeological artifacts, and from 1806 to 1814, the French excavated Pompeii.

Pompeii had been completely covered by a volcanic eruption in 79 A.D. The excavations uncovered a city that had been caught unaware. It provided a glimpse of an ancient civilization almost beyond belief to the 19th century. Beautiful houses with frescoed walls, atriums complete with fountains and mosaic floors, jewelry made with ancient unknown gold work methods, and everyday

items made with beautiful skill and craftsmanship—all these discoveries captured the imagination of the people.

Greek artifacts were discovered on the islands of Crete and
Rhodes. In 1848, Sir Austin Henry Layard wrote Minevia and Its
Remains, a book about the fascinating archaeological finds in the
ancient capital of Assyria. The archaeological motifs of the
Egyptians, Etruscans, Greeks, and Romans were popular first in
Europe, and then they spread to England. By the 1850s, the the-
ater was using the discoveries to authenticate scenery for plays.
The ancient motifs were further stimulated in 1862, by the display
of Castillani jewelry at The Great Exposition in London. They
attracted much attention, and the public went home convinced that
the ancient styles were the most suitable for jewelry designs.

By 1864, jewelry designs inspired by the finds had spread to the
United States.

Interest in archaeological findings continued to increase. The
"Treasure of Priam" was discovered by Heinrich Schlieman in
1869. In 1872, the British Museum bought some fine examples of
ancient jewelry from the Castillani Collection. This enabled the
British to study and admire the archaeological styles. The French
could satisfy their curiosity by viewing the Cavalier Company

Collection at the Louvre, and the Italians could study pieces by Augusto Castillani in the Capitoline Museum.

It was not until 1877 that people in the United States could boast of a collection of archeological finds. In the early 1870s, Luigi P. do Cesnola, a U.S. Consul at Larmoce, discovered the treasure vaults of the Temple of Kurium. An account of the discovery was published July 1872, in the Harper's New Monthly Magazine. Within the next five years, more discoveries were made on the island of Cyprus.

Revival jewelry was already in fashion by the time the Metropolitan Museum acquired Cesnola's finds. Ten years later (1887), the ancient style jewelry was still being worn. But instead of being made of gold, the designs were now executed in silver.

Popular Jewels
Jet

At the death of her beloved husband, Queen Victoria went into a period of mourning that was to last the rest of her life. This unexpected death left the English subjects shocked and grieved. All the nation went into mourning.

Jet was an obvious solution to the problem of jewelry suitable during this period. Victoria had first worn jet during the mourning period for William IV, her predecessor, and it was natural for her to wear it while in mourning for her husband.

Jet is a hard, coal-like material, a type of fossilized wood. The finest jet was mined in the town of Whitby, England. The industry started there in the early 19th century, and by 1850, there were fifty jet workshops. Because it lent itself well to carving and kept a sharp edge, it was used extensively. By 1873, there were more than 200 jet shops in this one small town.

Because jet is extremely lightweight, it was the perfect material for making the enormous lockets, necklaces, brooches and bracelets that were so popular in the 1860s and 1870s. The success enjoyed by the jet factories led to many imitations. French jet, which is neither French nor jet (it is black glass), was cheaper to manufacture. It gave the jet industry some competition; but because it is much heavier, it was used mostly in the making of beads and smaller items.

Today it is illegal to mine jet in Whitby. The jet is in seams in the walls of the cliffs on which parts of the town were built. Consequently, the very existence of the town was threatened by those who extracted the velvety substance. The two jet cutters in the town today have to rely on the pieces that wash up on the shore of this coastal town. This circumstance makes the jet of the Victorian era more precious than ever. Good, well-made examples of Whitby jet are sure to appreciate in value.

Diamonds

Diamonds were discovered in South Africa in 1867. A peasant boy, playing near a river, found a pretty stone and took it home. A traveler passing through the village saw the boy's prize and suspected what it might be. He was right; it was a diamond valued at $2,500. Word of the find spread, and the diamond rush began. Within a few years, diamonds were very much in fashion, and this new source was supplying the Paris demand.

Diamonds have always been coveted. The Greeks appreciated the stone's hardness and called it "Adamas," meaning unconquerable. Consequently, it was often worn into battle. The stones were not cut or faceted as they are today, but worn in their natural pointed shape.

These early diamonds were found in streams of India. These alluvial diamonds required no mining because the natural erosion of the earth uncovered them. Until 1871, alluvial diamonds were the only ones available to man.

(Photo courtesy of Christie's East, New York 6-7-99)

Antique diamond and ruby pendant brooch.

Price: $3,450

By chance it was discovered that diamonds were buried deep inside the earth in what is now known as "pipes." These pipes are thought to be part of extinct volcanoes. The rock surrounding the diamond is called "blue ground." It is estimated that an average of two tons of blue ground must be mined to find a single carat of diamonds.

Diamonds are judged by carat weight, cut, clarity, and color. Consequently, three stones each weighing one carat could vary thousands of dollars in price. A carat weighs two hundred (200) milligrams, which is equal to one hundred (100) points. Hence a half carat is fifty points, and twenty five points equal a fourth of a carat.

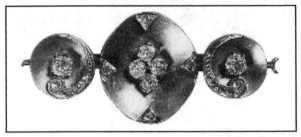

(Camille Grace)

1880s-1890s brooch, 18k gold with 6 diamonds, 1-7/8" x 7/8".

Price: $1,275

The cut of a diamond is very important. It takes an expert to decide the proper cut for each stone. The proper proportions will enhance the stone's brilliance and increase its value. Most diamonds today are brilliant cut and have fifty-eight facets.

The clarity of a diamond is determined by the purity of the stone. Flaws such as dark inclusions and feathers can greatly decrease the value. A diamond is considered to be flawless if there are no visible flaws when the stone is examined using a ten power loupe.

Diamonds come in a variety of colors. Some are colorless, many have a yellowish tinge, and a few have a bluish tinge. When fancy colors such as green, violet, brown, blue, red, and yellow are found in quality stones, they are very expensive and highly collectible. Since diamonds tend to pick up color from surrounding objects, a white background is best when determining a stone's true color.

From the 1880s through the 1920s, the Tiffany mounting was the most popular setting used for a diamond. Someone at Tiffany came up with a six-prong setting that became known as a ''Tiffany'' mounting. It became so fashionable that the average person would ask for it by name, and this infuriated the other jewelers. They did not like the fact that a customer had to use a competitor's name to describe the type of setting they wanted.

Because the diamond has always been highly prized, there have been many imitations. These include rock crystal, zircon, spinel, Strass glass, and diamond doublets. Today's popular imitations are cubic zirconia, YAG, and strontium titanate. Because these synthetic stones look very much like diamonds to the untrained eye, it is wise to buy from a reputable source.

Opals

In 1870, a huge opal field was discovered in Australia. This prompted Queen Victoria to try again to lift the veil of superstition that had befallen the stone. The novel, Anne of Geurstein, written by Scott and published in 1829, was responsible for the opal being considered bad luck. Lady Heromine, a character in the book, always wore an opal in her hair. Its iridescent glow seemed to reflect her every mood. When she came to a tragic end, the opal's mysterious powers were blamed.

The opal was one of Queen Victoria's favorite stones. She gave them as wedding gifts to her daughters and wore them herself. Still, the superstition remained. When Napoleon presented the Empress Eugenie with a parure of opals, she refused them. Even today some people think it is unlucky to wear an opal unless it is a birthstone. Others believe, as the ancients did, that the stone brings good fortune to its wearer.

There are three types of opals: precious, fire, and common. The precious is the kind most people associate with the word "opal." It has a beautiful multicolored iridescence that changes when exposed to different angles of light. The most common color of precious opal is white. There are also black opals, but they are very rare. Opals may also be found in colors of gray, blue, or green.

The fire opal is named for its orange color. It is not opalescent, and it does not have the rainbow-like colors. The best of this type are clear and transparent. Another variety of the fire opal is the Mexican water opal. It is usually light brown or colorless.

The so-called common opals are varied. There are agate opals, wood opals, honey opals, milk opals, and moss opals. Most of these the average person would never identify as an opal.

Because opals contain as much as thirty percent (30%) water, they require very special treatment. If a stone gets too dry, it tends to crack or lose its iridescent quality.

Garnets

Throughout the ages garnets have been worn and admired. Although the word garnet usually conjures up pictures of a wine red stone, they can be found in every color except blue. Actually, garnets are a group of stones that have the same structure, but differ chemically. The garnets most associated with the name are almadine and pyrope. They are also the most common.

The pyrope garnets were popular during the 1860-1889 period. Their deep rich color was a favorite accessory for the massive clothing of the 1860s and 70s. These Bohemian garnets, fashioned in lighter scale mountings, continued to be popular in the 1880s and 90s. They are red or reddish brown in color and tend to be more transparent than the almadine garnet. Most pyrope garnets are mined in Czechoslovakia, Australia, and South Africa.

The almadine garnet tends to have a slightly purplish tint. The most common variety of garnet, it is found in Brazil, India, Australia, Czechoslovakia, and Sri Lanka.

A lesser known variety of garnet is the demantoid. Its rich emerald green color and diamond-like luster make it the most valuable of garnets.

The garnet is the accepted January birthstone. Some believe that it empowers the wearer with truth, constancy, and faith. Ancient man wore it for protection against being struck by lightning. No matter what reason is chosen for wearing garnets, they always seem to be admired and enjoyed.

Mosaics

Mosaics were popular souvenirs for the Victorian traveler. Not only did they picture scenes that had been visited, but they were made using ancient methods made popular by the excavations. Most of these tiny works of art were done in Florence and Rome.

(Christie's East, New York 6-7-99)

Pietra-dura suite, brooch and earrings have floral mosaic centers.

Price: $1,500

The mosaics from Florence are commonly known as "petra dura." These works of art are made by cutting designs out of stones much as malachite and cornelian, and fitting them together in a black background stone. This was done so expertly that a magnifying glass is needed to verify that the design is indeed made from pieces and not painted. Flowers and birds were favorite motifs.

The mosaics from Rome have an entirely different look. They are made of tiny rectangular bricks of glass. As early as the eighteenth century, the Vatican was making pieces to sell to visitors. The motifs are typical Roman ruins and other familiar scenes of Rome.

Many designs were taken from mosaics found in the ruins of Pompeii. Again a magnifying glass is needed to fully appreciate the craftsmanship that went into creating these souvenir pieces.

Mosaics are highly collectible. The price depends on the material used for the mounting and the workmanship of the artist.

Pique and Tortoiseshell

The popular French definition of the word pique is "dotted" or "cracked." This is an apt description of the beautiful work done in tortoiseshell or ivory. The most frequently encountered pique is done in tortoiseshell, which comes from the hawksbill turtle. Even though this is the smallest of marine turtles, it usually weighs between 100 and 200 pounds. Both the mottled upper shell and the lower "yellow belly" are used for ornamental purposes.

Tortoiseshell is one of nature's natural plastics. It can be heated and molded or cut into many forms. For pique the shell is heated and a design is formed (star, cross, etc.). Into this design "dots" or "racks" are drilled. These minute spaces are inlaid with silver or gold rods. The hot tortoise shell emits a glue-like film which, along with the natural contraction caused by the cooling shell, snugly seals the metal.

Many lovely pieces were made using this process. Pique has been in and out of fashion since the 16th century. In the 19th century, it was popular in the 1820s and the 1870s. Today, it is highly collectible. When a piece comes on the market, it is quickly purchased by a collector. Since pique is not being reproduced, it most assuredly will continue to appreciate in value.

1890-1917

The "fin de siecle" (end of the century) mood that enveloped America created a desire for the dramatic in dress and jewelry. Designers endeavored to make the most of this by designing fashions that were exciting and risqué. Dress that accentuated the figure came into fashion. The princess-style dress was revived even though the dressmakers hated the time involved to fit it properly.

Accessories were becoming more daring. Also very much in fashion was the wicked look of the snake. Even with the sinister element, clothing and accessories had a light, delicate look. Bodices were soft and designers wasted no time in creating a profusion of lace pins.

Royalty still exerted an influence on fashion. As late as 1891, Queen Victoria's approval affected a fashion's acceptance. Because Queen Alexandra was attractive, she influenced fashion even before she became queen. High necklines and collars complemented her long, graceful neck. Realizing this, she wore them frequently. For evening, Alexandra favored choker type necklaces or "dog collars." Soon women all over England, Europe, and America were wearing them. Pearls were another of her favorites. This made them even more desirable to the general public.

Chatelaines had gone out of style in the 1860s, but Alexandra revived the fashion by wearing one.

King Edward was an avid sportsman. His horses won the English Derby on three occasions, and this was a constant source of pride. His passion for racing caused the horseshoe to become a decorative motif. Cuff links, fobs, pins, and brooches were just a few of the items that were either made in this shape or carried its motif.

The increase in women's activities led to changes in the wardrobe. Bicycling was a favorite pastime, and clothing materials were chosen with this fact in mind. With the hands busily engaged in keeping the cycle on the road, coin purses were attached to a chain and worn around the neck. Watches and lorgnettes were also worn in this manner. It is interesting to note that chains were rather long, so long that when sitting, the attached articles usually rested in the lap.

The whistle bracelet was another popular bicycling accessory. It was a "protective ornament" for women who took long rides by themselves. The shrill whistle could be heard for a distance of two miles. It was used to summon help in case of an emergency.

By 1910, there were 386,765 women working in offices. The business women or isolated farm wives could keep abreast of the

latest fashions by looking through mail order catalogs. The
Montgomery Ward Company and Sears Roebuck Company had cat-
alogues that could fulfill any woman's dreams. In 1909, Macy's
published a 450 page Spring and Summer Catalogue that was
mailed to thousands of homes.

Women who did not work outside the home were bombarded by
advertisements to sell products to their friends and neighbors.
Most of these companies offered jewelry as an incentive. A choice
of a "heavily plated chain bracelet with lock and key, or a solid
gold shell belcher birthday ring" was given for selling twelve, 12¢
packages of "Imperishable Perfume." Another perfume company
offered "a gold shell ring and a silver chain bracelet with lock
and key warranted for five years" for selling ten packs of
"Rosebud Perfume" at 10¢ each. If a lady wanted a "beautifully
engraved gold filled watch," she had only to sell 100 gold filled
"ladies beauty pins" at 5¢ each. McCall's Magazine encouraged
women to "raise clubs" by selling subscriptions. Each subscription was given a premium. Watches, opera glasses, and rings were
given according to the number sold. For example, a Waltham gold
filled hunting case watch was free with 48 subscriptions, but even
one subscription entitled the seller to a gold filled ring set with a
genuine opal. These offers enabled many women to wear jewelry
who did not have the money to buy it.

Opals had lost their unearned reputation for being unlucky. They were being used in the newest designs.

New stones were being used. "Like canines, every stone has its day," noted the Ladies' Home Journal in 1891, "At present, the Alexandrite appears to be in the ascendancy. This jewel comes from Siberia, and is of a beautiful dark green transparent color, which under any artificial light changes to that of pigeon blood ruby. The Alexandrite is cut like a diamond and is being used by the leading jewelers for lace pins, bracelets and other ornaments."

It was not long before the automobile began to influence fashion. A dustcoat with a belted or buttoned waist was a necessity. Scarves that covered the hat and tied under the chin were essential for women, and goggles were a "must."

The hobble skirt became popular between 1910 and 1915. It was a straight skirt that became narrow at the hem line. Walking was difficult, because only small steps were possible. Women felt very sleek and sophisticated in them, so they endured the inconvenience in order to be fashionable.

The sleek look was also becoming fashionable in jewelry. The effects of the Cubist art movement and the geometric machine designs were seen in the straight lines and rectangular shapes being used in jewelry motifs.

Throughout this time period, brooches continued to have a very delicate, light look. They were frequently decorated with enameling and pearls. Bar pins and circle brooches were also very fashionable. The jewelry from this time has a charm all its own.

Art Nouveau

Art nouveau had an important influence on the jewelry designers of the period. It provided a form of expression for them which seemed to be unlimited. All the forces of nature could be captured in the free-flowing asymmetrical lines.

(Photo courtesy of Sotheby's, New York 10-6-83)

Bracelet, art nouveau, gold and enamel, Arnould, France.

Price: $1,540

Characteristic motifs of art nouveau designs are flowing lines, exotic flowers, asymmetry, plant shapes, sinister looking reptiles, and women with mystical faces and long flowing hair. Materials used were varied. Many of them had little intrinsic value. Horn, copper, tortoise shell, ivory, carved glass, and shells were some of the most popular. Near colorless stones such as opals and moonstones were popular. All types of pearls were used. Semiprecious stones were more favored by the designers than diamonds.

Art nouveau jewelry is extremely popular at the present time. Because of this many pieces are being reproduced. Be sure to buy from a reputable dealer who will guarantee the authenticity of the piece.

Enameling

It is not surprising that the art nouveau jewelry designers made use of ancient enameling techniques. The scope and range of enameling could produce an endless variety of effects. One enamel could be applied on top of another to create the varied, flowing colors so indicative of the period. Colors could be opaque or transparent. The possibilities were unlimited, and enamel's durability made it suitable for everyday use.

Enamel is a glass-like mixture of silica, quartz, borax, feldspar, and lead. Metallic oxides are added to produce the desired color.

These materials are ground into a fine powder and applied to the article being embellished.

Firing at a temperature of about 1700 degrees Fahrenheit is required to melt the mixture and bond it to the article. Care must be taken since the melting point of the article should be higher than that of the enameling mixture. Each color is fired separately. The color with highest melting points is fired first. Those requiring progressively less heat are fired in succession. The methods of enameling are named according to the method used to prepare the article being decorated. The most popular of these are cloisonné, clampleve, basse-taille, and plique-a-jour.

For cloisonné (partition), a design is drawn on the article and traced with fine gold wire. This wire forms partitions into which the enamel mixture is poured. Since powdered enamel tends to shrink when fired, several firings are sometimes necessary for each color. After all colors are fired, the enameling is polished off even with the top of the wire.

Champleve (to cut out) is an enameling technique in which the designs are cut out from the background of the metal. The metal between these cut-out areas becomes an intricate part of the design. The hollowed areas are filled with enamel and fired in suc-

(Camille Grace)

1890-1917 brooch, sterling, cloisonné and bassetaille enameling, blue background and yellow center, white flowers with green stems. 1-1/2" dia.

Price: $225

cession of hardness. After firing is completed, polishing is required to finish the piece.

In Basse-taille (shallow cut) the designs are cut and engraved in the metal. But instead of just filling these depressions, the entire piece is covered with a transparent enamel. Many beautiful designs can be achieved using this method because the color varies with the depth of the design.

Plique-a-jour is an enameling method that was used to full advantage by the Art Nouveau designers. It is an especially delicate method in that the enameling has no backing—only sides. To achieve this feat the enameling mixture is used in a molasses type form. Sometimes a thin metal or mica backing is used and removed after firing. Cellini used a layer of clay to back his pieces while firing. Whatever material is used, the results are quite lovely. The enameling has the effect of stained glass or gem stones. These translucent enamels are seen at fullest advantage when held to the light.

Taille d' epergne, an ancient form of enameling, was popular in the mid-19th century. After a design was deeply engraved or cut into a metal, it was filled with powdered enamel. The piece was then fired and polished. Although any color could be used in taille d' epergne, the Victorians favored black or blue.

Niello is considered a form of enameling even though it is not a "true enamel." A mixture of sulphur, lead, copper, or silver is used instead of the powdered glass enamel. After the design is engraved into the metal, the niello mixture is applied. The piece is fired and then polished to remove the niello from all but the incised portion of the design. All niello is black; it is easy to distinguish from black enameling because it lacks sheen. Instead it has a metallic-like luster. Good examples of niello are found in the Siamese jewelry of the 1950s.

The metals used in enameling were as varied as the methods. For champleve and cloisonné, copper and bronze were often used. Gold and silver provided an excellent base for all enameling techniques. Although the metal used is of prime consideration when determining value, the execution of design and the clarity of colors are of the utmost importance. A piece well done in copper using several enameling techniques can sometimes be more valuable than one in gold using one color and technique.

Enameled jewelry is highly collectible. People who are aware of the time, effort, and talent that combine to create these tiny works of art appreciate and treasure them. Although little enameling is being done today in the United States, many lovely pins made in the early 1900s are still available at moderate prices. If you are interested in collecting enamels of this period, now is the time to buy.

Popular Jewels
Amber

Amber beads were popular during the 1890-1917 period and continued to be through the 1920s. According to Marilyn Roos, an amber dealer, it was a different form from what we see today. The inclusions and air bubbles were considered unattractive so the amber was melted to remove them before forming the beads. Sometimes the beads even had a celluloid core.

Amber is a fossilized tree resin. Over 50 million years ago trees taller than the Redwoods of today grew along the shores of the Baltic Sea. The Glacier Age caused them to be swept into the sea. There they solidified under ice and pressure. Scientists believe that the trees probably had a fungus of some type because the resin was so loose it even surrounded dewdrops. Amber often has insects, petals of flowers, seeds and bark locked inside. These add to the value of the gem.

One of the oldest gems known to man, amber has been revered through the ages. The Greeks called it "lectron," which is the root word for electricity. Ancient man wore it for protection against disease. As recently as the 1920s, doctors melted amber and mixed it with honey to make a remedy for throat ailments. People even believed that wearing an amber necklace would cure a goiter.

Although light yellow (honey colored) is the color most associated with the name, it can also be brown or red (cherry amber). Color varies according to the depth of water into which the tree fell. Amber can be translucent, opaque, or a mixture of both.

The "feel" of amber is very distinct. The best way to become acquainted with it is to actually handle a piece. It is so lightweight that long beautiful strands can be worn with ease.

(W. Baldwin)

1900-1920 pressed cut amber beads, 18" l, 5/8" dia.

Price: $225

Amber is not only a lovely accessory, but it can be a good investment. It can be worn with a feeling of safety no longer associated with diamonds. When buying amber, as with any fine gem, always deal with a reputable source. To ensure the beautiful luster of amber take care to protect it from hairspray and perfume. A bath in warm water and gentle detergent will keep it sparkling clean.

Celluloid, glass, and plastic have all been used to imitate amber.

Celluloid

A marvelous new material made it possible for people of modest means to have combs, bracelets, necklaces, and brooches that looked much more expensive than they actually were. Celluloid, the trade name given this material by its inventor John Wesley Hyatt in 1869, was widely used in the 1890-1917 period. Celluloid is an artificial plastic made from pyroxylin and camphor. Combs that looked like tortoise, bracelets and necklaces that could pass for ivory, and pins of every description were made from it.

Because celluloid was highly flammable, its use in jewelry manufacturing was discontinued when safer plastics became available. Since celluloid jewelry was made for a limited time, it stands to reason that these pieces will become more collectible and increase in value. At the present time, however, good bargains can still be found.

Pearls

Pearls were a favorite of Queen Alexandra, and women throughout the ages have prized them. A visit to most any art museum will evidence this fact with portrait after portrait of women wearing pearls with pride. They were used for necklaces, bracelets, earrings, and rings and were sometimes even sewn onto dresses for decoration.

Pearls are formed in mollusks. They begin when a tiny irritant enters the oyster. It reacts by secreting a substance called nacre to surround the intruder. The gradual building up of this substance creates the pearl.

The Oriental pearl is the most desirable of pearls. It does not necessarily come from the Orient but derives its name from the luster associated with pearls from that region. They are always formed by nature in sea water. The ones of best quality are found in the Persian Gulf.

Fresh water pearls are found in rivers all over the world. Between 1896 and 1899 pearls valued at over a half million dollars were found in the White River in Arkansas. Pearls are also found in edible clams and oysters, but these usually lack the luster of the more valuable ones.

Pearls come in many shapes and sizes. When a pearl becomes attached to the wall of a shell and forms a flat back, it is called a button pearl. Blister pearls are another malformation, and the name provides an apt description. Blister pearls and button pearls are quite lovely when set in earrings, brooches, and rings. Another malformed pearl is known as the Baroque pearl. It was perfect for the Art Nouveau jewelry designs and made the ideal appendage for the lavalieres that were so popular during this same time period.

The round pearl is the most desirable and hence the most valuable. It is ideally suited for the popular "string of pearls." Small round pearls that weigh less than a grain are called seed pearls.

Pearls come in a variety of colors: pink, cream, white gold, orange, and black. The color depends on the type of mollusk and the water in which it is found. Black pearls, which are really grey, are the most valuable.

Shapes, colors, and weights are all factors in determining the value of a pearl. Blemishes or any irregularities diminish the value. A perfect pearl is always allowed one blemish, because it can be drilled in that spot. It takes many years to collect a perfectly matched string of pearls. Consequently, they can be most expensive. Prior to the perfecting of cultured pearls, they were more costly than diamonds.

Cultured pearls are real pearls that man has helped nature develop. As early as 1883, Mr. K. Mikimoto was able to produce semispherical ones. It took many more years of experiments and the help of several men to perfect the round cultured pearl.

To produce a cultured pearl an irritant is placed inside the oyster. The natural reaction occurs, and the pearl is formed, but this takes many years. To hasten the process a round Mother of Pearl bead is now used as an irritant. Even with this head start, it takes from three to seven years to produce a cultured pearl.

There are many types of imitation pearls. The most common is a glass ball covered with essence d'orient, a liquid made from fish scales. Plastic is also used to imitate pearls, but it does such a poor job that it usually fools no one.

There are international laws and agreements concerning various aspects of the pearl industry. It is against the law to sell an imitation pearl as a natural pearl. Even cultured pearls must be so designated.

There is no other gem quite like a pearl. To keep this rare beauty, special attention is required. Because elements in the air cause deterioration, the average life span is only 100 to 150 years. That is not to say that in that length of time they will turn to dust; only that they will no longer have their inner sheen. To lengthen the life span, always take care not to expose them to perfume or hair spray. Never clean them with a commercial jewelry cleanser unless it specifies "safe for pearls." A gentle wiping with a soft cloth after wearing will prolong the luster and insure another generation the joy of wearing them.

Moonstones

The moonstone was a popular stone in the 1890-1917 period. It filled the designer's need for a stone with little color, and its moonish glow added a mystical touch to any piece it adorned.

(Camille Grace)

1890-1910 brooch, gold filled with 4 moonstones, 1-1/2" x 1-1/4".

Price: $125

The moonstone is a type of translucent feldspar. It was so named because of the blue white sheen that seems to glow from within. Some moonstones are colorless; others have a pearly look. They are even found as moonstone cat's eye.

Since the stone is a symbol of the moon, it had romantic associations. Like the moon it symbolized love, romance, and passion. Many felt that it had powers of persuasion in these areas.

Consequently, it was a favorite stone to give a sweetheart. The moonstone is one of the June birthstones, but it is seldom used today.

Peridot

King Edward VII considered the peridot his good luck stone. His preference made it popular throughout his reign. Because of its olive green color, the mineralogical name for peridot is olivine, although it is not uncommon to find yellow-green or even brownish peridots.

Peridots have been mined for over 3,500 years on the small island of St. John in the Red Sea. Other mines are located in Burma, Bohemia, Norway, Australia, Brazil, and South Africa. In the United States, peridots are found in Arizona, New Mexico, and Hawaii.

Because peridots are fairly soft and tend to be brittle, they are not too popular with today's jewelry designers. But a table or emerald cut stone mounted in yellow gold is quite beautiful. The magical properties ascribed to the peridot include the powers to overcome timidness.

(Photo courtesy Wm. Doyle Galleries, New York 12-7-89)

Art nouveau peridot, freshwater pearl, and gold pendant necklace. 14K yellow gold with kite and pear-shaped peridots and freshwater pearls.

Price: $2,800

1920-1930

The fashions of the twenties were as erratic as the times.
Everything was fast-paced and changing, and this was reflected by
the fluctuating styles. Hemlines yo-yoed up and down, waistlines
disappeared and then reappeared at the hip line, hairstyles went
from long to short and then back to shoulder length—all this in
ten short years!

Jewelry was used to compliment the dress and soften the effect
that short hair had on the features. Dangling earrings, long ropes
of beads, and a multitude of bracelets all added to the razzle-daz-
zle of the outfit. Everything that glittered or dangled captured the
imagination. Crystal and rhinestones became fashionable.

There were necklaces to adorn any neckline. Beads combining
crystal and jet were dramatic and therefore, fashionable. An illustrated jewelry catalogue for 1923 lists "fine faceted novelty beads"
in a choice of imitation jet, blue sapphire and crystal rondel, imitation jet with crystal rondel, transparent ruby, and aquamarine
with crystals. The beads were 34 inches long, and the tassels
added another four inches. Prices ranged from $1.50 to $3.
Today they would cost from $68 to $125.

Amber beads were popular. A twenty-inch necklace of genuine amber in a "clear light color" was priced at only $9, but a twenty-four inch Bakelite bead necklace in the "old amber color" was the same price. Evidently the new Bakelite was highly desirable.

There was an infinite variety of jewelry on the market.

By 1927, women were beginning to tire of the masculine look. When Lavin unveiled her new designs for feminine dresses made of soft materials, they were a welcome change. Greta Garbo also had a softening influence. Her starring role in "The Woman of Affairs" caused women to wear slouch hats and to let their hair grow longer.

Designers began to have an impact on clothing for the average woman. Madeline Veornet, Leanne Lavin, and Coco Chanel were designers whose creations were known and admired by American women. Reproductions of Chanel's jewelry collection adorned her creations. Designers were branching out into all fields of personal adornment.

Designers created special jewelry for "bathing costumes." There were "painted and waterproofed wooden balls for necklaces, bracelets and earrings!" The article stated, "some people will wear them and no doubt look excessively chic."

It took awhile for this new Paris trend to combine jewelry and clothing designs to filter down to the average woman. However, by 1936, the concept was so highly accepted that the Sears, Roebuck

(Photo courtesy of Sotheby's London 4-14-83)

1925 earrings, jade, onyx, and rose-cut diamonds, £825.

Price: $1,470

Catalogue featured dresses that came complete with accessories. A "hand smocked dress with matching bracelet and clips" was advertised as the "fashion of the hour," and cost a mere $3.98. The bracelet was described as a "lovely carved bracelet." The clips were of the same color and material. Another "4 star jubilee feature" was a "satin back crepe dress of cleanese with handmade scroll trim." A "stunning pin, bracelet and buckle" came with it. The advertisement stated they were "beautifully carved." They were all most likely made of Bakelite.

Pearls were by far the most popular necklace in the 1920s. The perfecting of the cultured pearl caused the price of oriental pearls to decline, but not enough to enable the average working girl to buy them. For her there were the "reproduction" or "indestructible" pearls. Pearls were always considered to be in good taste. An essential accessory for a woman's wardrobe, they were worn with both day and evening dresses.

Many new rhinestone ornaments were pictured in the catalog. A rhinestone flexible bracelet about 5/8" x 6-1/2" with a white metal back was $1. An oval cameo pin about 1-1/2" x 1-3/4" with three rhinestones on each side was $.79. Belt buckles and shoe ornaments in the modern style were the most pictured rhinestone ornaments.

Synthetic stones were highly advertised. The manmade sapphires and rubies were set in 10, 14, and 18 karat filigree mountings. Let this be a warning, a stone can be in a lovely 18K gold mounting obviously made in the twenties and still be synthetic. They were advertised to have "all the brilliance, all the hardness of genuine mined stones—the same rich color and the same sparkling luster." Prices ranged from $4.98 to $13.75.

Birthstones were very popular. Most were placed in white gold filigree rings, but they were also available in lavalieres and pins. A filigree "birth month bar pin" in 10K white gold with a "small round stone" was priced at $1.98. Today it would bring 20 to 50 times that. Almost all the birth month jewelry was in white gold because it resembled platinum, which was so popular at the time.

The dramatic look of onyx in a white gold mounting made it a favorite for rings. They were available in 14K gold and usually included a diamond set in the onyx.

Styles in wedding rings were changing. The gold wedding band had been replaced by one of platinum engraved with orange blossom flowers. For the first time, matching wedding and engagement rings were available. By 1928, jewelry companies were combining the wedding ring and the engagement ring into a bridal set.

Because the economy was depressed and money was tight, the important part jewelry could play in revitalizing an old outfit was stressed. Even though the 1931-32 Montgomery Ward catalogue featured fewer dresses and lower prices than in 1928-29, their jewelry section had been expanded. A new dress might cost two or three dollars, but an old one could be dressed up with a new 56" length of "unbreakable imitation pearls" for only 29 cents.

The emphasis was on costume jewelry. Evidently Montgomery Ward had a high concept of costume jewelry. Their 1931-32 catalogue advertised that "the smartest and most attractive of new costume jewelry creations" was made of genuine rock crystals combined with "sparkling genuine diamond centers."

For those who could not afford diamonds, the new smart silver jewelry with real "stones" provided a flashy look. The "real stones" were "genuine marcasites," and their glitter provided the glamorous look dictated by Hollywood designers. The jewelry had a slightly heavier look than that of the previous decade. The long dangling rectangular earrings and necklaces were definitely in the style now referred to as Art Deco. A necklace on a 15" chain with ear drops and bracelet to match, made of sterling silver and set with marcasites, was priced at $4.48.

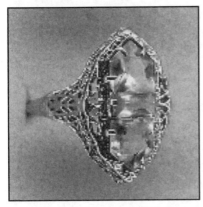

(Jewelry Box Antiques)

Circa 1920s-1930s ring, 14K white gold set with three aquas.

Price: $695

Marcasites were also used to surround other stones. Genuine Chrysoprase (jade green), genuine onyx (black), and genuine cornelians (burnt orange) were set in sterling silver and "studded with sparkling real marcasites." These were very popular, and a good many examples are still in existence today. A complete set consisting of a necklace, ear drops, bracelet, and gold ring sold for $7.98. Today, the same set would cost in excess of $450.

If a piece of jewelry was done in the new modern style, this fact was always brought to the attention of prospective buyers. They were available in a choice of Rose Quartz, Amethyst Quartz, and

Jade. The pendants sold for $2.48, and the bracelets were $5.98. Throughout the decade, the term modernistic was used to describe the styles now referred to as Art Deco.

Rhinestones continued to be popular throughout this time period. The 1935-36 Sears, Roebuck Catalogue called them the "most necessary, useful costume accessories for the fall and winter season."

Clips were a very versatile accessory. They could be worn on the dress, hat, or hand bag. Consequently, they became a necessity for the well-groomed woman.

Costume jewelry designs are indeed an indicator of what has captured the minds, hearts, and imagination of the people. In the 1920s, the discovery of King Tut's tomb made it fashionable to wear jewelry bearing his likeness. Many Egyptian motifs were incorporated into Art Deco designs. When Franklin D. Roosevelt became president of the United States, he and his family became the favorite subject for newspaper and magazine articles. Even his Scotch Terrier, "Fala," was photographed. By 1935 women were wearing pins in the shape of a Scottie.

Women were intrigued by things from the Orient. Lounging pajamas with an oriental look were worn for entertaining at home.

Jewelry made in China, and stones imported from the Orient became very fashionable.

The economy had an effect on ring designs. Smaller diamonds were placed in illusion settings to give them a larger look. In the twenties, wedding bands were often encircled with diamonds, but in the thirties the diamonds were only set across the top.

Art Deco

There is much discussion and confusion concerning art deco. Generally it is a term applied to a decorative style of the twenties and thirties. But the term was never used during the time in which the style was popular, thus adding to the confusion.

Perhaps the confusion as to what constitutes art deco can be attributed to the many varied influences that combined to produce the style. The Russian Ballet, Cubism, King Tut, the Bauhaus and the Paris Exposition all contributed to the collage that became known as art deco.

As in most period styles, the seeds of the style were sewn in the previous decade. When Dieghilev's Russian Ballet Company made its 1910 debut performance in Paris, it won the hearts and imagination of all Europe. The bold colors in the scenery and costumes designed by Leon Balst signaled a liberation of color for the "pastel" world. By the twenties, his bright emerald greens, vivid reds, and shimmering blues (along with his stenciled patterns and luxurious fabrics) had become incorporated into all fields of fashion and design.

Through the set designs of the Ballet Russes, many people were exposed for the first time to "modern art." Cubism and its offspring, orphism, neoplastecism, fauvism, and futurism provided the geometric lines and abstract designs for art deco style. The new art expressed a psychology of design for people living in a modern world filled with action and speed.

When Howard Carter discovered the opening to a tomb in Egypt on November 26, 1922, little did he realize the impact it would have on modern fashion. When the discovery was officially announced three days later, it was publicized throughout the world. Never had there been such a discovery! Newspapers were filled with descriptions of the many ancient objects made of gold. The riches of the young king were almost beyond belief.

By the time the burial chamber was opened in February 1923, King Tut and his world had already influenced fashion and design. Women were wearing Tut hats and jewelry bearing his likeness. Stones used in King Tut's jewelry, lapis lazuli, cornelian, and chalcedony became popular. Egyptian motifs such as the falcon, vulture, and vulture, and scarab were seen on everything from belt buckles to pendants. At first these unusual materials and designs were used in copies of the ancient articles, but it was not long before they were assimilated into the art deco style.

(Photo courtesy of Sotheby's, New York 12-7-83)

1930s brooch, art deco, platinum set with rubies, sapphires, emeralds, and black onyx. Oriental-style bird on flowering branch, branches highlighted with black enamel.

Price: $9,350

Art deco takes its name from the International Exposition des Arts Decoratifs, which was held in Paris in 1925. Nations from all over the world were invited to participate with the stipulation that they submit only those exhibitions executed in new modern designs. Any designs based on styles of the past or that incorporated those styles were strictly forbidden.

The exposition became the focal point for the new modernistic designs. They gained world acknowledgment. In the years that followed, the style became more defined.

Knowledge of all these varied influences on the art deco style shatters the veil of confusion and makes it easy to identify. Today, almost anything done in the art deco style is very collectible. Because of this demand, jewelry can be quite expensive. That is not to say that bargains cannot be found. They can, especially in costume jewelry.

Popular Jewels
Emerald

Emeralds have been popular since before the time of Cleopatra, but their rich green color made them especially desirable for the jewelry of the 1920s and 30s. The gem is at its best when used in the rectangular or square step cut that is also known as the emerald cut. It was well suited to the geometrical shape of Art Deco jewelry designs.

The emerald is part of the beryl group of colored stones. Prized for its medium light to medium dark green color, in larger sizes it is sometimes more expensive than a diamond of the same size. All genuine emeralds have inclusions referred to by gemologists as a "jardin." Often stones of the most desirable color also contain the most inclusions. These are more desirable than a pale stone with little "jardin."

The most beautiful emeralds come from Colombia. They are so esteemed that the finest emeralds from any location are known as Colombian emeralds. Other deposits are mined in Brazil, Rhodesia, Australia, South Africa, and India. In the United States, emeralds are found in North Carolina, Maine, and Connecticut.

Man has always been fascinated by the emerald. In ancient times it was believed that gazing at an emerald would restore eyesight. Many wore it because they believed it would heighten intelligence and help them to save money. Today, it is a favorite birthstone for people born in May, hopefully bringing them success and love.

Ruby

Rubies, both genuine and synthetic, were widely used in the 1920s and 1930s. Their bold red color helped create the dramatic effect that was so much in demand. The ruby is part of the corundum group of colored stones. To be termed a ruby, it must have a transparent red or purplish red hue. The lighter red stones are known as pink sapphires. "Pigeon's blood" red is the most desirable color and is identifiable by a slight blue cast in the pure red stone. These and other rubies are known as Burmese, regardless of where they were mined. Ruby deposits are found in Burma, Thailand, Ceylon, and Africa. In the United States, they are mined in Montana and North Carolina.

Biblical references attest to the high value placed on the ruby throughout the ages. A large ruby is sometimes more valuable than a diamond of comparable size. The ruby's hardness makes it a practical stone with a multitude of uses.

Fortunate is the person born in July, because the ruby is the birthstone for that month. Wisdom, wealth, and health are but a few of the many blessings that are believed to belong to the wearer of this lovely gem.

Marcasites

In the 1920s and 1930s, the average woman could add glitter and glamour to her life by wearing marcasites. Their reflective sparkles adorned pins, earrings, necklaces, bracelets, clips, and buckles.

(Camille Grace)

1930s brooch, silver with marcasites and aquamarine colored stone, 2" x 1".

Price: $245

The "stone" known as marcasite is actually pyrite. There is a mineral named marcasite, and, although it is similar in appearance, it is not suitable for jewelry. This case of mistaken identity is now commonly accepted. The iron sulfite, pyrite is cut into small pointed or rounded facets to create marcasites. Since their luster is metallic, their brilliance comes from light reflecting off the facets.

Marcasites were fashionable substitutes for diamonds as early as the 1700s. They were always mounted in silver as were the diamonds of that period. In the mid 1800s, they once again came into favor. The fashion waned until the glittering mood of the twenties revived it again.

Within the last year, marcasite jewelry has risen sharply in price. Better marcasites are set in and not just glued. Of course, the metal the "stones" are in and the design of the piece are also factors that greatly influence price. There are many new marcasite pieces on the market. Buying from a reputable dealer who will guarantee, in writing, the age of the piece is the best assurance for the new collector.

Ivory

Ivory, one of the oldest materials used for ornamental purposes, has been recognized throughout the history of civilization for its beauty and value. In the 1920s a resurgence of interest in African carvings brought with it a renewed interest in ivory.

As most people know, ivory is the tusk of the African elephant. But many do not realize that the tusks of the hippopotamus and walrus are also classified as ivory. Elephant ivory is distinguishable by its "cross hatched" or "engine turned" look when viewed under magnification. The other ivories have wavy grain lines. Once the ivory has been carved into bracelets, necklaces, and earrings, it is very hard to distinguish its origin.

The so-called vegetable ivories, the coroze nut from South America and the doum-palm nut from Central Africa, are often mistaken for genuine ivory. They are used to make beads and smaller items.

Ivory tends to yellow with age, but according to expert dealer Edward J. Tripp, this only adds to its value. It can be bleached, but this takes away value and beauty. He also cautions against subjecting ivory to extreme changes in temperature that could cause cracking or splitting. Since ivory is porous and is easy to stain, care should be taken to keep it away from anything that might discolor it.

Bakelite

Jewelry made of bakelite was popular during the 1920s and 1930s. This new plastic was invented in 1909 by Leo Hendrick

Baekeland (1863-1944). He came up with the resin while trying to develop a new type of varnish.

(Jewelry Box Antiques)

1930s clip, gold over brass leaves and clip with Bakelite grapes, 2" x 2".

Price: $45

Bakelite is a phenolic plastic and can be molded or cast. Jewelry items are molded. The name Bakelite is a trade name for the Bakelite Corporation. The same mixture is known as Durez when made by the Durez Company and other names when manufactured by other companies.

1932-1940s

The Retro Modern Style

The 1940-1950s time period had a variety of jewelry styles. Just as the 1890-1910 period had Arts and Crafts, Art Nouveau, and Edwardian all at the same time, the 1940-1950s had designs inspired by romantic Victorian pieces, and a new style that is now referred to as Retro Modern.

Since styles do tend to overlap, it is interesting to see jewelry of white gold filigree and the Victorian romantic style pictured along the side of Retro Modern pieces. As early as 1932, a subtle change of style was showing up in jewelry catalogs. By the late 1930s, the style now known as Retro Modern was very much in evidence. The new designs made use of stylized motifs and shiny finishes on pink, green, yellow, and rose gold. The designs were much flatter looking than the preceeding styles; they had a two-dimensional look.

Retro Modern is not a period style. It was not reflected in architectural styles or in the decorative arts other than jewelry. But it is a definite, recognizable style for jewelry design from the late 1930s throughout the 1940s. It is not as sleek and streamlined as

Art Deco. Many of the pieces have polished curves. The cone definitely replaced the geometric cube of Art Deco.

Rubies were often set in the rose gold that was so popular. Many pieces had several colors of gold incorporated into the design. Ladies' bracelet watches became very popular. The lids covering the dials were often encrusted with rubies and diamonds. Many watch dials were also finished in a rose or red gold.

One reason that yellow gold became popular again in the 1940s was because the government restricted the use of platinum, which was needed in munitions plants. The War Production Board had limited the use of silver, consequently "gold filled" was the available material for costume jewelry.

After Dior came out with the "New Look" in 1947, jewelry took on much larger proportions.

Retro Modern styled jewelry has become very much in demand in the last few years. As the demand increases so will the prices.

1940-1950

World War II had far reaching effects on the fashion industry. With France engaged in the war, American designers had to rely on their own expertise to capture the American woman's fancy. The styles were not as dramatic or "seductively named" as the ones originating in Paris, but the American designers presented "good wearable, saleable clothing. The chief trends of this ingenuity show in slender skirts with slits or 'back drops' which fall much lower behind than in front; 'front peplums' give fullness to tight skirts; the 'deep armhole cut' and 'soft shoulder'."

(Jewelry Box Antiques)

1940s child's bracelet, yellow gold filled with pink and green gold, expansion type with locket, locket 3/4"; bracelet 1/2" w.

Price: $125

The United States' declaration of war brought many changes in the American way of life. A War Production Board was formed to regulate production of goods and ensure that war needs would be met. Fashions were designed to use as little material as possible. At the same time, no dramatic changes were made so that last season's clothes would still be fashionable.

There were shortages in everything from cotton dresses to hosiery. Women used leg make-up instead of nylons. When stores were fortunate enough to receive shipments, there were always more customers than stockings.

The jewelry industry was also experiencing its share of shortages. The September 5, 1942 Business Week reported: "Sales are at high level, but present bread-and-butter stock can't be replenished. The most serious shortage is metal. The supply of silver plate and of inexpensive jewelry made from base metals is now strictly limited to inventories that manufacturers and retailers have on hand. There will be no more when these are exhausted. Sterling silver has been widely used to replace the baser and scarcer metals." Consequently, if a piece of jewelry is marked 1/20 12K on Sterling or G. F. on S. S., it was probably made during these years. The War Production Board also limited use of imported silver.

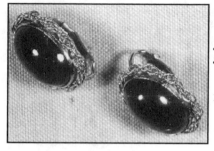

(W. Baldwin)

1940s earrings, 14K gold with cabochon garnets, clips 3/4" x 7/8".

Price: $495

In spite of these limitations, jewelry sales continued to soar. Business Week, April 17, 1943, explained it this way: "With the workers unable to spend their bulging bankrolls on automobiles, refrigerators or silk shirts, jewelry sales (including silver, watches, and clocks) last year hit an all time high of $790,000,000 showing a 30% increase over 1941 and considerable gain over the biggest previous year."

In September 1944, order L-45 was rescinded, eliminating these restrictions on gold and platinum. The jewelers were jubilant. The federal excise tax on jewelry had been raised from 10% to 20% in April, and it was hoped that the easing of restrictions might stimulate sales.

After the war, women had money to spend—and spend it they did. Costume jewelry became big business. Many designers switched to the costume jewelry industry during the Depression. Their expertise caused the industry to blossom.

(Jewelry Box Antiques)

Circa 1940s ring, 14K pink, yellow and green gold, set with blue zircon.

Price: $475

In 1946, Providence, Rhode Island, was the costume jewelry capital of the United States. Coro Incorporated, with 2,000 employees and sales of $16,000,000, was headquartered here. This undisputed leader in the industry was founded in 1902 as Cohn and Rosenberger. Later, the company was renamed using the first two letters of each name. Coro's high priced line was sold under the name of Corocraft.

(Jewelry Box Antiques)

1932-1945 bracelet, 10K pink and green gold set with cultured pearls, approx. 1/2" w.

Price: $430

Costume jewelry was produced in all price ranges. Trifari, Drussman & Fishel was the style leader. Their jewelry was priced from $10 and up. R.M. Jordan was a leader in the medium priced jewelry: $1 to $20. Monet was known for its tailored jewelry, and Forstner was the leading producer of the popular snake chains.

By 1947, Western Wear started to make the news. Dior created the biggest fashion sensation of the decade when he presented his "New Look" in 1947. Women had grown tired of the narrow skirts and squared shoulders of the war years. Dior offered a new feminine look with long (12 inches off the floor) full skirts, small waist, and rounded soft shoulders.

Nylon was also a welcomed addition to the wardrobe. It had been on the market in the form of stockings, parachutes, and toothbrushes for years, but new developments in weaves and dyes made it the perfect "wash and wear" fabric.

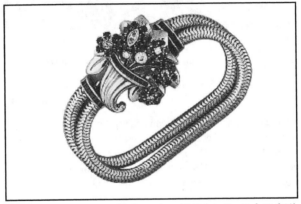

(Photo courtesy of Sotheby's, New York 10-6-83)

1945 bracelet, 14K yellow gold with pink gold cornucopia with yellow gold leaves, centrally set with one marquise-shaped diamond, one old mine yellow diamond, four small round diamonds, one round yellow diamond and numerous round and calibre-cut sapphires and rubies, missing watch movement

Price: $1,430

The jewelry used to compliment this new style was huge. It took on larger proportions, just as it did in the 1860s when skirts were widened. Massive rings were so in style that Life Magazine featured a full page on them in April 1952.

Huge earrings were also popular. Look Magazine, May 31, 1955, included an article on "Whopper Earrings." The newest styles were "bigger than silver dollars." Look jokingly called them "ear muffs—summer style." Large pearl buttons, "gold saucers," and bouquets of flowers were a few of the many motifs.

(Jewelry Box Antiques)

Retro Modern pin, gold filled with faux pearls, citrine paste and foil "stones," worn in the movie "Mr. & Mrs. Bridge," 3 x 4" overall.

Price: $145

Antique Jewelry

Jewelry 100 Years Old and Older

Bar Pins

Victorian Gold Bar Pin

Bar pin, citrine, garnet & peridot, Victorian Renaissance Revival style, five collet-set pear-shaped drops of citrine, garnet & peridot, each suspended from a box-set rose-cut diamond w/a pearl accent on either end, 18k yellow gold mount, signed "Giuliano," w/original box (repair to back) **$2,185**

Bar pin, diamond & platinum, set w/19 old European-cut diamonds, engraved gallery.. **$1,725**

Bar pin, diamond, set w/a row of ten old mine-cut diamonds, the center suspending a knife-edge bar w/old mine-cut diamond terminal, French assay mark, Edwardian **$1,150**

Bar pin, gold (15k yellow), navette-shaped, centered w/an octagonal-cut peridot, flanked on either side by foliate devices set w/half-pearls & two rubies, hallmarked "G," Victorian, w/fitted box (ILLUS.) **$1,035**

*Antique
Natural Pearl
Bee Pin*

*Victorian
Bar Pin*

Bar pin, pearl, a row of natural pearls w/model of a bee at the center w/a natural pearl & faceted ruby body, ruby eyes & rose-cut diamond-set wings, the bee in silver-topped 18k yellow gold on an 18k yellow gold pin w/safety mechanism, ca. 1890 (ILLUS.) **$1,725**

Bar pin, pearl & citrine, 14k yellow gold mount centered by a marquise citrine w/oval citrine terminals outlined by freshwater pearls, two missing, Victorian (ILLUS.) **$316**

Bracelets

*Etruscan
Gold Bangle*

*Art Nouveau Style
Bangle Bracelet*

Bracelet, bangle-type, 18k gold, Victorian Etruscan Revival style, hinged knot design w/ball terminals, overall bead & wiretwist decoration (ILLUS.) **$2,415**
Bracelet, bangle-type, art nouveau style pierced & chased foliate design in 14k yellow gold, 7 1/2" (ILLUS.) **$1,035**

*Citrine, Diamond &
Enamel Bracelet*

Bangle Bracelet

Bracelet, bangle-type, citrine, diamond & enamel, hinged design centering a large, faceted, heart-shaped citrine surrounded by old mine- & rose-cut diamonds w/two triangular-shaped citrines on the sides, each decorated w/rose-cut diamonds set in trefoil designs, mounted in 14k yellow gold w/royal blue enameled background, 6 1/2" (ILLUS.) **$3,450**

Bracelet, bangle-type, diamond, enamel, platinum & gold, the tested 14k yellow gold mount set on the top portion w/a filigree platinum chase-work floral design set w/93 round old European- and rose-cut diamonds weighing about 1.175 carats within a cobalt blue guilloché enamel field (ILLUS.) **$2,760**

Diamond & Sapphire Bangle Bracelet

Bracelet, bangle-type, diamond, sapphire & enamel, centered by a collet-set diamond flanked by eight diamonds w/sapphire terminals, further set w/old European-cut diamonds framed w/blue enamel, hinged platinum-topped 14k yellow gold mount, solder evident. ca. 1966 (ILLUS.) **$3,220**

Bracelet, bangle-type, gold (18k), Archaeological Revival style, hinged design w/three curved sections decorated w/Greek letters, alternating w/carved carnelian scarabs, w/wiretwist accents, monogram for Castellani, ca. 1875 .... **$8,625**

*Victorian
Pietra Dura
Bracelet*

Bracelet, bangle-type, gold & pietra dura, the hinged 10k rose gold mount surmounted by an oval hardstone plaque inlaid w/a bouquet of flowers flanked by gold leaves, Victorian (ILLUS.) **$575**

Bracelet, bangle-type, hallmarked sterling, rose quartz stone set in silver bezel w/silver floral design in center of stone, flexible graduated closure, ca. 1880, 1 3/4" w.................... **$200-$235**

Bracelet, bangle-type, sapphire & diamond, Etruscan Revival style, bead-set w/three sapphires & two round diamonds, accented w/rosettes & beads on edge, 18k yellow gold, interior engraved "Lung-Tsing, 1889," Victorian, in original box **$3,680**

Diamond & Gold Toggle Bracelet

Gold Bracelet w/Emeralds & Diamonds

Bracelet, charm, gold-filled fancy link chain, swiveling oval agate charm, ca. 1890-1910 .... **$250-$300**

Bracelet, diamond & gold, a horseshoe & toggle design bead-set w/old European-cut diamonds, silver-topped gold mount w/open curved link chain, 15k gold, English hallmarks, Victorian (ILLUS.) **$1,725**

Bracelet, emerald, diamond & gold, articulated barrel-shaped links w/the 16 center link section set w/an emerald flanked by rose-cut diamonds, ca. 1880, Victorian, w/original box (ILLUS.) **$2,875**

Gold & Enamel Hand Bracelet

Victorian Multicolored Gold Bracelet

Bracelet, enamel & 18k yellow gold, flexible gold & white enamel links w/foliate repoussé spacers completed by a hand clasping a basket of blue enamel flowers, surmounted by pink stones, French assay mark, chips & repair to enamel, Victorian (ILLUS.) **$2,300**

Bracelet, gold (14k multicolored), designed w/13 mottled "patchwork" plaques, each joined by small straight pins & highlighted w/two small sapphires & a diamond, hallmark for A.J. Hedges & Co., Victorian, ca. 1880s (ILLUS.) **$1,725**

*Antique Gold
Snake
Bracelet*

*Gold
Bracelet*

Bracelet, gold (14k yellow), designed as a coiled snake of flexible braided gold wire w/ruby eyes (ILLUS.) **$1,725**
Bracelet, gold (14k yellow), flexible plaque design alternating round floret links w/concave barrel-shaped stations, ca. 1900 (ILLUS.) **$1,380**

Diamond & Emerald Bracelet

Gold Snake Bracelet

Bracelet, gold (18k), diamond & emerald, four openwork plaques centered by bezel-set old mine-cut diamond & emerald clusters flanked by diamond & emerald peacocks, each plaque joined by cabochon emerald links, French assay & hallmarks (ILLUS. of part) **$1,495**

Bracelet, gold (18k), snake form, flexible woven design w/sapphire & rose-cut diamond-set head & eyes, minor dent near tail, European hallmark (ILLUS.) **$6,325**

Gold & Enamel Snake Bracelet

Victorian Gold & Enamel Bracelet

Bracelet, gold (18k yellow), enamel & diamond, designed as a hinged flexible coiled snake, the body w/guilloché pink enamel & adorned w/six old mine-cut & rose-cut diamonds set in silver, enamel damaged, Victorian (ILLUS.) **$4,750**

Bracelet, gold & enamel, the hinged rectangular plaques inlaid w/champleve enamel in white, navy & rust, 18k yellow gold mount, Victorian, 7 3/4" l. (ILLUS.) **$805**

*Etruscan
Revival
Style Lapis
Bracelet*

*Lapis Lazuli
& Diamond
Bracelet*

Bracelet, lapis & 18k yellow gold, Etruscan Revival style, center bezel-set round lapis flanked by two oval lapis-set links within gold wiretwist frames, gold bead & floral filigree detail, French import mark, 7" l. (ILLUS. of part) **$1,035**

Bracelet, lapis lazuli & diamond, an open, flexible design w/six ornate sections, each centering a round cabochon-cut lapis lazuli capped w/a rose-cut diamond w/gold fleur-de-lis designs & rose-cut diamonds on each side, attached to round snake chain borders, mounted in 18k yellow gold, two diamond points missing, 7 1/4" l. (ILLUS. of part) **$2,300**

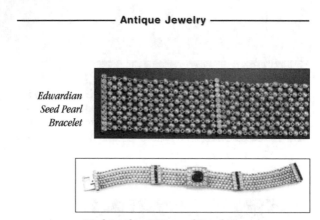

*Edwardian
Seed Pearl
Bracelet*

Pearl, Sapphire & Diamond Bracelet

Bracelet, pearl, mesh design of seed pearl & platinum links, bezel-set diamond spacers w/millegrain accents, Edwardian, 7 3/4" l. (ILLUS. of part) **$8,625**

Bracelet, pearl, sapphire & diamond, flexible, strap type, designed w/seven rows of natural seed pearls centering a cushion-shaped, faceted sapphire, surrounded by a square frame of 14 old mine- & old European-cut diamonds, decorated w/three small rectangular-shaped plaques each w/a centerline of square French-cut sapphires flanked by two rows of small round diamonds, mounted in platinum w/18k white gold catch, ca. 1900, approx. 6 1/2" l. (ILLUS.) **$12,075**

*Antique Gold
Bracelet/Brooch*

Bracelet/brooch, gold, ruby & diamond, wide mesh bracelet w/diamond accents w/detachable brooch of old mine-cut diamonds & cushion-cut rubies, pinched collet settings, ropetwist accents (ILLUS.) **$5,750**

Bracelets, bangle-type, 14k gold, designed as identical hinged bangles, the tops surmounted by rose & textured gold ornaments, ca. 1870, Victorian, pr. **$3,105**

Bracelets, bangle-type, enamel & 14k gold, hinged cuff-style, engraved w/black tracery enamel foliate motifs, Victorian, pr. **$1,265**

Bracelets, bangle-type, gold (14k), hinged design decorated w/applied multicolor 14k gold butterfly & floral motif, coiled gold wire border, 14k yellow gold mount, dated 1883, signed "E.W. Schurmann, Philadelphia," pr. (minor dents to back) **$2,990**

Bracelet, star sapphire & diamond, a hinged bangle, top centered by a cabochon star sapphire flanked by old mine-cut diamonds, set in 18k yellow gold w/black & white enamel detail, hallmarks for Carlo Giuliano **$5,750**

Brooches

*Aquamarine &
Diamond Brooch*

Brooch, amethyst, pearl & diamond, Arts & Crafts style, five bezel-
set amethysts, enhanced by baroque pearls & an old mine-cut
diamond, surrounded by platinum leaves in a 14k yellow gold
mount w/scroll & bead accents, attributed to Edward
Oakes **$4,025**

Brooch, aquamarine & diamond, centered by an emerald-cut
aquamarine within an open wirework, millegrain & rose-cut diamond frame w/four green gold florets & collet-set aquamarine
terminals, 14k yellow gold mount, Russian hallmarks, Edwardian, one diamond missing (ILLUS.) **$2,990**

Brooch, carved moonstone, depicting the profile of a classical figure, cushion-cut ruby & diamond highlights, 18k yellow gold
wiretwist & beaded frame, Edwardian (some minor surface
scratches) **$1,955**

Diamond Corsage Brooch

*Art Nouveau
Diamond Brooch*

Brooch, diamond & 14k white gold, a starburst design set of old mine-cut diamonds.. **$1,380**

Brooch, diamond, a floral & leaf design, decorated w/old mine- & rose-cut diamonds, the five flowerheads en tremblant, mounted in silver-topped 18k yellow gold, several detachable sections, ca. 1830 (ILLUS.).. **$6,900**

Brooch, diamond, art nouveau style, graceful open-work w/lozenge-shaped design centering a large old mine-cut diamond w/old mine- & rose-cut diamond accents, one small rose-cut diamond missing, mounted in platinum-topped 18k yellow gold (ILLUS.) **$5,060**

Diamond Flower Brooch

Diamond & Pearl Bow Brooch

Brooch, diamond, flower design
centered by a collet-set old European-cut diamond, surrounded
by numerous collet & bead-set diamonds, platinum-topped 18k
gold, signed "Marcus & Co.," Edwardian (ILLUS.) **$19,550**

Brooch, diamond & pearl, four-loop bow design set w/approxi-
mately 153 old mine-cut diamonds, suspending a natural pearl
drop, diamond-set cap, silver-topped 18k yellow gold mount,
European hallmarks (ILLUS.) **$17,250**

*Delicate Early
Butterfly Brooch*

*Art Nouveau Style
Portrait Brooch*

Brooch, diamond, ruby, garnet, moonstone, gold & platinum, butterfly-shaped, the 14k yellow gold & platinum top openwork mount set w/two oval & one round cabochon moonstone weighing about 9 carats surrounded by 42 old mine- and European-cut diamonds weighing about 1.15 carats, the eyes set w/two round faceted rubies weighing about .10 carats, the back of the head set w/one round faceted demantoid garnet weighing about .20 carats, early 20th c., 2" w. (ILLUS.) **$6,325**

Brooch, enamel & 18k yellow gold, art nouveau style portrait brooch, scalloped shell shape w/pink iridescent champlevé enamel, rose-cut diamond accent, French assay mark (ILLUS.) **$1,610**

Arts & Crafts Moonstone Brooch

Dragonfly Brooch

Brooch, enamel, modeled as a dragonfly, cabochon emerald & rose-cut diamond body decorated w/green to blue shaded plique-a-jour enamel, wings set en tremblant & highlighted by rose-cut diamonds, platinum-topped 14k gold (ILLUS.) **$4,140**

Brooch, enamel, moonstone & 18k yellow gold, Arts & Crafts style, the circular shape decorated w/an overall vine motif against a shaded blue enamel ground, centered by a bezel-set moonstone, some enamel loss near edges, signed "Tiffany & Co." on applied plaque (ILLUS.) **$5,750**

Brooch, enamel, openwork design of a lily w/burgundy enameling, green enameled leaves, an old mine-cut diamond at the top

*Gold & Enamel
Ribbon Brooch*

of stem, a free-hanging pearl drop at the base, mounted in 18k, yellow gold .. **$1,265**

Brooch, gemstone & pearl, Arts & Crafts style, floral spray design prong-set w/various colored gems in shades of lilac, yellow, pink & green, including colored sapphires, kunzite, emerald & amethyst w/seed pearl accents, gilt silver mount, by Dorrie Nossiter...................................... **$2,760**

Brooch, gold (22k yellow), enamel & diamond, a floral engraved ribbon design w/blue enamel knot set w/old mine-cut diamonds, suspending a blue enamel locket, the scalloped edge accented w/gold & center-set w/diamonds set in a star shape, ca. 1860 (ILLUS.) **$4,025**

Brooch, gold, enamel & diamond, a blue enamel shield-shaped medallion w/18k gold & diamonds applied in a floral form topped w/a crown of gold & seed pearls & inlaid w/gemstones, ending in a ribbon design w/a center diamond, 19th c., 1 1/2 x 2" **$1,288**

Miniature Portrait Brooch

Egyptian Revial Scarab Brooch

Brooch, gold, Etruscan Revival style, bar pin top designed as the chariot of the sun w/lion's head terminals, suspending a capped tassel w/bead, palmette & ovoid drops, overall granulation & millegrain accents, signed "Giacinto Melillo, Napoli" (designed w/two figures of Victory, one missing, one detached) **$8,050**

Brooch, gold, miniature portrait-type, the circular plaque depicting Marie Antoinette, surrounded by 18k yellow gold feather motif frame accented by pearl & rose diamond flowers, French hallmark (ILLUS.) **$690**

Brooch, hardstone & enamel, Egyptian Revival design of two polychrome enamel falcon wings centered by a collet-set hardstone scarab & flanked by two serpent heads, collet-set diamond

Victorian Micromosiac Brooch

accents, 14k yellow gold mount, signed "Schumann Sons"
(ILLUS. on previous page) **$2,070**
Brooch, micromosaic, center malachite ground w/micromosaic
of the Vatican within a gold wiretwist & scalloped frame, 18k yel-
low gold mount, Vatican hallmarks, Victorian
(ILLUS.) **$2,300**
Brooch, micromosaic, oval, depicting a group of poly-chrome
bathing birds perched on a gold-colored tureen set in a cobalt
blue hardstone plaque, surrounded by a later 18k gold frame,
Victorian (chips to stone & loss to mosaic) **$1,093**

*Art Nouveau
Moonstone & Enamel
Brooch*

*Moonstone & Sapphire
Brooch*

Brooch, moonstone & enamel, art nouveau style centered by an oval moonstone within a foliate blue green enamel & 18k yellow gold mount w/sapphire accents, signed "Tiffany & Co.," boxed (ILLUS.) **$17,250**

Brooch, moonstone & sapphire, Arts & Crafts style, four bezel-set moonstones joined by a foliate design of collet-set sapphires & seed pearls, 14k yellow gold, attributed to Edward Oakes (ILLUS.) **$2,645**

Victorian Pearl & Diamond Brooch

Brooch, natural pearl & diamond, composed of three rosettes, each centering a natural round pearl surrounded by old mine-cut diamonds separated by diamond-set trefoil designs, the center rosette suspending three large old mine-cut diamonds in a free-hanging frame of small pearls & diamonds w/a free-hanging old mine- and rose-cut diamond accented bow design drop on either side, each terminating w/a pear-shaped pearl drop decorated at the top w/rose-cut diamonds, center portion detachable to be worn as a pendant, mounted in silver & silver-topped 18k yellow gold, three small rose-cut diamonds missing, ca. 1865 (ILLUS.) **$14,950**

Opal & Diamond Brooch

Brooch, opal & diamond, foliate design set w/cabochon opals, rose-cut diamonds & demantoid garnet accents, silver & 14k yellow gold mount (ILLUS.) **$1,265**

Brooch, opal, emerald & garnet, butterfly design, opal body, emerald head, green garnet eyes, the wings set w/rubies, emeralds & diamonds in an 18k gold & silver-top mounting **$2,645**

Brooch, pearl & diamond, wing design center set w/a round old European-cut diamond surrounded by six seed pearls, the wings

Seed Pearl Wing Form Brooch

Serpent & Starburst Brooch

pavé-set w/split pearls, 14k yellow gold mount, ca. 1900, Victorian (ILLUS.) **$1,093**

Brooch, pearl, emerald & ruby, designed as a coiled emerald & pearl-set serpent w/pearl in fangs, surmounting a starburst set w/rubies & pearls w/large center prong-set pearl, 18k yellow gold mount, English gold mark, solder to back, 19th c. (ILLUS.) **$1,725**

Brooch, pearl & gemstone, a cruciform design set w/five split pearls & four round emeralds within a square frame of 36 old mine-cut diamonds, the corners in a fleur-de-lis motif w/red stone accents, silver-topped 18k yellow gold mount, French hallmarks **$1,610**

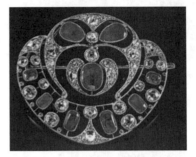

Art Nouveau Ruby & Diamond Brooch

Brooch, pietra dura, oval hardstone centered by a white rose, white & green floral buds within a 14k gold triple wiretwist frame (later clasp) **$460**

Brooch, pietra dura, the oval hardstone centered by a red & white flower within an 18k yellow gold wirework frame **$374**

Brooch, ruby & diamond, art nouveau style, an open frame w/a stylized wreath design centering a free-hanging oval faceted ruby flanked by two curved rows of old mine-cut diamonds topped w/an old mine-cut diamond, suspended from a pair of pearl-shaped faceted rubies & diamonds, the lower portion decorated w/six rectangular cushion-cut rubies slightly tapering in size, w/old mine- and rose-cut diamonds between the rubies & in the borders, mounted in platinum & 18k yellow gold, signed by Vever, Paris, ca. 1900 (ILLUS.) **$10,925**

Arts & Crafts Jeweled Wreath Brooch

Brooch, sapphire & diamond, centered by a cushion-shaped sapphire within a diamond-set bezel, surrounded by round diamonds in an openwork foliate design & geometric frame, platinum mount, Edwardian **$7,475**

Brooch, sapphire & diamond, five cushion-shaped sapphires in yellow gold prong settings surrounded by prong- & bead-set old mine-cut diamonds, mounted in silver & yellow gold, detachable clasp & retractable bail **$13,800**

Brooch, sapphire, emerald, ruby & moonstone, Arts & Crafts style wreath design w/prong-set faceted & cabochon sapphires, emeralds & moonstones & clusters of wire-set pearls, highlighted by a sapphire & ruby insect set in 14k yellow gold, gilded silver leaves & mount, by Dorrie Nossiter, England (ILLUS.) **$8,625**

Tiffany Jeweled
Brooch/Pendant

Brooch/pendant, diamond, flowerhead design, set throughout
w/49 old mine-cut diamonds, diamond-set bail, silver-topped
gold mount (one diamond missing) **$2,300**

Brooch/pendant, diamond, pearl, garnet & sapphire, set
throughout w/multicolored natural pearls, fancy color diamonds,
pink stones, demantoid garnets & centering an oval pink sapphire, platinum-topped 18k yellow gold, late 19th c., signed
"Tiffany & Co." (ILLUS.) **$63,000**

Cameos

Garnet Cameo Brooch

Cameo brooch, carved garnet, profile of a woman within a gold
& silver mount, surrounded by 30 old mine-cut diamonds
spaced by six pearls, French gold marks, removable back, signed
at neck "LEBAS" (ILLUS.) **$7,475**
Cameo brooch, carved sard-onyx, the profile of a woman in high
relief, within a 14k yellow gold oval frame set w/split pearls,
Victorian (repair to back, clasp replaced) **$1,093**
Cameo brooch, carved shell depicting the profiles of three classical males & one classical female centered by a ram's head within
a 14k gold foliate frame w/bead & wiretwist accents (minor lead
solder) **$575**

*Three Muses
Cameo Brooch*

Cameo brooch, carved shell, depicting the Three Muses, the center muse within a floral canopy, 14k yellow gold mount, Edwardian (ILLUS.) **$460**
Cameo brooch, depicting a woman in profile within a pearl, rose-cut diamond & foliate frame, 18k gold mount, ca. 1875 .... **$3,795**
Cameo brooch, hardstone, depicting a cherub playing a lyre, framed by pearls, 14k yellow gold foliate mount, Victorian (cameo nicked) **$1,610**

*Fine Hardstone
Cameo Brooch*

Cameo brooch, hardstone & gold, a tested 14k yellow gold oval framed composed of delicated chased C-scrolls enclosing a hardstone cameo carved in high-relief w/a profile bust of a classical woman, her hair dressed w/leaves & berries, a sleeping ram mounted on her shoulder, early 20th c., 1 3/4 x 2 1/4" (ILLUS.) **$1,725**

Cameo brooch, shell, 14k yellow gold lattice & beadwork decorated mount set w/a large oval cameo depicting two classical women within a floral landscape, one feeding a duck, the other attending a cherub, 3 x 4" **$575**

*Agate Cameo & Pearl Brooch &
Earrings*

Cameo Brooch/Pendant

Cameo brooch & earrings, agate, the brooch depicting a
woman in profile, surrounded by prong- & box-set pearls, suspending a fringe of pearls, together w/matching pair of earpendants, 18k yellow gold mount, European & export hallmarks, the
set (ILLUS.) **$1,610**

Cameo brooch/pendant, hardstone, oval onyx cameo depicting
the bust of a classical female within a 14k gold foliate frame
accented w/26 old mine-cut diamonds, the reverse w/beveled
glass compartment, suspended from a bow further set w/11 dia-
monds (ILLUS.) **$3,565**

*Victorian
Agate Cameo
Earrings*

Cameo earrings, carved agate, pearl & gold, depicting a female bust within an oval frame in engraved 18k yellow gold w/seed pearl accents, suspended from an engraved gold bow, one pearl missing, lead solder to backs, later findings, Victorian, pr. (ILLUS.) **$690**

Cameo & Garnet Pendant/Brooch

Cameo necklace, carved jasper, the festoon design featuring four oval cameos w/14k yellow gold frames, completed by an 18k yellow gold trace link chain, the clasp labeled "Amitie," boxed **$1,380**

Cameo pendant/brooch, shell & garnet, 14k yellow gold lattice & beadwork decorated mount set w/a large oval cameo depicting a gladiator & a woman riding a horse-drawn chariot, cherub holding a cornucopia within a clouded field, the frame set w/seven oval buff top garnets, 3 1/2 x 4" (ILLUS.) **$805**

*Victorian
Cameo Pin*

Cameo pin,
necklace, ear-
rings & hair
comb, the pin w/four mythological figural oval & round cameos,
a tortoiseshell hair comb w/six oval cameos & the necklace of
oval cameos, depicting mythological scenes, the frames accented
w/green & white enamel & ropetwist accents, 18k yellow gold, in
original box together w/pair of cameo earrings, Victorian, the set
(ILLUS. of pin) **$7,475**
Cameo ring, diamond, pearl, moonstone & gold, the tested 14k
yellow gold mount set w/a circular carved moon-stone cameo
depicting a face of a young girl surrounded by six old mine-cut
diamonds weighing about .60 carats alternating w/six seed pearls
measuring 2.5 mm, last quarter 19th c., size 7.............. **$1,725**

Cuff Links

*Late Victorian
Cuff Links*

Cuff links, coin, Classical Revival style, each bezel-set coin depicting the profile of a classical Roman warrior within an 18k gold wiretwist frame, pr. **$1,093**

Cuff links, demantoid garnet & diamond, double-sided, each side w/a looped petal form centering a round faceted demantoid garnet w/small rose-cut diamonds set in the petals & borders, mounted in silver-topped 18k yellow gold, ca. 1895, pr. (ILLUS.) **$2,185**

Cuff links, gold (18k) & pearl, prong-set freshwater pearls connected by figure eight links, signed "Tiffany & Co.," ca. 1910.. **$920**

*Gold Bacchus
Cuff Links*

Cuff links, gold (18k yellow), chased & engraved Bacchus
design, collet-set old mine-cut diamond accent, pr.
(ILLUS.) **$1,725**

Cuff links, gold (18k yellow), double-sided, art nouveau style,
one side depicting a high relief female profile within a floral
design, accented w/small rubies & sapphires, reverse designed
from a navette-shaped bar w/high relief floral design
pr. **$1,955**

Cuff links, gold (18k yellow) & lapis, Arts & Crafts style double-
sided oval plaques within gold frame, beaded accents, signed
"F.G. Hale," pr. (minor repair to one) **$1,955**

Cuff links, quartz, rectangular frame w/bezel-set inlaid golden
quartz, 14k rose gold mount, Victorian, pr. **$489**

Cuff links, star ruby & 14k yellow gold, art nouveau style, two
bezel-set cabochon star rubies attached to a gold twist link, links
possibly later, signed "Marcus & Co.," pr. **$518**

Earrings

Arts & Crafts Jeweled Earrings

Earrings, coral, topaz, zircon, garnet & tourmaline, Arts & Crafts
style, designed as a cluster of
prong-set faceted gemstones,
including topaz, zircon, garnet &
tourmaline, w/pearl & gold bead accents, surrounding a coral
cabochon & suspending a carved coral pear-shape framing a
gem-set drop, by Dorrie Nossiter, England, crack to one bottom
stone, pr. (ILLUS. of one) **$2,070**

Earrings, diamond, a cascade of flexible old European-cut diamond-set crescents suspending a pear-shaped diamond surrounded by a frame of diamonds, millegraining, mounted in platinum w/later yellow gold plating, 1 1/4" l., pr. **$3,910**

Pavé-set Diamond Earrings

Earrings, diamond & emerald, topped by a square-cut emerald, suspending a round old mine-cut diamond, mounted in yellow gold, pr. **$18,400**

Earrings, diamond, foliate-set diamond tops, silver-topped gold mounts suspending spheres set w/approx. 336 round pavé-set diamonds, pr. (ILLUS.) **$7,475**

*Edwardian Basket
Earrings*

Earrings, diamond, seed pearl, gold & platinum, a 14k yellow gold & platinum top mount w/an arched design & set w/11 rose-cut diamonds weighing about .15 carats & one seed pearl, suspending a basket of flowers tassel set w/four seed pearls & 25 rose-cut diamonds weighing about .30 carats, Edwardian, 1" l., pr. (ILLUS.) **$2,300**

Earrings, diamond & silver, each set throughout w/pavé single-cut diamonds, brown diamond accent, rose-cut ruby eyes, 18k yellow gold posts, pr. **$1,725**

*Victorian Gold &
Diamond Earrings*

Earrings, gold (14k yellow), enamel & diamond, an old
European-cut diamond set in the center of a round enamel gold-
trimmed disk suspending an oval pendant enamel & gold foliate
design, further suspending a small diamond-set drop, Victorian,
pr. (ILLUS.) **$575**
Earrings, gold (18k yellow), engraved day/night style, pyramid-
shaped terminals suspending detachable kite-shaped drops,
pr. **$3,795**
Earrings, gold & turquoise, Etruscan Revival style, the round tops
set w/buff-top turquoise, accented w/black enamel, suspending
tapering gold pendants, 18k yellow gold, 2 3/4" l., pr. .. **$2,300**

Lavalieres/Necklaces/ Pendants

Edwardian Lavaliere

Lavaliere, diamond & platinum, a bow design surmounted by a foliate spray, suspending fringed flexible tails, set throughout w/round diamonds, platinum mount, minor gold solder to back, Edwardian (ILLUS.) **$1,265**

Lavaliere, diamond, centered by a prong-set fancy yellowish brown old European-cut diamond surrounded by a scroll design of prong- & bead-set European-cut white diamonds interspersed w/fancy yellows, suspending diamond-set drops mounted on a knife-edge bar, completed by a double trace link platinum chain, 16" l. **$8,625**

*Morganite &
Diamond
Lavaliere*

Lavaliere, diamond, open-work foliate mount w/collet- & bead-set diamonds, silver-topped yellow gold mount w/beaded accents, suspended from a silver box link chain w/diamond accent, Edwardian, 11 1/2" l. (break to mount) **$2,760**

Lavaliere, morganite & diamond, rectangular morganite terminal, diamond-set bow motif shoulders, suspending a faceted pear-shaped morganite, collet-set diamond accents, completed by a fancy link platinum chain, Edwardian, 15 1/2" l. (ILLUS.) **$2,645**

Victorian Gold Locket

Locket, gold (14k) & enamel,
the top w/white guillocheé
enamel surmounted by a sapphire & rose-cut diamond
sautoir motif set in silver, completed by a 14k gold trace link
chain, Russian hallmarks,
Edwardian (minor enamel loss to edges) **$1,725**

Locket, gold (14k yellow), decorated w/an applied cross design
in black enamel & rose-cut diamonds (repair to back) .. **$316**

Locket, gold (14k yellow), shield shape decorated w/applied
wiretwist & beaded accents, hinged top opens to reveal hidden
locket, minor dents, Victorian (ILLUS.) **$316**

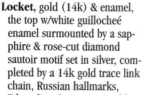

Gold Pendant Locket

Locket, gold, an oval shape w/an applied design of gardening tools, a flower basket & a hat, engraved multicolor 18k gold, French hallmarks, in fitted box (ILLUS.) **$2,185**

Locket, gold, Art Nouveau style, round shape depicting an American Indian accented by a diamond, repoussé & hand-chased, verso initialed **$748**

Pearl & Ruby Portrait Locket

Locket, pearl & ruby, a circular design w/h.p. signed portrait of a child on porcelain, surrounded by a row of cushion-shaped, faceted Burmese rubies, framed by a row of natural half pearls that taper in size, seed pearl & ruby accents, hair compartment on reverse, circular bail decorated w/six additional pearls, mounted in 14k yellow gold, ca. 1810, together w/original fitted leather box (ILLUS.) **$2,415**

*Art Nouveau
Locket Pendant*

Locket pendant, gold (18k yellow), Art Nouveau style, circular form depicting bust portrait of woman w/upswept hair & wearing a diamond melée choker, scrolled vine & floral border (ILLUS.) **$1,380**

Locket/pendant, memorial-type, pavé-set, turquoise w/Gothic Revival pearl initial, pavé turquoise terminals w/rose-cut diamond accents suspended from a bail w/simulated diamonds, gilt-metal mount, (solder evident), verso w/beveled glass compartment w/14k yellow gold trace link chain w/12 bezel-set light blue opaque glass beads, Victorian, 36" l. (bezels are gilt-metal, chipped glass) **$920**

Amethyst & Pearl Festoon Necklace

Necklace, amethyst, pearl & 14k gold, festoon-type, the pearl, amethyst, trace line & S-scroll chain suspending three pear-shaped amethysts hanging within pearl-set, shield-shaped drops, the center suspending a larger amethyst, Edwardian, 15 1/2" l. (ILLUS.) **$1,610**

Necklace, aquamarine, centered by an oval aquamarine within a seed pearl & diamond frame, platinum-topped 18k yellow gold mount, completed by a platinum curb link chain, Edwardian, 18" l., ... **$1,265**

Necklace, amethyst & pearl, choker-type, a 14k yellow gold single line necklace w/64 circular yellow gold links, each set w/a half seed pearl, the center w/five floral circular links, each set w/one

Amethyst & Seed Pearl Choker

half seed pearl surrounded by 12 smaller
seed pearls suspending a removable 14k
yellow gold floral pendant set w/a large
oval faceted amethyst surrounded by 42
half seed pearls, joined by a 14k yellow
gold rectangular box tongue-in-groove
clasp set w/two half seed pearls, Europe,
ca. 1900, 15 1/2" l. (ILLUS.) **$1,840**
Necklace, black onyx, gold & seed pearl, rectangular carved
black onyx links connected by circular gold links w/a shield-
shaped center pendant medallion overlaid w/delicate floral-
shaped lily design in gold & seed pearls, the reverse opens w/a
gold-mounted crystal door w/a velvet-lined compartment containing blond hair, in original silk-lined leather case, ca. 1865,
medallion 1 1/2 x 2", overall 21" l. **$1,650**

*Plique-a-Jour
Enamel Necklace*

Necklace, enamel, art nouveau style, lavender & green iridescent enamel flowers w/green, pink & white plique-a-jour enamel leaves, accented throughout w/rose-cut diamonds & pearls, 18k yellow gold mount w/later faux pearl chain (ILLUS.) **$1,265**

Necklace, enamel & pearl, art nouveau style choker, eight pansy links in translucent yellow, green & violet shaded enamel, the center motif suspending a flexible pendant designed w/a collet-set diamond & two freshwater pearls, edged by a fine trace link chain accented by freshwater pearls set at intervals, 13" l. **$2,990**

Necklace, English paste riviere, the graduated collet-set white pastes mounted in silver-topped 18k yellow gold, ca. 1800 .... **$1,495**

Garnet & Diamond Necklace

Necklace, garnet & diamond, openwork pendant set w/a demantoid garnet, further set throughout w/rose- & old mine-cut diamonds, suspending a pear-shaped rose-cut diamond drop, completed by fine platinum chains accented w/rose-cut diamond trefoils, Edwardian (ILLUS.) **$6,038**

Necklace, gemstone & pearl, Arts & Crafts style, designed in the manner of an echelle w/descending faceted citrine drops framed by clusters of prong-set multicolored gemstones, pearls & carved emerald leaves w/similar citrine & gemstone clasp, silver mounts, completed by a strand of pearls linked w/twisted gold wire, by Dorrie Nossiter, England, 15" l. **$11,500**

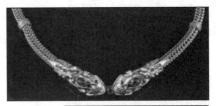

*Gold Snake
Necklace*

Etruscan Revival Necklace

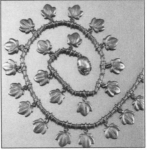

Necklace, gold (18k yellow) &
Favrile glass, Arts & Crafts
style, designed w/14 blue iridescent scarabs mounted on
gold bases & edged by open
scrolling frames, signed
"Tiffany & Co.," 15" l. **$40,250**

Necklace, gold (18k yellow), open mesh links set w/four textured
spacers, completed by two brushed gold snake heads set
w/cabochon rubies & faceted emeralds & rubies, 15" l.
(ILLUS.) **$1,380**

Necklace, gold (18k yellow), Victorian Etruscan Revival style,
barrel-shaped links suspending stylized ivy leaf drops threaded
through a loop-in-loop chain, completed by a scarab clasp, 16"
l. (ILLUS.) **$3,450**

Jade & Enamel Necklace

Necklace, jade & enamel, Arts & Crafts style, elliptical-shaped jade within conforming enamel scrolled links joined by trace link chains, similarly set pendant suspending three jade drops, 18k gold, some enamel loss, signed "Tiffany & Co.," 18" l. (ILLUS.) **$31,050**

Necklace, kunzite, negligee-type, the fancy link yellow gold-wash chain interrupted by collect-set faceted round kunzites, pear-shaped kunzite terminals, ca. 1900, 37 1/2" l. **$1,150**

Necklace, lapis & 18k gold, Arts & Crafts style, designed w/ten slightly curved lapis plaques accented by floral vine motifs, 14 1/2" l. **$6,325**

Micromosaic Necklace

Necklace, micromosaic & gold, depicting a dove on a branch w/pink & white flowers against a teal ground, within a 14k yellow gold frame w/wiretwist & beaded accents, later 14k box-link chain, damage to frame, 17" l. (ILLUS.) **$661**

Necklace, onyx & pearl, the pendant in a shield shape surmounted by a foliate design in seed pearls, black enamel bail, suspended from an onyx link chain w/pearl accents, 14k yellow gold mount, Victorian, 24" l. **$920**

Necklace, pearl, a graduated mixture of natural, ten year & cultured pearls completed by a silver-topped gold clasp set w/an old mine-cut diamond, 18" l. **$2,530**

Necklace, pearl, choker-type, six strands of natural pearls completed by a sapphire, ruby, emerald & rose-cut diamond clasp, w/GIA certificate, 13 3/4" l. **$1,840**

*Victorian
Gold & Pearl
Necklace*

Necklace, pearl & gold, pearl-set links w/a central fringe of floral motif drops, 14k yellow gold, later ropetwist chain, Victorian, 14 1/2" l. (ILLUS. of part) **$805**

Necklace, sapphire & pearl, 14k yellow gold single line oval link necklace w/seven central floral motifs, six set w/split cultured pearls alternating w/five oval mixed-cut sapphires, the center sapphire surrounded by four split cultured pearls suspending garland tassels set w/split cultured pearls, ca. 1900, 16" l. **$1,380**

Necklace, silver plated coiled chain, graduated crystal dangles in individual cups, ca. 1890, 16" l. .... **$145-$175**

Necklace, sterling silver & citrine, art nouveau style, sterling silver chain w/center designed w/collet-set cabochon citrines & citrine beads on double chain, the large center citrine flanked by a scrolled sterling frame & suspending multiple chains, two citrine beads & a center teardrop-shaped citrine..................... **$1,035**

Necklace, topaz & chrysoberyl, festoon style centered by a cushion-cut pink topaz surrounded by collet-set round- & rhomboid-

Arts & Crafts Gold & Tourmaline Necklace

cut green chrysoberyl, gold bead accents, completed by foxtail & curb link chains, ca. 1860, 15" l. **$2,185**

Necklace, tourmaline, Arts & Crafts style, the center oval plaque set w/graduated tourmalines surrounded by Montana sapphires & edged w/various color natural pearls, joined by a triple strand of 18k yellow gold chains, clasp signed "Tiffany & Co.," together w/extra links, in original Tiffany box (ILLUS.) **$49,450**

Necklace & pendant, citrine, the necklace designed as a band composed of 21 graduated oval faceted citrines, suspending a pendant of quatrefoil design center set w/a round citrine & surrounded by four large & four smaller oval citrines, the set **$2,760**

*Diamond,
Enamel & Pearl
Pendant*

Pendant, diamond, pearl & enamel, a scalloped circular form
decorated w/a six petal flower pattern centering a cultured pearl
& further set w/old mine- & rose-cut diamonds in a geometric
design on pastel green plique-a-jour enameling, diamond decorated bail, mounted in platinum (ILLUS.) **$4,140**

Pendant, diamond, wreath design w/collet-set diamonds on a
platinum grille, edged w/rose-cut diamond leaves & surmounted
by a diamond-set bow, platinum & seed pearl fine link chain,
Edwardian, 20" l. **$1,495**

*Etruscan Revival
Portrait Pendant*

Pendant, enamel & gilt, portrait-type, miniature, Etruscan Revival style, depicting two children in polychrome enamel, ropetwist, floral & beaded accents, locket back, gilt mount (ILLUS.)...................... **$1,725**

Pendant, gold (18k yellow), diamond & enamel, Jerusalem cross set w/18 table-cut diamonds suspending a baroque pearl, the verso decorated w/champlevé enameling in green, gold, light blue & yellow (minor enamel loss) **$13,225**

Pendant, gold (18k yellow) & enamel, art nouveau style, shield shape centering a woman in a blue guilloché enamel bonnet w/diamond necklace & earrings, against a background of polychrome plique-a-jour enamel squares, framed in diamond-accented flowers decorated w/en cabochon enameling, diamond-set bail, Swiss hallmarks... **$2,415**

Fine Early Lalique Glass Pendant

Pendant, molded glass, diamond & pearl, art nouveau style, a rectangular plaque of opalescent mold-blown glass w/a scene depicting a group of robed figures w/gold faces, within a frame of small rose-cut diamonds, the frame accented on each side w/a double rose-cut diamond, the diamond at the base suspending a natural pearl drop, mounted in silver-topped 18k yellow gold, signed by Lalique & w/French hallmark, w/original fitted box, ca. 1900 (ILLUS.) **$16,100**

Pendant, opal & enamel, art nouveau style, centered by an oval opal within an open-work foliate design in pink jubilee enamel, diamond & opal accents, signed "Mrs. Newman, Goldsmith and Court Jeweller, 10 Savile Row," some damage to opals, in fitted box **$2,875**

*Edwardian Diamond &
Enamel Pendant*

Pendant, pearl, Arts & Crafts style, centered by a winged cherub within a pearl frame, freshwater pearl drop, completed by a fancy knot link chain, boxed **$3,910**

Pendant, pearl & diamond, large baroque pearl set w/V-shaped band of rose-cut diamonds, cap w/tapered rows of rose-cut diamonds, French import assay marks, ca. 1900 .... **$1,840**

Pendant, pearl & turquoise, shield form set throughout w/pearls & buff-top turquoise, 18k gold & silver mount, Victorian, together w/an 18k gold snake chain **$633**

Pendant, platinum, enamel & diamond, quatrefoil form, centering a disk of cobalt blue guilloché enamel surmounted by a diamond quatrefoil accent, within a rose- & full-cut diamond filigree mount, suspended from a fine trace link chain w/pearl accent, Edwardian (ILLUS.) **$3,220**

*Imperial Topaz &
Diamond Pendant*

Pendant, sapphire & diamond, snowflake design centered by a
cushion-cut pink sapphire, surrounded by prong-set round pink
sapphires & collet-set diamonds, rose-cut diamond accents, suspended from a pinch-set diamond bail, silver-topped 14k yellow
gold **$4,025**

Pendant, topaz & diamond, bow form above oval mixed-cut
Imperial topaz surrounded by old mine-cut diamonds, completed by a yellow diamond briolette, platinum-topped 14k yellow
gold, minor abrasion, lead solder, one diamond missing,
Edwardian (ILLUS.) **$17,250**

Pendant, turquoise, gold & diamond, the openwork cartouche
outline & foliate motif frame set w/an oval Persian turquoise
cabochon & two old mine- & round rose-cut diamonds, suspending a teardrop-shaped turquoise cabochon **$1,265**

Art Nouveau Diamond Pendant Necklace

Pendant necklace, diamond, art nouveau highly stylized butter-fly-shaped outline w/delicate openwork, intricately set w/round-& rose-cut diamonds, one free-hanging in the center, mounted in platinum-topped 18k yellow gold w/double wire loops on the back w/white gold chain attached on each side,
17 1/2" h. (ILLUS.) **$4,830**

Pendant/brooch, diamond & silver, the silver openwork star-form mount set w/one old mine-cut diamond weighing about .80 carats surrounded by three tiers of forty smaller old mine-cut diamonds weighing about 4.10 carats, ca. 1850,
1 1/2" d. **$1,955**

Pendant/brooch, glass & gold, centered by an oval plaque of engraved gold & green glass under mica, peacock motif, 18k yel-low gold rosette border, from Pertabgarh, Northern India, ca. 1820-40 (some loss to gold on plaque) **$316**

Enamel Pendant/Compact   *Victorian Gold Pendant/Locket*

Pendant/compact, enamel & diamond, centered by a triangular neoclassical painted porcelain plaque depicting outdoor scene w/maidens, framed by single-cut diamonds, verso w/blue guilloché & white enamel decoration, opens to reveal two powder compartments, diamond-set bail, platinum-topped yellow gold, Edwardian (ILLUS.) **$3,738**

Pendant/locket, gold (18k yellow), a shield-form pendant locket w/applied wiretwist detail & pearl accent, completed by a double oval link chain of reeded design w/14k rose gold six-pointed star decoration, the pendant & chain 18k yellow gold, some dents to back of locket, Victorian (ILLUS.) **$1,725**

Pins/Stickpins

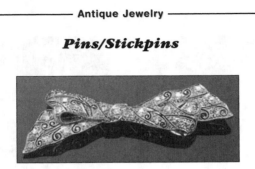

Edwardian Diamond Bow Pin

Pin, diamond bow design set w/28 bead-set old European-cut diamonds, open swirl accents, platinum mount, Edwardian (ILLUS.) **$2,645**

Pin, diamond & ruby, model of a dragonfly centered by an old mine-cut diamond, weighing approx. .61 cts. w/diamond-set wings & ruby-set back, platinum-topped 18k yellow gold mount **$4,370**

Pin, enamel, art nouveau style, designed as the head of a woman against an iridescent pale blue enamel background, rose-cut diamond accents, circular 18k yellow gold mount w/scalloped edge, signed "G. Charles" **$1,725**

Pin, enamel & diamond, clover design centered by an old mine-cut diamond, leaves decorated w/purple & white enamel & edged w/seed pearls, pearl-set stem, 14k gold, hallmark for Crane & Theurer, Edwardian.. **$805**

Edwardian Demantoid Garnet Pin

Pin, enamel, pearl, & 14k yellow gold, art nouveau style, modeled as an orchid w/light greenish yellow & purple openwork petals highlighted w/a baroque pearl & old European-cut diamond, retractable bail **$1,265**

Pin, garnet & diamond, a collet-set demantoid garnet w/diamond & pearl accents, further rose-cut diamond & platinum decoration, 14k yellow gold mount, Edwardian (ILLUS.) **$1,840**

Pearl & Diamond
Crown Pin

Pin, gold (14k) & enamel, art nouveau style four-leaf clover
shape, light shading to dark green leaves centering an old
European-cut diamond, completed by a polished gold stem, hallmark for Crane & Theurer **$1,380**

Pin, gold (14k yellow), emerald & diamond, oval form centered
by a cushion-cut emerald, surrounded by 11 round old mine-cut
diamonds & enhanced w/black enamel (one diamond
missing) **$3,450**

Pin, gold (18k yellow), Arts & Crafts style centered by a cabochon
oval feldspar flanked by four seed pearls, naturalistic motif
frame, signed "Tiffany & Co." **$6,900**

Pin, gold-plated, art nouveau style figure of nude on leaves w/vine
background, ca. 1895, 2" .... **$65-$90**

Pin, multi-gem & 14k yellow gold, diminutive model of a flower
basket, set w/seed pearls, rubies & demantoid garnets, diamond-
set platinum leaves, wiretwist handle, Edwardian (minor lead
solder) **$1,265**

Pin, pearl & diamond, crown design, the points set w/two old
European-cut diamonds & three white & grey pearls, the gallery
in an alternating pattern of four old European-cut diamonds &

Diamond & Natural Pearl Pin

three purple, rose & golden-pink pearls, edged by collet-set old mine- & rose-cut diamonds, 18k gold mount (ILLUS. on previous page) **$4,025**

Pin, pearl & diamond, oval form w/scalloped edge & scroll motif, center set w/natural pearl & numerous old mine-cut diamonds, millegrain & platinum mount, Edwardian (ILLUS.) **$3,450**

Pin, pearl & sapphire, the oval shape set w/seed pearls in an openwork grillework design framed by a double row of pearls & accented at the top, bottom & both sides w/two prong-set sapphires, 14k yellow gold mount, Edwardian **$978**

Pin, shell cameo, classic female profile w/ornate frame, extended pin, ca. 1880, 1 3/4" .... **$135-$155**

Pin, zircon & onyx, a circular blue zircon set within an onyx, old mine- & rose-cut diamond frame, Edwardian **$1,898**

Stickpin, diamond & garnet, designed as a pavé-set diamond horse & demantoid channel-set horseshoe, platinum on 14k gold, Edwardian (one garnet missing) **$1,265**

Stickpin, enamel, art nouveau style in the form of a sweet pea blossom decorated w/lavender & white enamel, old European-cut diamond accent, 14k yellow gold **$920**

Stickpin, enamel & diamond, designed as a pansy in shaded yellow & pale lilac, centered by an old mine-cut diamond, 18k yellow gold mount (minor enamel loss to edges) **$345**

Stickpin, enamel & gold (14k), art nouveau style depicting the head of a Byzantine woman in polychrome guilloché enamel (minor enamel loss) **$546**

Stickpin, gold, art nouveau style, tested 18k yellow gold mount depicting at the top two embracing nude figures, Lalique, France, ca. 1900, 3 1/2" l. **$4,370**

Stickpin, gold & diamond, 14k yellow gold buttercup-form mount set w/one old mine-cut diamond weighing about .60 carats, late 19th c., 2 1/2" l. **$719**

Stickpin, moonstone & 14k gold, oval, carved moon-stone of a gentleman's face, ca. 1900 .... **$1,840**

Stickpin, moonstone, the circular design w/carved moonstone depicting the man in the moon & stars, surrounded by fou faceted red stones, silver mount, ca. 1900 .... **$259**

Stickpin, opal, carved as a scarab & set w/four modified fleur-de-lis prongs, 14k gold, Edwardian **$633**

Stickpin, sapphire, bezel-set w/a pear-shaped sapphire mounted in 14k yellow gold, signed "Tiffany & Co.,"
Edwardian **$978**

Rings

Gentlemen's Cat's Eye Ring

Ring, cat's eye, gentlemen's, centered by a round double-sided cabochon chrysoberyl, 14k yellow gold dragon motif mount (ILLUS.) **$9,200**

Ring, diamond, ballerina style centered by an old mine-cut diamond, surrounded by baguette-cut diamonds, platinum mount **$4,140**

Ring, diamond, centered by an old European-cut yellow diamond within a diamond-set platinum mount, Edwardian, accompanied by GIA report **$37,950**

Ring, diamond, gentlemen's, gypsy-set old European-cut diamond, approx. 1.56 cts., 14k yellow gold mount..................... **$5,175**

Ring, diamond & platinum, centered by a round old mine-cut diamond, approx. 1.71 cts. flanked w/six baguette-cut diamonds w/additional six round diamonds set above & below the center stone, approx. total .50 cts. **$4,312**

Three Stone Diamond Ring

Ring, diamond & sapphire, by-pass style w/a prong-set sapphire measuring approx. 8.25 x 5.21 mm., & an old mine-cut diamond weighing approx. 1.90 cts., gold mount **$5,405**

Ring, diamond, sapphire, emerald & 18k gold, cocktail ring centered by a cushion-shaped old mine-cut diamond weighing approx. 1.98 cts., surrounded by three step-cut emeralds, approx. 3.08 tcw. & a cushion-, oval- & square-cut sapphire, approx. 5.21 tcw., further enhanced by smaller bead-set sapphires, collet-set diamond accents & bead-set diamond shoulders mounted in platinum **$5,750**

Ring, diamond, three stone navette shape, centered by a cinnamon color circular-cut diamond, further enhanced w/similarly

Jeweled Snake Ring

cut yellow & colorless diamonds, flanked by diamond trefoils & swags, platinum-topped 18k gold, obliterated hallmark, possibly for Tiffany & Co., Edwardian (ILLUS. on previous page) **$14,950**

Ring, emerald & diamond, centered by an oval cabochon emerald, surrounded by 16 old mine-cut diamonds, 18k white gold mount (surface nicks & scratches) **$14,950**

Ring, garnet & diamond, three-stone design centered by an oval green demantoid garnet, flanked by prong-set old European-cut diamonds, 18k yellow gold scroll mount, English hallmark (repair to shank) **$4,888**

Ring, garnet, ruby & diamond, designed as a coiled snake w/a demantoid garnet, ruby & diamond bead-set head & tail, 14k yellow gold mount (ILLUS.) **$1,495**

Unusual Child's Face Ring

*Edwardian Diamond
Filigree Ring*

Ring, gold (14k bicolor), crystal, diamond & sapphire, the rose & yellow gold mount w/a carved frosted crystal depicting a young child's face wearing a bonnet set w/six old mine-cut & one round brilliant-cut diamond, ribbon below the child's chin set w/11 rose-cut diamonds, shank portion of ring is of a later date, ca. 1900 (ILLUS.) **$1,265**

Ring, gold (14k yellow), platinum & diamond, filigree platinum reticulated mount set w/41 old mine- & old European-cut diamonds, Edwardian (ILLUS.) **$1,265**

Ring, gold (18k yellow) & diamond, Arts & Crafts style, centered by a cluster of collet-set old European-cut diamonds within an oval millegrain frame, scroll accents, flanked by two collet-set diamonds **$2,530**

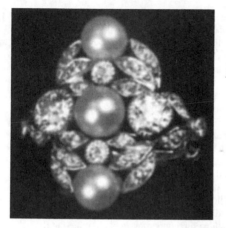

*Pearl &
Diamond Ring*

Ring, gold, turquoise & diamond, dinner-type, 18k yellow gold
floral-designed mount set w/an oval cabochon turquoise stone
measuring 5.6 x 7.2 mm surrounded by 14 old mine-cut diamonds weighing about .45 carats, ca. 1900, size 6 .... **$489**
Ring, pearl & diamond, centered by an old European-cut diamond flanked by pearls, 14k gold mount, Edwardian.... **$2,185**
Ring, pearl & diamond, the center vertically-set w/three pearls
further set w/four collet-set diamonds & old European-cut diamond trefoils, platinum-topped 14k gold mount, Edwardian,
w/finger guard (ILLUS.) **$2,645**

Ring, pearl, garnet & diamond, Arts & Crafts style, bezel-set blister pearl surrounded by four old mine-cut diamonds & eight demantoid garnets, floral motif shoulders, 14k yellow gold mount (demantoids abraided) **$1,725**

Ring, peridot, citrine & aquamarine, Arts & Crafts style, the bombé design featuring a prong-set round peridot surrounded by seven prong-set citrines & seven smaller aquamarines, gold bead accents, silver gilt mount, by Dorrie Nossiter, England **$978**

Ring, sapphire & diamond, centered by a cushion-cut intaglio sapphire within a framework of 24 rose-cut diamonds (later shank) **$4,945**

Ring, sapphire & diamond, centered by an oval cabochon sapphire flanked by two gypsy-set old European-cut diamonds, engraved 18k yellow gold mount **$2,760**

Ring, sapphire & diamond, floral design center set w/round faceted blue sapphire surrounded by eight old mine-cut diamonds, platinum mount, ca. 1900 .... **$1,840**

Ring, spinel & diamond, set w/an oval prong-set red spinel & a crimped collet-set spinel, highlighted by seven collet-set old mine- & old European-cut diamonds, 14k gold openwork shield-form mount **$1,840**

Ring, turquoise & diamond, marquise cabochon turquoise framed by 16 old mine-cut diamonds, 14k yellow gold mount...... **$863**

Ring, white gold, diamond & sapphire, 14k white gold filigree setting containing three mine-cut center diamonds bordered by one small round-cut diamond on each side & flanked by a small triangular sapphire above a band on each side, ca. 1900 .... **$1,120**

Sets

Etruscan Revival Gold Bracelet

Enamel Pansy Brooch

Bracelet & brooch, gold, Etruscan Revival style, the bracelet w/five canatille star-bursts joined by trace links, matching brooch, some discoloration to gold, solder evident to backs, the set (ILLUS. of bracelet) **$1,035**

Brooch & earrings, enamel, the brooch designed as a pansy w/shaded purple enamel petals, centered by a prong-set old

*Victorian
Gold
Grapevine
Suite*

mine-cut diamond, 14k yellow gold mount, together w/matching
pair of earrings w/screw backs, hallmark for A.J. Hedges & Co.,
tiny chip to brooch & one earring, the set
(ILLUS. of brooch on previous page) **$1,380**
Brooch & earrings, gold (14k yellow), a grapevine design
brooch w/gold repoussé leaves accented w/seed pearls, matching
earrings, Victorian, repairs, the set (ILLUS. of part) **$546**

Micromosaic Scarab Brooch

Brooch & earrings, gold (18k yellow) & mosaic, the brooch a
rectangular form w/scrolled & leaf design suspending a circular
micromosaic plaque w/scarab design, together w/pair of matching earrings, ca. 1860, the set (ILLUS. of brooch) **$1,955**

Gold & Amethyst Brooch & Earrings

Brooch & earrings, gold (18k), the shield-shaped brooch
designed w/overlapping gold sections accented w/seed pearls &
amphora-shaped drops, matching earrings, Swedish import assay
marks, Victorian, the set **$1,265**

Brooch & earrings, gold, diamond & amethyst, Rococo Revival
style brooch w/cabochon amethysts within scrolling 14k yellow
gold mount w/collet-set old European-cut diamonds, matching
earrings, the set (ILLUS. of part) **$1,380**

Earrings & pendant, diamond, the earrings each centrally set
w/an old mine-cut diamond surrounded by ten smaller old mine-
cut diamonds, the pendant-drop set w/an old mine-cut diamond

*Diamond
Earrings &
Pendant*

solitaire attached to a fine curb link 16" l. chain, the set
(ILLUS.) **$5,405**
Locket & earrings, enamel & gold, an 18k yellow gold locket
designed w/an enamel portrait of an angel, wings outlined in
onyx & composed of rose-cut diamonds, the platinum-topped
bail set w/two rose-cut diamonds, together w/pair of earpendants
depicting an angel (originally cuff buttons), Victorian, the
set **$1,840**
Necklace & bracelet, tortoiseshell & 18k yellow gold, the neck-
lace composed of alternating gold & tortoiseshell curb links,
together w/matching bracelet, pieces combine to form one necklace, necklace 16 3/4" l., bracelet 7 5/8" l. (two worn
links) **$2,185**

*French
Victorian
Jewelry
Ensemble*

Necklace, bracelet & earrings, enamel, pearl & gold, consisting of French hallmarked 18k yellow gold serpent & leaf necklace, the leaves highlighted w/green enamel, alternating w/openwork serpent links suspending a removable serpent & leaf pendant-brooch w/four leaves highlighted w/green guilloché enamel centering a floral-designed set w/five baroque & one simulated pearl (one pearl missing), w/a matching bangle bracelet & earrings, last quarter 19th c., necklace 15" l., set of 4
(ILLUS.) **$1,840**

Necklace & earrings, onyx, the necklace w/shaped onyx links surmounted by seed pearl decoration suspending an oval pendant w/reverse hair locket, similar earrings, Victorian, the set (chips to glass, later findings) **$978**

Gold & Enamel Necklace, Buckle/Brooch & Earrings

Necklace, earrings & brooch, gold, enamel & diamond, the necklace designed w/an alternating pattern of fancy links set w/numerous rose-cut diamonds outlined in cobalt blue enamel, 14" l., together w/matching earrings, the pendant brooch mounted w/two pear-shaped rose-cut diamonds in buttercup mountings surrounded by diamonds & decorated w/blue enamel scrolls, the set (chip to one rose-cut) **$4,025**

Necklace, earrings & belt buckle/brooch, gold (18k bicolor) & enamel, parure comprising a necklace w/detachable pendant, day/night earpendants & belt buckle/brooch, all matching pieces w/fruit & floral motif basse taille enameling w/acorn gold highlights, 18k yellow gold w/18k green gold inlay, French hallmarks, in original fitted leather box, the set (ILLUS. of part) **$8,625**

Vintage & Collectible Jewelry

Early 20th Century to 1950s

Bar Pins

*Art Deco
Diamond Bar
Pin*

Bar pin, diamond, art deco style, an openwork platinum mount w/pointed ends set w/old mine-cut diamonds, beaded accents, signed "Tiffany & Co." **$4,600**

Bar pin, diamond & 14k yellow gold, five bezel-set old European-cut diamonds, approx. total wt. 4.42 cts., highlighted by 74 diamond melée, approx. 1.03 cts., w/bead & millegrain mount **$5,175**

Bar pin, platinum & diamond, art deco style, central diamond-shaped motif set w/an old mine-cut diamond, surrounded by 54 graduated old mine- & rose-cut diamonds, ca. 1920-30, 3 1/4" l. (ILLUS.) **$2,185**

*Ruby &
Diamond Bar
Pin*

*Sapphire &
Diamond
Bar Pin*

Bar pin, platinum & diamond, art deco style, set w/round diamonds within an open-work platinum mount w/millegrain accents, 14k yellow gold clasp **$863**

Bar pin, ruby & diamond, yellow gold & silver scrolled openwork design alternately set w/five rubies & four round diamonds (ILLUS.) **$920**

Bar pin, sapphire & diamond, art deco style, 12 square sapphires set in groups of three spaced by six old European-cut diamonds, platinum mount w/millegrain accents (one sapphire missing) **$920**

Bar pin, sapphire & diamond, art deco style, centered by a transitional-cut diamond flanked by calibré-cut sapphires within a diamond-set mount w/millegrain accents, missing two diamonds (ILLUS.) **$863**

Art Deco Sapphire & Diamond Bar Pin

Bar pin, sapphire & diamond, art deco style, long narrow form set in the center w/three old European-cut diamonds, accented w/four French baguette-cut sapphires w/diamond-set flower heads, flanked by 12 French baquette-cut sapphires, mounted in platinum w/a 14k yellow gold pin, ca. 1930s (ILLUS.) **$4,485**

Bar pin, sapphire & diamond, centered by a cushion-cut sapphire, measuring approx. 10.01 x 9.23 x 4.49 mm., flanked by four square-cut sapphires & four old European-cut diamonds, approx. total diamond wt. .96 cts., platinum mount, signed "Cartier Paris/Londres No. 9372," French platinum mark... **$7,475**

Bar pin, sapphire & pearl, art deco style set w/nine round faceted blue sapphires alternating w/eight baroque pearls, 14k yellow gold mount, ca. 1935 .... **$431**

Bracelets

Bakelite Cuff Bracelet

Bracelet, Bakelite & faux pearl, cuff-style, hinged design w/an abstract foliate motif of carved green Bakelite set w/faux golden pearls (ILLUS.) **$2,185**

Bracelet, Bakelite "School Days" charm-type, the links designed as rulers suspending seven plastic, Bakelite or felt school-related charms **$345**

Bracelet, bangle-type, garnet, hinged design set w/three rows of faceted garnets, gilt-metal mount **$288**

Muscial Instrument Charm Bracelet

Bracelet, bangle-type, gold (14k yellow), pearl & amethyst, the top portion of the bracelet set w/five oval faceted amethysts alternating w/eight graduated cultured pearls, ca. 1950 .... **$374**

Bracelet, bangle-type, jadeite, mottled apple green, interior measurement 60 mm. ca. 1920, China (cracked) .. **$4,500-$6,500**

Bracelet, bangle-type, onyx & diamond, art deco style, channel-set alternating pattern of French-cut onyx & old European- & single-cut diamonds, platinum-topped 18k yellow gold mount, 7" d. (out of round, solder evident due to sizing) **$2,300**

Bracelet, bangle-type, onyx, emerald & diamond, onyx bangle surmounted by a geometric design of calibré-cut emeralds & old European-cut diamonds set in platinum, millegrain accents, signed "Ghiso," accompanied w/statement that bracelet was made by Alberto Ghiso (one emerald missing, some abraided) **$5,463**

Bracelet, charm-type, gold, the oval link chain suspending seven musical instrument charms, two marked "Italy" & two signed "Tiffany & Co.," all in 14k yellow gold, 7" l. (ILLUS.) **$805**

Bracelet, crystal, sapphire, diamond, gold & platinum, art deco style, the 14k yellow gold & platinum top flexible mount w/five square links each w/a sunburst-etched frosted crystal panel & set

*Art Deco
Style
Diamond
Bracelet*

w/one round old European-cut diamond weighing about .08
carats alternating w/five oval openwork links each set w/one
square French-cut blue sapphire weighing about .10 carats, ca.
1930, 7 1/2" l. **$1,840**

Bracelet, diamond, art deco style, wide design w/three repeated
rectangular-shaped sections, each centrally set w/an old
European-cut diamond having a total weight of approx. 2.0 cts.,
each section pavé-set w/round diamonds, including open, rectangular-shaped links & barrel-shaped connectors, the diamonds
having a total weight of approx. 18 cts., mounted in platinum,
two small stones missing, 7 3/4" l. (ILLUS. of one
section) **$16,675**

Bracelet, diamond & emerald, flexible, strap-type having a repeated eye-shaped motif set w/round diamonds & bordered by round
diamonds, separated by two pairs of baguette-cut emeralds,
mounted in platinum, ca. 1920, 7" l. (two of the 14 emeralds are
simulated **$5,290**

Bracelet, diamond & emerald, flexible, w/a repeating motif composed of two triangle-shaped, faceted emeralds set base to base
on a slightly bombé background of pavé-set old European-cut
diamonds, mounted in platinum, ca. 1925, 7 1/2" l. (three emeralds replaced w/emeralds simulants) **$4,830**

Art Deco Diamond Bracelet

Diamond & Platinum Bracelet

Bracelet, diamond, emerald & platinum, art deco style, center plaque set w/a marquise diamond, flexibly-set throughout w/72 single- & full-cut diamonds, calibré-cut emerald accents, 7" l. (one emerald missing) **$5,463**

Bracelet, diamond, onyx & platinum, art deco style, centered by an old European-cut diamond flanked by flexibly set geometric plaques decorated w/72 diamonds, millegrain accents, 6 5/8" l. (one onyx missing) **$8,338**

Bracelet, diamond & platinum, art deco style, centered by a bead-set round diamond, accented w/46 round diamonds in a pierced, square link bracelet w/29 bead-set round diamonds, one diamond missing (ILLUS.) **$3,738**

Bracelet, diamond & platinum, centered by a spray of eight marquise & bead-set diamonds framed by straight baguettes, flanked by an openwork, graduated flexible band set throughout w/bead-set diamonds, ca. 1950, 6 1/4" l. (ILLUS.) **$3,335**

Bracelet, diamond & ruby & platinum, art deco style, designed w/geometric plaques set w/round diamonds, enhanced by channel-set ruby links, together w/two extra plaques, in fitted box for Cartier, 6 1/2" l. **$12,650**

*Garnet
Bracelet*

Bracelet, diamond, sapphire & platinum, art deco style, centered by an old European-cut diamond & approximately 140 full-cut diamonds & 22 calibré-cut sapphires in flexible geometric plaques, fancy engraved gallery, 6 1/2" l. **$5,463**

Bracelet, emerald & diamond, the central portion containing a square emerald-cut Columbian emerald, flanked on each side w/a row of tapering, calibré-cut emeralds bordered by round single-cut diamonds w/a single row of old mine-cut diamonds on either side, mounted in platinum, 6 3/4" l. **$11,500**

Bracelet, garnet, graduated shaped hinged plaques set throughout w/faceted garnets, together w/extra link, gilt-metal mount, solder evident, some stones missing, 6 1/4" l. (ILLUS.) **$489**

Bracelet, gold (18k tricolor), wide flexible mesh design of polished honeycomb links engraved in a geometric & floral pattern, 7 1/2" **$1,380**

Bracelet, hemitite & gold, Art Moderne design w/cut-corner 18k yellow gold square plaques centered by domed hematite cabochons, alternating w/reeded white gold rectangular links, French gold mark & maker's mark, signed "G. Fouquet, No. 20461," ca. 1930, 7 1/2" l. (rectangular links show minor evidence of gold solder, probably from original construction) **$35,650**

Moonstone &
Sapphire
Bracelet

Elegant Ruby
& Diamond
Bracelet

Bracelet, moonstone & sapphire, oval moonstones & collet-set sapphires mounted in fancy 14k yellow gold links, signed "Yard" for Raymond Yard, 6 3/4" l. (ILLUS.) **$2,300**

Bracelet, platinum, diamond & ruby, designed w/three diamond-set flowers, the middle flower centered by a round brilliant-cut diamond, approx. 2.10 cts., the two side flowers centered by an old European & an old mine-cut diamond, approx. total wt. 1.50 cts., round & French-cut diamond links, approx. total 11.00 cts., diamond flower clasp, round ruby highlights, one small diamond missing, accompanied by a letter of authenticity from Oscar Heyman (ILLUS.) **$25,300**

Bracelet, reverse intaglio crystal, equestrian theme consisting of a horse head, fox head & dog head links attached by stirrup & horse-shoe motif links, 14k yellow gold, dated 1924, 6" l. **$863**

Reverse-painted Crystal Bracelet

Sterling Silver Dove Bracelet

Bracelet, reverse-painted crystal, rectangular plaques depicting four different scenes, a woodcock, a grouse, a quail & a pheasant in flight, spaced by alternating gold leaf-shaped & crossed shotgun-shaped links, 14k gold frame, hallmark (ILLUS.) **$920**

Bracelet, sterling silver, square form leaf & bead decorated links alternating w/openwork oval links centering a model of a dove, No. 14, signed "Georg Jensen," Denmark, 7" l. (ILLUS.) **$1,035**

Bracelet, sterling silver, seven rows of lozenge-shaped links w/beaded edge between links on first & last rows, No. 86, designed by Harald Nielsen, signed "Georg Jensen," Denmark, ca. 1945, together w/bill of sale from Georg Jensen, 1 1/4" w., 7 1/2" l. **$2,645**

Bracelets, Bakelite, "Philadelphia Bracelet," hinged bangle-type, amber w/multicolor spiky teeth **$3,565**

*Modern Wood &
Ivory Bracelet*

Bracelet/ring, gold & gemstone, eight hinged engraved circular links that convert from a bracelet to a ring, the clasp forming the top of the ring w/two interchangeable gemstones, one a blue zircon, the other a citrine, French hallmarks **$805**

Bracelets, wood, ivory & 18k gold, hinged contemporary style, one w/a nephrite bar, the other w/a hematite bar, signed "Amalia del Ponte," numbered "2/50" & "3/50" & dated "1967," in original felt & leather box from Sculpture to Wear, New York, pr. (ILLUS.) **$2,415**

Brooches

*Art Deco
Diamond
Plaque
Brooch*

Brooch, citrine & gold, Retro style, centered by a prong-set emerald-cut citrine highlighted by five round diamonds & eight round rubies within a bicolor 14k yellow gold scroll design **$1,150**

Brooch, crystal, diamond & onyx, art deco style bow design w/etched crystal center, edged in calibré-cut onyx & diamonds, set in platinum, gold pin stem (two onyx missing) **$2,070**

Brooch, diamond, art deco style, oblong plaque-form, centering an old European-cut diamond weighing 1 ct. flanked by straight baguette-cut diamonds within an intricate frame of round & baguette-cut diamonds w/a total weight of 10.80 cts. for the round diamonds & 3.90 cts. for the baguettes, mounted in platinum w/an 18k white gold catch, French hallmarks (ILLUS.) **$6,900**

*Diamond & Enamel Lily
Brooch*

Brooch, diamond & enamel,
designed as a lily w/two
pavé-set diamond leaves,
polychrome guilloché enam-
el leaves & stem, further accented by 16 diamond stamen, 18k
yellow gold, some loss to enamel, marked "Italy"
(ILLUS.) **$3,220**

Brooch, diamond & enamel, modeled as a beetle, the wings in
green guilloché enamel, body, antennae & feet w/round diamonds set in silver, cabochon emerald eyes, sapphire accents,
14k yellow gold mount, Russian hallmarks **$1,725**

Brooch, diamond & onyx, art deco style, centered by a collet-set
European-cut diamond, flanked by an onyx & diamond-set tapering design, platinum mount w/millegrain accents, French hallmark (one onyx missing, minor solder to gallery) **$8,050**

Brooch, diamond & platinum, art deco style, the oblong platinum
filigree mount set w/one round old European-cut diamond
weighing about .60 carats surrounded by 70 graduated round
old European-cut diamonds weighing about 1.50 carats, ca.
1930, 3/4 x 2" **$1,955**

Diamond Leaf Brooch

Brooch, diamond & platinum, art deco style, the platinum open-work mount centered w/one round brilliant-cut diamond weighing about .40 carats set w/60 round brilliant-, old European- and single-cut diamonds weighing about 2.50 carats suspending three teardrop tassels, the center of each suspending a fancy light to fancy brownish-yellow natural-colored briolette-cut diamond weighing about two carats surrounded by 49 round brilliant-cut diamonds weighing about 1.05 carats, 1 1/4 x 2" **$9,200**

Brooch, diamond & platinum, leaf design w/center diamond weighing approx. 1.00 cts., pavé-set w/245 old European-cut diamonds, approx. total wt. 9.80 cts. (ILLUS.) **$11,500**

Brooch, diamond & sapphire, art deco style, lozenge-shaped bow design mounted w/old European-cut diamonds & calibré-set French-cut sapphires, ca. 1925 .... **$3,220**

Diamond & Sapphire Brooch

Art Deco Citrine Brooch

Brooch, diamond & sapphire, art deco style, platinum oval reticulated filigree ribbon design set w/54 round old European- & single-cut diamonds & 22 square & rectangular cut sapphires, ca. 1930, 3/4 x 2" (ILLUS.) **$3,220**

Brooch, diamond, sapphire & citrine, art deco style, the lozenge shape centered by a pear-shaped citrine flanked by three collet-set round citrines, w/French-cut sapphire terminals & round sapphire accents, within an openwork platinum mount bead-set w/old mine- & single-cut diamonds (ILLUS.) **$3,450**

*Emerald &
Diamond Brooch*

*Starburst Design
Brooch*

Brooch, emerald & diamond, two rectangular &
two pear-shaped collet-
set emeralds within an
openwork geometric design set throughout w/rose-cut diamonds, silver-topped 14k yellow gold mount (ILLUS.) **$690**
Brooch, emerald, ruby & sapphire, clip-type, set w/cabochon
emerald surrounded by cabochon rubies & carved sapphires, ca.
1940s, French assay & hallmark "H.L," Cartier,
Paris **$8,625**
Brooch, gold (14k bicolor), aquamarine & ruby, designed as a
rose & yellow gold starburst centered by a step-cut aquamarine,
enhanced by six round-cut rubies (ILLUS.) **$546**

Crown & Stickpin Brooch

Brooch, gold (14k bicolor) & gemstone, designed as a butterfly w/diamond & colored gemstone accents, rose & yellow gold openwork mount, hallmarked **$1,380**

Brooch, gold (14k rose), ruby & diamond, the flower design set w/round rubies & diamonds, 14k rose gold foliate mount, ca. 1940 .... **$1,265**

Brooch, gold (14k yellow), crown design w/seven points, each set w/a cultured pearl w/seven stickpins protruding from crown, variously set w/rose-cut diamonds, paste baroque & seed pearls, a large buff-top amethyst & a round faceted aquamarine, ca. 1950 (ILLUS.) **$460**

*Gold Abstract
Bow Brooch*

Brooch, gold (18k yellow), amethyst & turquoise, designed as a bouquet w/prong-set amethyst petals w/turquoise accents & gold stems w/textured gold leaves, hallmarks for Andre Poirier, Paris **$3,335**

Brooch, gold (18k yellow), modeled as an abstract bow, the terminals bead-set w/round diamonds & channel-set w/emerald baguettes, French hallmarks (ILLUS.) **$748**

*Gold &
Diamond Floral
Brooch*

Brooch, gold
(18k yellow),
opal & diamond, modeled as two violets, the larger flower-head
set en tremblant, w/prong-set black opals & pavé bead-set round
diamond petals mounted in 18k yellow gold, the leaf also pavé
diamond-set, signed "W.T. Ltd.," hallmarks, w/fitted box **$2,185**

Brooch, gold (bicolor) & gemstones, Retro style butterfly design
set w/diamonds & colored gemstone accents, 14k rose & yellow
gold openwork mount, American hallmark **$1,380**

Brooch, gold & coral, designed as an 18k yellow gold branch
w/four coral acorns (solder evident) **$805**

Brooch, gold & diamond, floral circle design, prong set w/seven
round brilliant-cut diamonds, 14k yellow gold mount, hallmark
(ILLUS.) **$978**

Lily of the Valley Brooch

Jade & Diamond Brooch

Brooch, jade, diamond & quartz, lily of the valley design w/carved jade leaf, flowers of carved quartz suspending prong-set round diamonds, 14k gold mount, marked "Made in Austria" (ILLUS.) **$1,495**

Brooch, jadeite jade & diamond, art deco style carved jade plaque bordered on both ends w/old mine-cut diamonds, weighing approx. 3.75 cts., mounted in platinum-topped 18k white gold w/14k white gold pin (ILLUS.) **$13,800**

Water Lily Brooch

Onyx & Diamond Brooch

Brooch, mixed metal, modeled as a waterlily w/beaded center & leaves, chased & engraved 18k yellow gold, hammered silver leaves & lilypads, signed "Janiyé" (ILLUS.) **$345**

Brooch, moonstone & diamond, Retro-style, stylized floral spray set w/ten moonstones, 20 prong-set sapphires & 31 bead-set diamonds, platinum-topped 14k yellow gold mount, signed "Trabert & Hoeffer Mauboussin, Reflection, No. 4383" **$5,175**

Brooch, onyx & diamond, art deco style, a calibré-cut onyx set in an openwork design edged w/37 round diamonds, platinum mount (ILLUS.) **$3,450**

Brooch, onyx & diamond, art deco style, onyx circle w/diamond-set 14k white gold bow accent **$518**

Opal Brooch

Pearl Brooch

Brooch, opal, garnet & ruby, centered by an oval bezel-set opal within platinum & diamond open-work mount w/millegrain decoration set w/demantoid garnet & ruby florets, repair to back (ILLUS.) **$4,600**

Brooch, pearl & silver, circular form set w/11 grey & cream pearls, flanked by an additional pearl at each end & alternating w/engraved leaves, scrolled vine holding center pearl, signed "S.I." w/hallmark for Mikimoto, ca. 1950s (ILLUS.) **$1,725**

Brooch, platinum & diamond, art deco style, oval form set w/graduated old European-cut diamonds, rectangular terminal centered by an old mine-cut diamond surrounded by diamonds, platinum mount **$2,875**

Art Deco Double Clip Brooch

Art Deco Ruby & Diamond Brooch

Brooch, rock crystal & diamond, designed as a leaf accented w/21 circular-cut diamonds, platinum-topped 14k yellow gold, minor chips to crystal, Tiffany & Co. **$2,070**

Brooch, ruby & diamond, art deco style, double clip-type, designed w/eight oval cabochon rubies & set throughout w/bead-set circular-cut diamonds, 12 baguette diamond accents, platinum mount (ILLUS.) **$6,325**

Brooch, ruby & diamond, art deco style w/a center sugar loaf cabochon-cut ruby within a finely worked open frame decorated w/rose-cut diamonds, each end w/an old European-cut diamond, all within a border of small old European- and old mine-cut diamonds, two diamonds missing, mounted in platinum & 18k yellow gold (ILLUS.) **$10,120**

Brooch, sapphire & 14k yellow gold, designed as a Scottie dog, the body covered w/a coat of blue sapphires in various shapes, sizes & colors, collar & eye accented w/diamond melée **$2,645**

Retro Bicolor Sapphire Brooch

Abstract Design Brooch

Brooch, sapphire & gold, Retro style stylized 14k yellow & rose gold bow centered by three bead-set diamonds mounted in platinum, circular & calibré-cut sapphire terminals, inscription on back (ILLUS.) **$1,725**

Brooch, silver glazed earthenware & fused glass, abstract design in shades of green & blue glaze, ceramic backing, abstract silver mount, impressed on reverse "Elsa" for Elsa Freund, ca. 1960 (ILLUS.) **$1,093**

Brooch, star sapphire & diamond, art deco style, bezel-set center star sapphire framed in old European-cut diamonds, platinum mount, signed "M. & Co." for Marcus & Co.................... **$9,200**

Brooch, sterling silver & enamel, open amorphic form accented w/cobalt blue enamel, No. 323, by Henning Koppel for Georg Jensen **$633**

*Sapphire & Diamond
Brooch/Pendant*

Brooch, sterling silver & chrysoprase, shield form w/purplish blue enamel surmounted by a buff top pyramid-shaped chrysoprase, suspending three chrysoprase teardrops, hallmarks for Theodor Fahrner & Patriz Huber, imported by Murrie/Bennet & Co. (minor enamel loss) **$2,070**

Brooch, sterling silver & lapis, designed as a flower centered by a collet-set round lapis, three curving leaves & bead accent, hallmark for Georg Jensen, No. 71 .... **$403**

Brooch, sterling silver, oval, scalloped & beaded edge w/openwork center decorated w/abstract grapevine design, No. 177, signed "Georg Jensen" **$546**

Brooch/pendant, jade & diamond, art deco style, pierced & carved jadeite in the form of a gourd surrounded by an oval platinum frame set w/round diamonds & channel-set faceted onyx, diamond-set bail & slide, suspended from a black cord, w/box, 19" l. **$5,463**

Brooch/pendant, sapphire & diamond, centered by a square sugarloaf sapphire suspended within a geometric & openwork platinum grille set throughout w/single & old European-cut diamonds, 14k white gold pin stem, ca. 1920s (ILLUS.) **$1,380**

Clips

Art Deco Flower Basket Clip

Fine Diamond 'S' Clip

Clip, diamond, emerald, ruby & sapphire, art deco style, designed as a flower basket encrusted w/circular & baguette diamonds, cabochon sapphire, carved emerald & ruby highlights, platinum mount (ILLUS.) **$4,313**

Clip, diamond & platinum, stylized 'S' form, the platinum mount set w/14 round brilliant-cut diamonds weighing about 4.90 carats, six emerald-cut diamonds weighing about 4 carats, two pear-shaped & four marquise-cut diamonds weighing about 2.90 carats, ca. 1960, 1 1/2 x 2" (ILLUS.) **$5,750**

Gold, Ruby & Diamond Christmas Tree Clip

Clips, diamond & platinum, art deco style, designed as chevrons centering a large round-cut diamond & enchanced w/numerous round brilliant-cut & emerald-cut diamonds, approx. 8.00 cts., pr. **$21,850**

Clips, diamond & platinum, ribbon & scroll design set w/146 bead- & collet-set round brilliant- & single-cut diamonds, ca. 1940, pr. **$4,025**

Clip, gold (18k yellow), ruby & diamond, modeled as a stylized Christmas tree, the base set w/11 graduated old mine- & old European-cut diamonds, the body composed of circular swirls set w/42 round faceted rubies, ca. 1950, 1 1/2" w., 3" h. (ILLUS.) **$1,495**

Turquoise & Aventurine Clip

Clip, moonstone & tourmaline, art deco style, the geometric design surmounted by carved moonstone flowers w/collet-set diamond accents & carved green tourmaline leaves, 14k white gold, hallmark for Krementz (chip to one leaf) **$575**

Clip, turquoise & aventurine, flower design w/collet-set turquoise petals framing a round matrix turquoise completed by a carved aventurine leaf, 18k yellow gold mount, stamped "AVI Spain" (ILLUS.) **$978**

Clip brooch, diamond, art deco style circular design w/a cascade motif, decorated w/two large old mine-cut diamonds w/a total weight of approx. 2.5 cts., w/old mine-, old European- & a few rose-cut diamonds, pavé-set within the circle & old mine single-cut diamonds bead set in the cascade, pin on back which allows it to be worn in two directions together w/hinged pendant bail, mounted in platinum w/18k white gold pin, accompanied w/thin neck chain, French hallmarks **$4,255**

Cuff Links

Gold Pistol Cuff Link

Cuff links, gold (14k yellow), modeled as a pistol w/revolving barrel, stamped "Jost," pr. (ILLUS. of one) **$748**

Cuff links, gold, an 18k yellow gold scaly fish w/tiny ruby eyes suspended from a bamboo-form gold bar, Tiffany & Co., by Jean Schlumberger, ca. 1960, 1" l., pr. **$1,495**

Cuff links, gold, moonstone & enamel, art deco style, a 14k yellow gold twin-oval mount set w/two oval cabochon moonstones measuring 7 x 10 mm, within a green to white enameled border, ca. 1935, pr. **$1,093**

Cuff links, mother-of-pearl & enamel, the circular disk centrally set w/a cabochon blue stone, edged in cobalt blue enamel, mounted in 14k yellow gold, hallmark for Krementz, pr. **$345**

Cuff links, Satsuma pottery, round, each set w/Satsuma design of a bamboo tree in green & gilt, ca. 1925, Japan, pr. .. **$200-300**

Cuff links, silver, bird & berry motif, hallmark for Georg Jensen, No 43, ca. 1933-44, pr. **$374**

Earrings

Elegant Diamond Earrings

Earrings, agate & 14k yellow gold, Revival style, banded agate teardrop w/ropetwist & bead cap suspended from a gold roundel centered by a ropetwist flowerhead, 2 5/8" l., pr. **$345**

Earrings, amethyst & diamond, art deco style, a faceted & fluted amethyst tear-drop suspended from a platinum & diamond link chain, screw-on, signed "Tiffany & Co.," pr. **$2,185**

Earrings, aquamarine & diamond, art deco style, oval aquamarine tops suspending a row of bead & collet-set diamonds in millegrain & platinum mounts terminating in claw-set pear-shaped aquamarines, pr. **$3,565**

Earrings, diamond, each set w/a round brilliant-cut diamond weighing approx. 3.0 cts., suspended from a row of three hexagonal-cut diamonds having a total weight of approx. 0.50 ct., freehanging from an old mine-cut diamond weighing approx. 0.50

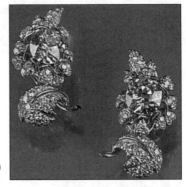

Elaborate Diamond Earrings

ct., having a total weight of approx. 8.0 cts., mounted in platinum w/18k white gold posts, French hallmarks, pr. (ILLUS. on previous page) **$21,850**

Earrings, diamond & pearl, bezel-set old European-cut diamond tops suspending a fall of four bezel-set & seven bead-set diamonds terminating in a South Sea pearl drop measuring approx. 14.90 x 13.80 mm., platinum mount, pr. **$2,530**

Earrings, diamond, platinum & 18k gold, each centered by an old mine-cut diamond approx. 10.98 x 10.37 x 6.40 & 10.95 x 10.30 x 6.42 mm., set in an 18k gold basket design & surrounded by dimaond & platinum trefoils, flanked by pavé-set diamond leaves, designed by Jean Schlumberger for Tiffany & Co., pr. (ILLUS.) **$90,500**

Earrings, emerald & diamond, a pavé-set diamond snake coiled around a cabochon emerald, approx. total diamond wt. 0.72 cts., approx. total emerald wt. 3.45 cts., flexible tail, red stone eyes, 18k white & yellow gold mount, clip-back posts, pr. **$920**

Emerald Earrings

Earrings, emerald, diamond & platinum, designed w/bezel-set circular old mine-cut diamond tops, suspending diamond-set trefoils & similarly styled caps terminating in tumbled pear-shaped emerald beads, ca. 1920s, missing end finials on terminals, in original S.J. Phillips fitted box, pr. (ILLUS. of one) **$16,100**

*Elegant Art Deco Jade
Earrings*

Earrings, jade & diamond,
art deco style, a large carved
mottled green & white jadite
jade disk accented w/rose-cut diamonds in scrolled designs, suspended from round & rose-cut diamonds, mounted in platinum
& 18k yellow gold, jade has some hairline cracks, ca. 1926,
w/maker's mark, w/leather box, pr. (ILLUS.) **$5,060**

Earrings, moonstone & 14k rose gold, day/night style, set w/mar-
quise-cut moonstones & faceted round sapphires, detachable
moonstone & sapphire-set drop, pr. **$1,380**

Earrings, moonstone & ruby, center set w/a prong-set round
moonstone, surrounded by round rubies, 14k yellow gold
mount, pr. **$633**

Earrings, onyx, carnelian & marcasite, art deco style, the marcasite-set terminals suspending a rectangular carnelian plaque &
ovoid onyx drop w/marcasite accents, sterling silver mount,
pr. **$403**

Fine Natural Pearl Ear Pendants

Earrings, pearl, large pear-shaped natural pearl drops, each topped w/a round brilliant-cut diamond attached to a button-shaped pearl ear pad surrounded by round diamonds, can be worn independently without the detachable drops, mounted in 14k white gold, ca. 1930, w/original leather box & EGL report stating the pearls are saltwater natural pearls, pr. (ILLUS.) **$57,500**

Earrings, platinum & diamond, designed as abstract bowknots set w/82 full-cut & baguette diamonds, ca. 1950, pr. **$2,875**

Earrings, ruby & diamond, four graduated bezel-set circular-cut diamonds, approx. total wt. 1.00 cts. suspending seven marquise-cut & pear-shaped ruby drops, approx. total wt. 4.50 cts., within a platinum-topped 18k yellow gold openwork mount w/diamond accents, pr. **$4,025**

Necklaces/Pendants

Art Deco Diamond & Ruby Necklace

Necklace, amber, comprised of butterscotch colored "rock" amber alternating oval & elliptical beads, purchased in 1922, 39" l. (some cracks) **$316**

Necklace, aquamarine & platinum, art deco style large teardrop-shaped aquamarine pendant suspended from a platinum-topped 14k gold floral engraved box & rectangular link chain, hallmark for Allsopp & Allsopp, 15 1/2" l. **$3,738**

Necklace, diamond & ruby, art deco style featuring a slightly graduating row of square-cut calibré rubies & round brilliant-cut diamonds, 18k white gold mounting, approx. diamond wt. 3.00 cts. (ILLUS.) **$2,185**

Diamond & Chrysoprase Choker

Necklace, diamond, green chrysoprase & platinum choker-type, the double chain alternating 62 collet-set round- & 62 marquise-cut diamonds totalling approx. 11.50 cts., centering a modified oval openwork section w/a marquise-cut diamond, approx. 2.50 cts., & two square-cut, eight baguette-cut & two half-moon-shaped diamonds, total approx. 2.60 cts., defined by carved green chrysoprase accents, approx. 26.1 dwt. (ILLUS.).......... **$16,675**

*Art Deco Carved
Emerald & Diamond
Necklace*

Necklace, emerald &
diamond, art deco
style, a large pendant
in the Oriental
flower vase motif
designed from
carved Columbian
emeralds & round
diamonds, w/black
enamel & cabochon-
cut emerald accents,
joined by a black
enamel loop to a
similarly designed emerald, diamond & black enamel chain,
mounted in platinum, numbered, w/French hallmarks & maker's
mark, ca. 1925, Mauboussin, Paris (ILLUS.) **$167,500**

*Gold & Diamond
Necklace*

Necklace, gold (18k yellow) & diamond, designed w/an open circle & oval drop w/prong-set diamonds suspended from a pavé-set terminal, completed by a double barrel link chain w/collet-set diamonds, approx. total diamond wt. 2.40 cts., obliterated signature for Cartier, ca. 1950s (ILLUS.) **$4,025**

Necklace, jade, lariat-type, oval-shaped jade within 14k gold & enamel frame suspending two teardrop-shaped jade drops suspended by a black cord, ca. 1930 .... **$920**

Necklace, jadeite, diamond & seed pearl, art deco style, composed of delicately woven seed pearls w/four oval pierced & carved green jadeite plaques & suspending another larger elongated oval pierced & carved jadeite pendant w/a floral design, accented w/small round brilliant- and rose-cut diamonds, mounted in platinum, 17" l. **$10,580**

Art Deco Sterling Marcasite Necklace

Abstract Design Necklace

Necklace, pearl, 81 cultured pearls measuring approx. 8.40 to 8.90 mm., 14k gold clasp, 32" l. **$805**

Necklace, sterling silver, abstract open form links, designed by Henning Koppel, hallmark for Georg Jensen, ca. 1947, 15 1/2" l. (ILLUS. of part) **$1,150**

Necklace, sterling silver & amethyst, designed w/overlapping silver arcs suspending teardrop cabochon amethyst, signed "Antonio, Taxco, Mexico" **$920**

Necklace, sterling silver, quartz & marcasite, art deco style, designed w/marcasite-set hinged silver links centered by an abstract knot terminating in a faceted fancy shape smoky quartz, green stone accents, hallmarks for Theodor Fahrner (ILLUS.) **$6,900**

Art Deco Style Crystal Pendant

Pearl enhancer, gold (18k yellow) & diamond, the stamped polished triangular form mount w/scalloped edge & set w/52 round brilliant-cut pavé-set diamonds.................................... **$1,035**

Pendant, crystal, diamond & platinum, art deco style, the crystal reverse intaglio depicting a dancer within an openwork frame w/bead-set round diamonds, diamond-set bail (ILLUS.) **$2,990**

Pendant, diamond & pearl, art deco style, designed as an openwork bell-shaped cap bead-set w/old European- and full-cut diamonds & a row of channel-set square-cut sapphires, diamond-set bail, platinum mount, suspending a multi-strand seed pearl tassel, Tiffany & Co. partially obliterated signature **$3,220**

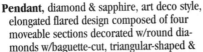

*Art Deco Diamond &
Sapphire Pendant*

Pendant, diamond & sapphire, art deco style,
elongated flared design composed of four
moveable sections decorated w/round diamonds w/baguette-cut, triangular-shaped &
calibré-cut sapphires set in geometric designs, attached to a fine
link chain w/rectangular-shaped, barrel clasp decorated w/two
small diamonds, two triangular-shaped & two baguette-cut sapphires, platinum mounting & chain, approximately 21 1/2" l.
(ILLUS.) **$4,830**

Pendant, jade & diamond, art deco style, the jade carved &
pierced in a floral design, accented w/collet-set diamonds & surmounted by a diamond-set cap, cabochon sapphire accent, suspended from a rose-cut diamond bail & black cord w/rose-cut
diamond terminals, pendant signed "Cartier New York," clasp
signed "Cartier," numbers obliterated, 27" l. **$8,050**

Art Deco Pendant

Sapphire & Diamond Pendant

Pendant, jadeite, white, rectangular w/dragon & cloud decoration on both sides, 36.1 mm. x 29.3 mm., China.... **$1,000-$1,500**

Pendant, onyx, diamond & platinum, art deco style, centered by an old European-cut diamond within an onyx circular frame, further enhanced by three collet-set old European-cut & 36 rose-cut diamonds within a pierced & millegrain mount, suspended from a trace-link chain, 16" l. (ILLUS.) **$2,300**

Pendant, sapphire & diamond, art deco style, flexible bail suspending a lozenge shape plaque set throughout w/old European- & single-cut diamonds, calibré-cut sapphire accents, millegrain & platinum (ILLUS.) **$3,565**

*Art Deco
Tourmaline
& Diamond
Pendant*

Pendant, sterling silver, abstract geometric form suspended from a torque, signed "Ed Wiener," ca. 1949 .... **$2,990**

Pendant, sterling silver & amethyst, centered by an oval faceted amethyst within a circular foliate frame, hallmark for Theodor Fahrner, completed by a twisted curb link silver chain, 28" l. **$374**

Pendant, tourmaline & diamond, art deco style, centering a pinkish-purple tourmaline carved in a three-dimensional floral design w/a small diamond pistil, in a frame of old mine-cut (one replaced w/an old European-cut) & baguette-cut diamonds mounted in platinum & 18k white gold (ILLUS.) **$9,200**

Stone-set Pendant & Chain

Pendant & chain, gold & semi-precious stone, egg-form, tested 18k yellow gold mount set w/eight oval cabochon multi-colored & lace agate stones each measuring 9 1/2 x 13 mm, together w/an 18k yellow gold rope chain, ca.1950, 20" l. (ILLUS.) **$230**

Pendant/brooch, citrine, pearl, coral & gold, Art Nouveau style, the 18k yellow gold delicate scrolling leaf mount set w/a large heart-shaped scotch-colored citrine weighing about 50 carats flanked by two leaping silver panthers, the top set w/four fresh-water pearls, the bottom suspending a yellow gold, orange coral & baroque pearl tassel, ca. 1960, 2 x 4' **$1,265**

Pins/Stickpins

*Art Deco
Coral &
Onyx Pin*

*Diamond & Garnet
Dragonfly Pin*

Pin, coral, onyx & diamond, art deco style geometric buckle design of coral w/onyx & diamond highlights, platinum mount (ILLUS.) **$2,990**

Pin, diamond & garnet, dragonfly design w/demantoid garnet-set tail, scrolled openwork wings w/collet- & bead-set diamonds, ruby eye accents, platinum-topped 18k yellow gold mount (ILLUS.) **$4,313**

Figural Bee Pin

Pin, diamond, pearl & platinum, art deco style, 'S'-form, the platinum mount in the form of an elongated S set w/seven round old European- and mine-cut diamonds weighing about 1.05 carats alternating w/12 rose-cut diamonds, the ends set w/two oblong pearls, one natural, the other cultured & added at a later date, together w/the original fitted box, dated 1922, 1 1/2" l **$1,265**

Pin, diamond & sapphire, art deco style, bow design centered by a collet-set old European-cut diamond surrounded by smaller bead-set old European-cut diamonds, edged w/channel-set cali-bré-cut sapphires, silver mount, gold pin stem, European hallmarks **$2,415**

Pin, enamel, butterfly design, the silver-topped wings set w/pearls, opals, colored gemstones & diamond accents, bordered by orange guilloché enamel, 19k yellow gold mount, Portuguese hallmarks **$633**

Pin, gold (18k yellow), mother-of-pearl & ruby, a three-dimensional bee design w/four round, faceted rubies set in the body, round brilliant-cut diamond-set eyes & antennae, mother-of-pearl wings accented w/twisted gold wire, French hallmark, maker's mark & signed "Chaumet" (ILLUS.) **$2,185**

Art Deco Moonstone Pin

Pin, gold & pearl, "Golden Mink," designed as a textured 14k yellow gold mink w/sapphire eye accents, surmounting three baroque pearls, signed "Rotter" **$259**

Pin, gold & pearl, mistletoe design w/pearl berries, brushed 18k yellow gold leaves & branches, numbered & signed "Buccellati" **$863**

Pin, gold, Retro style bow of 14k pink & green gold, stamped "H.S.B." **$374**

Pin, gold & silver, sterling silver eagle surmounting a shield atop two crossed anchors in 14k yellow gold, signed "Tiffany & Co." **$460**

Pin, moonstone, flower design set w/round moonstone petals, red stone center accents, 14k yellow gold stem, leaf & mount, hallmark for Wordley, Allsopp & Bliss, Newark **$489**

Pin, moonstone, sapphire & platinum, art deco style, centered by a sugarloaf moonstone, flanked by square-cut sapphires, edged w/rectangular moonstones, all channel-set, oval moon-stone terminals, wiretwist filigree accents, yellow gold pin stem, signed "Tiffany & Co.," 3" l. (ILLUS.) **$24,150**

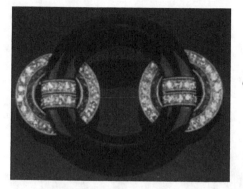

*Art Deco
Circle Pin*

Pin, onyx, diamond & ruby, art deco style, onyx circular plaque
w/round diamond & calibré-cut ruby terminals, platinum mount,
minor chip to onyx, signed "J.E. & Co." for J.E. Caldwell & Co.,
No. K-5045 (ILLUS.) **$9,775**

Pin, pearl, onyx & diamond, art deco style bow design centered by
a cultured pearl w/collet- & bead-set pavé-set diamond accents,
engraved platinum mount **$978**

Pin, ruby & diamond, designed as a circular band of channel-set
rubies & single-cut diamonds surmounted by a diamond floret,
platinum & millegrain mount **$2,760**

Pin, sapphire & diamond, circular design w/an alternating pattern
of round sapphires & old European-cut diamonds, approx. total
diamond wt. .60 cts., platinum-topped 14k yellow gold
mount **$1,380**

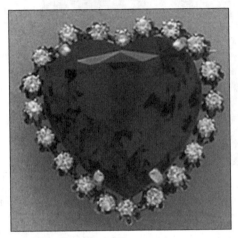

Amethyst Heart-shaped Pin

Pin, sterling silver, modeled as a pansy, hand-hammered w/beaded accents, signed "Georg Jensen, No. 113" **$374**
Pin/pendant, amethyst & diamond, heart-shaped amethyst surrounded by 20 prong-set round diamonds, 14k yellow gold mount (ILLUS.) **$862**

Diamond & Sapphire Pin/Pendant

Pin/pendant, diamond & sapphire, center set round diamond w/rose-cut diamonds in the circular white gold openwork design & framed by 12 round sapphires (ILLUS.) **$1,840**
Stickpin, enamel, designed as a beagle head, diamond eye, 14k yellow gold engraving & chasing, hallmark **$575**

Emerald & Diamond Stickpin

Stickpin, emerald & diamond, art deco
style, cushion-cut emerald in a pierced & platinum millegrain
mount edged w/12 old mine-cut diamonds (ILLUS.) **$1,495**

Stickpin, sapphire & diamond, art deco style, circular form set
w/29 channel-set sapphires & 35 rose-cut diamonds, the inner
rings swivel to reveal opposite color combination, maker's mark
on pin stem, French assay marks, signed "Cartier Paris Londres,
No. 2432" **$4,140**

Rings

Edwardian Diamond Ring

Ring, aquamarine, diamond & platinum, Retro-style, dinner-type, the platinum four-prong A-box mount set w/one rectangular emerald-cut aquamarine weighing about 6.35 carats flanked by three round brilliant-cut & two baguette diamonds weighing about .35 carats, J.E. Caldwell, Philadelphia, ca. 1940, size 9 .... **$1,725**

Ring, diamond, 14k yellow gold & platinum-topped oval mount set w/three round old European-cut diamonds framed by 20 old mine-, old European- & single-cut diamonds, ca. 1910, Edwardian (ILLUS.) **$1,035**

Ring, diamond, art deco style, center fancy color diamond flanked by two old European-cut diamonds in a pierced platinum mounting set w/diamonds in the gallery, hallmark for Jung & Klitz **$28,750**

Ring, diamond, centering an old European-cut diamond weighing approx. 5.50 cts. w/24 small round, single-cut diamond accents, mounted in platinum **$13,800**

Ring, diamond, collet-set oval old European-cut yellow diamond, approx. 1.75 cts., framed by concentric rows of calibré-cut emeralds & sapphires, platinum mount **$2,875**

Ring, diamond, gentlemen's Masonic ring w/a bezel-set old European-cut diamond, 14k yellow gold & enamel mount **$2,300**

Ring, diamond & gold, tested 18k yellow & white gold mount centered by one oval old mine-cut diamond weighing about 2.75 carats flanked by two smaller old mine-cut diamonds each weighing about 1.30 & 1.50 carats, size w/ball spacers 5 3/4 .... **$14,950**

Ring, diamond, men's twin-stone design w/two old European-cut diamonds weighing approx. 1.35 cts. & 1.23 cts., bead-set in squared white gold mountings, 14k yellow gold mount, marked "F.R. Co." **$6,038**

Ring, diamond & platinum, art deco solitaire, the platinum four-prong mount set w/one round old European-cut diamond weighing about 1.25 carats flanked by two marquise & ten single-cut diamonds weighing about .40 carats & three straight baguette emeralds weighing about .15 carats, ca. 1920-30, size 6 (one emerald missing) **$3,680**

Ring, diamond & platinum, reticulated mount set w/an old European-cut diamond weighing approx. 1 ct. flanked by four smaller round old European-cut diamonds weighing approx. 2 cts., surrounded by six round brilliant-cut, six marquise, two pear-shaped & 14 baguette diamonds weighing approx. 2.80 cts. **$6,900**

Ring, diamond, Retro style, centering two round diamonds, one old European- and one round brilliant-cut w/a total weight of

Ruby & Diamond Ring

1.50 cts., decorated on one side w/five round & six baquette-cut diamonds & on the opposite side w/four baquette-cut diamonds within a frame of eight round-cut diamonds w/a total weight of 1.30 cts. for the baquettes & .60 cts. for the rounds, mounted in platinum **$4,370**

Ring, diamond & ruby, bombé cross-over design centering a round faceted ruby approx. 3.37 cts. on one side & an old mine-cut diamond approx. 2.44 cts. on the other side, w/pavé-set round brilliant-cut diamonds w/total weight of approx. 7.75 cts., mounted in platinum (ILLUS.) **$13,800**

Ring, diamond solitaire, centered by an old European-cut diamond, approx. 3.75 cts., futher set w/ten bead-set diamonds in a scroll design, 14k white gold mount **$10,350**

Diamond Ring

Ring, diamond solitaire, gentlemen's, Retro style, 18k white gold box illusion mount set w/one old mine-cut diamond (ILLUS.) **$2,760**

Ring, diamond solitaire, gentlemen's, Retro style centering a round old European-cut diamond, 14k yellow gold mount, ca. 1940 .... **$4,830**

Ring, diamond, solitaire, men's, centered by a claw-set old European-cut diamond weighing approx. 0.95 cts., 14k yellow gold mount (minor chips) **$1,150**

Ring, emerald & diamond, art deco style set w/an octagonal square-cut emerald flanked by 18 single-cut diamonds, platinum mount, ca. 1920-30 .... **$1,840**

Ring, emerald, diamond & platinum, center set w/a square-cut emerald weighing approx. 5.25 cts., surrounded by 16 round old European-cut diamonds weighing approx. 2.40 cts., the shoulders of the ring set w/six smaller round old European-cut diamonds weighing approx. .10 cts. **$5,290**

Ring, gold (14k white) & diamond, art deco style, set w/one round old European-cut diamond approx. 1.05 cts., flanked by

Art Deco Diamond Dinner Ring

two smaller old mine- & European-cut diamonds, approx. .40 cts., ca. 1930 (ILLUS.) **$1,495**

Ring, jadeite, set w/oval-shaped cabochon of mottled apple green, approx. 14.7 mm. x 10.8 mm. x 5.9 mm., 14k gold mount, post-World War II, China **$1,000-1,500**

Ring, onyx & diamond, centered by an emerald-cut onyx measuring approx. 4.85 x 14 x 18.50 mm., flanked by ten old European-cut diamonds, approx. 1.40 cts., further set w/six colorless sapphires (scratch to onyx) **$2,300**

Ring, opal & diamond, art deco style, an oval opal edged by four collet-set old European-cut diamonds, eight diamond accents, platinum mount w/engraved & chased shoulders (minor scratches to opal) **$1,495**

Ring, pearl & diamond, shield shape, centered by a cultured pearl measuring approx. 6.20 mm., framed by eight old European-cut diamonds, approx. total wt. 0.80 cts., further surrounded by nine cultured pearls each measuring approx. 3.20 mm., 14k yellow gold mount **$1,093**

Ring, pearl & emerald, art deco style, centered by a cultured pearl flanked by table-cut emeralds, diamond shoulders, pierced & millegrain platinum mount (one emerald cracked) **$3,450**

*Art Deco Diamond
Dinner Ring*

Ring, platinum & diamond, art deco style, dinner-type, platinum braided design mount centered by a bezel-set round old European-cut diamond surrounded by 34 round old mine- & old European-cut diamonds, ca. 1930 (ILLUS.) **$2,415**

Ring, platinum & star sapphire, art deco style, centered by a star sapphire flanked by bead-set & tapered baguette-cut diamonds **$4,025**

Ring, ruby, diamond & gold, Claddach-style, the tested 14k yellow gold mount set w/a pear-shaped diamond weighing about .50 carats & one pear-shaped ruby weighing about .35 carats surrounded by 30 old mine-cut diamonds weighing about .75 carats, ca. 1930, size 4 3/4.. **$2,530**

Ring, ruby, diamond & platinum, art deco eternity band-style, the platinum channel mount set w/21 single-cut diamonds weighing about .35 carats alternating w/21 square-cut rubies weighing about .70 carats, ca. 1920-30, size 6 1/2 .... **$1,035**

Ring, ruby & diamond, Retro style, designed w/a cluster of rubies & a cluster of round-cut diamonds, wide reeded bypass 14k yellow gold mount **$1,955**

Ring, sapphire, art deco style, centered by an oval sapphire within a single-cut diamond-set platinum mount, millegrain accents (solder evident, two small diamonds missing) **$5,750**

Ring, sapphire & diamond, art deco style, centering an emerald-cut sapphire weighing 3.70 cts. decorated on each end w/two small triangular sapphires, within a frame of old round single-cut diamonds w/three additional diamonds in each shoulder, mounted in platinum **$3,680**

Ring, sapphire & diamond, centrally designed w/two rows of faceted calibé-cut sapphires w/a row of round brilliant-cut diamonds forming a border on each side, having an approx. total diamond weight of 0.50 ct., mounted in platinum, numbered & signed "Cartier," ca. 1930 .... **$6,325**

Ring, sapphire & diamond, designed w/stepped bars of channel-set square sapphires & round diamonds, platinum mount, ca. 1940s **$2,760**

Ring, star sapphire, centering a round cabochon-cut star sapphire weighing approx. 17 cts., mounted in platinum, ca. 1935, signed "Tiffany & Co.," w/original leather box **$3,680**

Sets

Art Deco Bracelet & Brooch

Bracelet & brooch, gold (18k yellow), art deco style, flexible belt design w/three rectangular & oval interlocking links, together w/matching brooch converted from one of the bracelet links, ca. 1930, bracelet 6" l., the set (ILLUS.)........................ **$1,380**

Bracelet & necklace, gold (14k yellow), a floral & scroll link necklace together w/a bracelet of similar design, No. 251, signed "Georg Jensen," necklace 19 1/2" l., bracelet 7 1/2" l., the set **$3,738**

*Leaf-shaped
Brooch*

Brooch & dress clips, gold (18k), sapphire & diamond, the
openwork brooch designed as a leaf set w/sapphire & diamond
florets, diamond-set platinum-topped stem, together w/two
matching dress clips, the set (ILLUS. of brooch) **$5,175**

Brooch & earrings, citrine & diamond, the brooch designed as a
four-leaf clover w/heart-shaped citrine leaves centered by a circular-cut diamond w/a bead-set diamond stem, 14k yellow gold
mount, matching earrings, the set **$546**

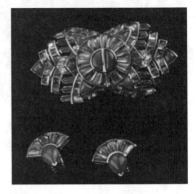

*Art Deco Brooch &
Earrings*

Brooch & earrings, jade, moonstone & diamond, art deco style,
a double-clip brooch (one moonstone missing) & matching pair
of clip earrings, platinum mounts, signed "Seaman Schepps," the
set (ILLUS.) **$8,338**

Brooch & earrings, sterling silver, the brooch of asymmetric
design w/bead accents, No. 235, signed "Sigi, Taxco," together
w/pair of matching earrings designed w/asymmetric pendant
drop decorated w/two beads & suspended from round silver
bead, screw-on, the set **$460**

Dress set, mother-of-pearl, a pair of cuff links w/center pearl
accent, together w/four matching vest buttons & three shirt studs,
platinum-topped 14k gold mount, the set **$633**

*Garnet &
Seed Pearl
Necklace*

Earrings & pendant, aquamarine, prong-set emerald-cut aquamarine earrings & similar pendant suspended from a 20" l. 14k
white gold box-link chain, 14k white gold mounts, the
set **$403**

Necklace & earrings, garnet & seed pearl, the necklace set
w/faceted garnet clusters, the center three accented by seed
pearls, together w/a matching pair of clip earrings, gilt silver
mounts, ca. 1950s, hallmark, the necklace 14" l., the set (ILLUS.
of part) **$1,035**

Necklace & earrings, opal & diamond, the necklace centered by an opal suspended within a blue enamel engraved plaque w/diamond accents, further suspending a similiar drop, the fine 10k yellow gold chain w/old mine-cut diamond floral links spaced by opal-set plaques, together w/silver-topped gold mount earrings, the set **$2,300**

Necklace & earrings, sterling silver & enamel, the necklace designed w/stylized links & light blue enamel, w/matching earrings, NO. 5372, signed "Margot de Taxco," the set **$403**

Necklace & earrings, sterling silver, the necklace of hinged retangular plaques decorated w/an applied foliate design, together w/matching earrings, signed "USA Georg Jensen Inc.," earrings No. 419B, necklace No. 429B, the set **$633**

Necklace & earrings, sterling silver, the necklace w/rectangular links w/oval floral cartouche spaced by trapezoid shape links, signed "Georg Jensen, No. 60B," together w/clip earrings designed as round balls set within open circles, signed "Georg Jensen, No. 91," the set **$633**

Collecting
Costume Jewelry

Costume jewelry...what is it? To say that it's jewelry made of inexpensive materials is only part of the story. It's a personal adornment old as mankind. In early historic times shells, animal bones, teeth, and feathers were used as personal ornaments. Ancient civilizations produced jewelry made of glass, ceramics, iron, copper, and bronze.

During the mid-to-late 19th century, mass production made it possible for the average woman to purchase inexpensive jewelry. Daytime jewelry of the 19th century was the forerunner of 20th century costume jewelry. Hair jewelry, jet, gutta percha, bog oak, black glass jewelry, pinchbeck as well as gold-filled and sterling silver jewelry were popular. Shell cameos were available in gold-filled and silver mountings as well as in precious 14k and 18k gold. Garnet jewelry set in gold-plated brass, copper, gunmetal, silverplate on copper, celluloid, and enamel on sterling were some of the materials used in daytime jewelry.

Sears Roebuck catalogs enabled almost every woman to afford at least one piece of finely made inexpensive jewelry. Amber and coral beads, gold-filled and sterling lockets, and gold-filled festoon necklaces set with "fine imitation diamonds" could be purchased for less than $3. Gold-filled and rolled gold-plated bangle bracelets, expansion bracelets, and chain link bracelets were also available at these low prices. Daytime jewelry imitated the designs of precious jewelry and the more "real" it looked, the better.

During this time it became stylish for some women to show off their wealth with precious jewelry. The more precious jewelry someone wore, the richer she was, and rich women, and those who aspired to be, looked down at inexpensive jewelry as "sham jewelry" or "imitation jewelry."

Two art movements of the late 19th and early 20th century helped make non-precious jewelry more acceptable to fashionable women. The Arts and Crafts and art nouveau artisans felt that their art was an expression of the design and the materials used weren't as important as the design itself. Their work showed that beauty and craftsmanship were not limited to expensive metals and precious stones. Jewelry was made of glass, ivory, enamels, tortoise-shell, and freshwater pearls.

Rene Lalique, a jewelry craftsman of the time, used glass and a variety of semi-precious gemstones in his designs. These art designs made jewelry of inexpensive materials more acceptable to the public, but it wasn't until after World War I that costume jewelry was created and became widely accepted.

After the grim reality of a world war, to show off one's wealth became socially inappropriate. Dress designer Coco Chanel saw costume jewelry as the mark of the post-war liberated woman who dressed to please herself and not to display her wealth. She designed original and conspicuously fake costume jewelry to complement her clothing collection. She did not try to disguise the fact that these art forms were made of inexpensive materials and that they did not imitate precious jewelry. She also went against the conventions of the time by mixing precious and costume jewelry as accessories for her clothing collections.

Art deco became the major art and design movement of the 1920s. Geometric forms and bright colors replaced the snake-like gale-swept curves and pastel colors of art nouveau. Art deco motifs emphasized speed and movement and were influenced by Native American, African, Egyptian, Chinese, and Japanese art.

Elsa Schiaparelli and other dress designers also began designing their own jewelry for their costume designs and, by 1933, the term "costume jewelry" came into use. During the 1930s costume jewelry, originally a fun fashion accessory, became a fashion necessity for the Depression-poor public. An inexpensive clip or pin could extend the wardrobe for a woman who couldn't afford new clothing, and many makers of costume jewelry helped to meet this need. Coro, founded in the first decade of the 20th century, pro-

duced thousands of different designs each month. Its production
ranged from higher end fashion jewelry to very inexpensive jewelry
marketed in dime stores. The United States division of Coro discontinued production in the 1970s and the Canadian division in
1996.

Trifari was founded in 1918 as a maker of hair ornaments. In the
1920s women bobbed their hair, and when combs became passe,
Trifari turned to making costume jewelry. By 1930 designer Alfred
Philippe joined the company. His designs made costume jewelry
become totally acceptable to fashion-conscious women when First
Lady Mamie Eisenhower, wife of president Dwight D. Eisenhower,
commissioned him to design sets of costume jewelry for both of
her inaugural balls in 1953 and 1957. In doing so, she became
the first wife of a president to wear costume jewelry to her inaugural ball. Trifari continues making lovely costume jewelry designs
today.

Eisenberg originally started as a women's clothing firm in 1880.
An attractive piece of jewelry made with Swarovski crystals was
attached to each dress to appeal to customers and increase sales.
By the 1930s theft of the pins from the dresses became so great
that Eisenberg made a separate line of costume jewelry to sell to
the public. Eisenberg is still in business today and continues making fine rhinestone jewelry.

Miriam Haskell founded her own jewelry company in 1924 in New York City. Her designs were not mass produced but each one was made by hand. Many designs featured beads, seed pearls, and rhinestones put together with tiny wires on an openwork metal background. Her very pretty, detailed style was continued by her assistant, Frank Hess, in 1953 when she fell ill. Miriam Haskell jewelry is still being made today.

Wartime restrictions of metals affected the costume jewelry industry during the 1940s. Metals such as brass, copper, chrome, and nickel were commandeered by the government for the war effort. Sterling silver, which was not needed for the war, became a base metal for costume jewelry and was also plated with gold. Other materials including plastic, glass, leather, fabric, and straw were used to meet the increased public demand for costume jewelry.

The 1950s and 1960s were prosperous decades for the nation and for the costume jewelry industry as well. People were very fashion-conscious and had money to spend, and women looked for designer names as indicative of good quality costume jewelry.

By the 1970s, women no longer followed the fashion trends, and many costume jewelry makers went out of business, but some survived and are still in business today.

During the 1980s, celebrities such as Princess Diana of England, Madonna, and Michael Jackson helped revive an interest in costume jewelry. Collecting vintage costume jewelry became the hot new hobby and continues into the 21st century.

Originally not meant to last any longer than the clothing it accessorized, costume jewelry did survive as many women continued to wear it and saved it for its beauty. More than merely jewelry made of inexpensive materials it is art, design, and fine craftsmanship. It is a reflection of its time and representative of art and design movements of those times. It's a wonderful 20th century accessory that continues to be made today. But best of all, costume jewelry is not only meant to be collected, but to be worn and enjoyed!

Marion Cohen

Costume Jewelry

Bracelets

Gold-plated & Faux Gemstone Bracelet

Bakelite & Brass Bangle Bracelet

Bracelet, antique gold-plated links, four large ornate links set w/large faux gemstones & trimmed w/multicolor rhinestones, signed "Marino," 2 3/8" w. (ILLUS.) .... **$80-$100**
Bracelet, bangle-type, Bakelite, alternating sections of Bakelite & brass, 3 1/4" (ILLUS.) **$175**

Monet Bangle Bracelet

Faux Gemstone Bangle Bracelet/Watch

Bracelet, bangle-type, hinged, gold-plated, large rhinestone end ornaments can be removed & bracelet can be refitted w/black enamel & pearl ornaments, signed "Joan Rivers," mint condition in original box & velvet pouches .... **$150-$175**

Bracelet, bangle-type, hinged, gold-plated, matte finish, squared top, purple marquise rhinestone designs, signed "Monet," 1 1/2" w. (ILLUS.) .... **$150-$175**

Bracelet, bangle/watch, hinged, textured gold-plated finish, large faux emerald center w/marquise cabochon faux gemstones, opens to reveal watch under emerald center (ILLUS.) .... **$185-$220**

Bracelet with Rose Charms

Vendome Charm Bracelet

Bracelet, charm, brass, chain w/six rose charms (ILLUS.).......... **$55-$75**
Bracelet, charm, gold-plated multi-chain, filigree enclosed red beads, green "jade style" beads, basket style charm of green "jade" beads, red rhinestone trim, signed "Vendome" (ILLUS.) .... **$65-$90**
Bracelet, charm, gold-washed sterling, chain links w/15 assorted charms .... **$150-$185**
Bracelet, charm, heavy sterling silver chain w/15 assorted motif charms .... **$165-$195**
Bracelet, cuff-style, sterling silver, three openwork flowers w/raised centers, 1 1/2" w. .... **$135-$155**

Cini Floral Bracelet

Bracelet, gold-filled links, five hinged links set w/oval shell cameos on circles, signed "Sammartino Bros.," ca. 1910, 1" w. .... **$375-$400**

Bracelet, gold-plated links, square motif, Retro design center w/two rows of vertical baguettes, signed "Trifari," 1" w. .... **$175-$200**

Bracelet, gold-plated open-work links w/leaves, red baguette flowers w/clear pavé-set rhinestone center, signed "Trifari," 5/8" w. .... **$125-$150**

Bracelet, link, gold-filled circles alternating w/large emerald cut royal blue stones, 5/8" w. .... **$95-$115**

Bracelet, rhinestone, art deco style links set w/clear & blue stones, signed "TKF" (old Trifari mark), 1" w. ...... **$175-$200**

Bracelet, rhinestone, double row of large clear stones, center emerald-cut stones w/overlaid rhinestone-set ovals, signed "Eisenberg," 3/4" w. .... **$150-$175**

Bracelet, rhinestone, hand-set clear openwork links, large oval red rhinestone centers, round red rhinestones accents, signed "Kramer," 1" w. .... **$175-$200**

Bracelet, slide-style, gold-plated, Victorian style motifs strung on double chain, pearl spacers, faux turquoise, jade & cultured pearl centers, thick oval clasp w/faux goldstone & three hanging chains w/pearls, 5/8" w. .... **$70-$95**

Bracelet, sterling silver, links of flower & leaves motif, signed "G. Cini," 1" w. (ILLUS.) .... **$250-$275**

Clips

Art Deco Style Clip

Clip, gold-plated, bird motif, movable wings w/clip on each wing, large snakechain tassel in mouth, tag marked "Claire McCardell," 4" .... **$165-$185**

Clip, gold-plated, Retro style open fan style top, center blue baguettes, hanging tassel, signed "Kreisler," 2 3/4" .. **$95-$120**

Clip, rhinestone, art deco style oval iridescent green art glass stones in inverted teardrop shape, large emerald green baguettes, trimmed w/clear square stones, 3" (ILLUS.) .... **$90-$120**

Grape Cluster Clip

Clip, rhinestone, art deco style w/red cabochon stones designed as a cluster of grapes, red & clear baguettes leaves & stem, 3 1/4" h. (ILLUS.) .... **$90-$120**

Clip, rhinestone, flower & leaves design, large clear unfoiled emerald cut center stones, large marquise-set drop, pear-shaped & round stones trim, signed "Eisenberg Original," 2 1/2" w., 4 1/4" h. .... **$375-$425**

Leo Glass Ornate Filigree Clip

Clip, rhinestone, gold ornate inverted teardrop-shaped filigree set w/large cabochon amber stones, signed "Leo Glass," 2 1/4" (ILLUS.) .... **$75-$100**

Clip, rhinestone, large clear & emerald marquise stones in ribbon style Retro design, signed "Eisenberg Original," 3" **$275-$300**

Clip, rhinestone, large swirled feather motif, clear marquise stones, signed "Eisenberg Original," 3" h. .... **$275-$300**

Rhinestone Bow Clip

Clip, rhinestone, openwork bow design w/large oval pink, purple & aqua rhinestones, pavé-set clear stones on "ribbon," 2 1/4 x 3 1/4" (ILLUS.) .... **$125-$150**

Clip, rhinestone, pavé-set w/clear marquise stones in openwork white metal, 2 5/8" .... **$75-$100**

Shield-shaped Clip

Rosenstein Flower Design Clip

Clip, rhinestone, shield shape design w/three large red cabochon marquise center stones & oval & diamond shaped red, green & blue stones, small clear stones trim, 2 x 2" (ILLUS.) .... **$75-$100**

Clip, sterling & gold-washed, large openwork flower, cluster of green glass teardrops in center, w/clear rhinestones set in tips extending from center, signed "Nettie Rosenstein," 3 x 3 1/2" (ILLUS.) .... **$275-$325**

Carved Bakelite Leaf Clips

Clip, sterling, scallop shape, marcasites set, center cabochon-set faux blue topaz, 1 3/4" .... **$95-$125**

Clip/compact, green enamel on chrome, opens to reveal compact w/puff, 1 5/8" d. .... **$195-$225**

Clip/lorgnette, folded sterling silver lorgnette behind white metal marcasite set clip, Retro design, 1 1/4 x 2" when folded .... **$325-$350**

Clips, Bakelite, marbleized butterscotch yellow circles, densely carved leaves, 1 3/4" d., pr. (ILLUS.) .... **$85-$110**

Clips, enameled, duette, blue enameled birds on floral branch, pavé-set rhinestone-set heads, signed "Coro Duette," 3 1/4" .... **$265-$300**

Clips, Bakelite, marbleized yellow w/light brown inlay design, 2", pr. .... **$95-$115**

Clips, glass & enamel, large red glass spheres w/red enameled ribbon style coils & clear rhinestone accents, signed "Coro Duette" .... **$85-$110**

Art Deco Rhinestone Duette Clips

Clips, gold finish, antiqued, wings motif set w/faux cabochon rubies, 2 1/2", pr. .... **$70-$85**

Clips, gold-plated, chatelaine style, pavé-set rhinestone keys on hearts, connected w/chain, pearls in center .... **$75-$95**

Clips, gold-plated, sweater-type, leaf motif connected w/chain, pearls in center .... **$20-$25**

Clips, rhinestone, art deco bow motif, larger emerald, triangle rhinestone accents, 1" h., pr. **$35**

Clips, rhinestone, bow motif, pavé-set rhinestones, 3/4", pr. .... **$30-$45**

Clips, rhinestone, duette, pavé-set openwork art deco design, signed "TKF (Trifari) Clipmates," 2 5/8" (ILLUS.) .. **$175-$200**

Clips, sterling, sweater-type, circles connected w/chain links w/original flannel storage case, signed "Tiffany & Co." .... **$95-$125**

Earrings

Pear-shaped Earrings

Earrings, crystal & sterling, drop-style, two crystal beads on sterling chains hanging from art deco design, ca. 1930, screw-on, 2 1/8" l., pr. .... **$75-$100**

Earrings, glass beads, black beads wired to silver background, signed "Schiaparelli," clip-on, 1 1/4", pr. .... **$150-$175**

Earrings, glass stones, white free-form style shape, clear rhinestone background, signed "Jomaz," 1 1/8" d., pr. ...... **$75-$95**

Earrings, gold-plated, drop-style, gold-plated leaves connected w/rhinestone strips, large rhinestone center, one behind the other in three-dimensional effect, signed "Hobé," slip-on, 3 1/4" l., pr. .... **$75-$95**

Earrings, metal & plastic, nine multicolored plastic hoops that can be interchanged on gold-plated metal clips, signed "Kenneth Lane," together w/original black cylindrical box, also signed "Kenneth Jay Lane," 1 3/4" l., the set..................... **$150-$175**

Earrings, pearl, large pearl ball hanging from three baguette rhinestone "chain," 2 1/4", pr.................................... **$45-$65**

Earrings, rhinestone, drop-style, light blue top, large black pear-shaped drops w/Aurora Borealis finish, screw-on, 1 1/2", pr. (ILLUS.) .... **$45-$65**

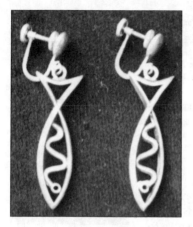

Sterling Fish Motif Earrings

Earrings, rhinestone, green, fleur-de-lis style, signed "Eisenberg," clip-on, 1", pr. .... **$75-$100**

Earrings, sterling silver, drop-type, marcasite-set graduated crescents w/bow motif top, unsigned Alice Caviness, clip-on, 1 3/4", pr. .... **$80-$100**

Earrings, sterling silver, drop-type, openwork fish motif, screw-on, 1 3/4", pr. (ILLUS.) .... **$60-$75**

Earrings, sterling silver flowers, screw-on, 1" d., pr. .. **$60-$75**

Earrings, white metal, pear-shaped, center grey iridescent pear-shaped stone in textured frame, clip-on, 1", pr. .... **$25-$35**

Lapel Watches

Horse Head Form
Lapel Watch

Lapel pendant watch, 800 standard silver set w/marcasite, marcasite-set bow pin w/center swiveling drop to hold watch which can detach & be added to 30" marcasite accented chain, 17 jewel, w/original cylindrical box, signed "Bucherer" .... **$350-$400**

Lapel watch, enameled, cloisonné, yellow background, pink roses & green leaves, watch suspended from bow motif by chains, watch swivels to read time, second hand, signed "Crawford," w/original blue velvet box, 2" l. .... **$240-$265**

Lapel watch, gold-filled flower spray w/watch set as a flower on stem, second hand, watch signed "Louis," pin signed "Carl-Art," 2 1/2" .... **$200-$225**

Lapel watch, gold-filled, heart-shaped watch suspended from Retro ribbon style pin, second hand, signed "Selbro," 2 1/2" .... **$175-$200**

Lapel watch, gold-plated, Retro style horse head motif, watch w/works visible on reverse, signed "Monocraft" (old Monet mark), 2 1/4" (ILLUS.) .... **$150-$175**

Floral Spray Lapel Watch

Lapel watch, sterling silver & marcasite, floral spray design w/watch set as flower, second hand, signed "Merit," 3" (ILLUS.).. **$265-$295**

Lapel watch/pendant, silver (800) & marcasite, bow pin w/swivel drop suspending detachable watch, attaches to matching 30" marcasite-set chain, signed "Bucherer," w/original box .... **$400-$425**

Necklaces

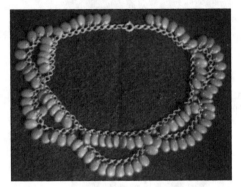

*Collar Style
Glass Bead
Necklace*

Necklace, antiqued goldplate, Renaissance style, purple marquise stone links & snakechain, ornate center moftif w/center purple stones, signed "Sandor," 16" l. .... **$135-$155**

Necklace, Bakelite, 2" black owl slide, white trim on 48" gold-tone snakechain, ca. 1930 .... **$165-$190**

Necklace, beads, coral glass, collar style, hanging from gold-plated swag design chains, ca. 1955, 15" l. (ILLUS.) .... **$100-$150**

*Ornate Glass
Bead Necklace*

Necklace, beads, double strand purple glass beads w/two very ornate overlaid beaded purple glass drops w/pink rhinestones & pink glass flowers, the center drop w/bow designs, custom made by Ian St. Gielar, 20" l. (ILLUS.) .... **$1,200-$1,500**

Necklace, beads, graduated amber, yellow & marbleized brown oval beads, 29" l. .... **$135-$155**

Necklace, beads, graduated coral & red beads on sterling silver chain, 16" l. .... **$180-$220**

*Art Deco Carnelian & Enamel
Necklace*

Necklace, beads, yellow art glass w/multicolored dots, long
faceted beads alternating w/white metal spacers, double
teardrop-shaped drops, ca. 1925, 25" l., drops
4 1/2" .... **$150-$175**

Necklace, carnelian & enamel, art deco style, carved glass car-
nelians & enamel links w/Chinese writing, ca. 1930s
(ILLUS.) .... **$100-$125**

Necklace, enamel, cloisonné on sterling, green enamel links w/4"
drop w/watch which reverses to yellow rose design, ca. 1930,
chain 22" l. .... **$155-$185**

*Flower Motif
Necklace*

Necklace, gold-plated, carved red beads, large oval pearls alternating w/gold-plated chains, signed "Miriam Haskell,"
31" l. .... **$200-$250**

Necklace, gold-plated double chain suspending seven square-shaped enameled flower motifs w/center black oval stones framed by pearls, stone & pearl accents, signed "Hobé," 15" l.
(ILLUS.) .... **$200-$250**

*Jomaz
Collar
Necklace*

Necklace, gold-plated, inverted triangular links, large center faux emerald on each, purple & clear rhinestone trim, signed "Jomaz," 14 1/2" l. (ILLUS.) .... **$250-$300**

Necklace, gold-plated & rhinestone, Renaissance style design w/red rhinestones in center of two pearl links, pendant of red center stone w/pearl trim, two links leading to large oval stone in center of pearls & red stone motif w/three 4" hanging drops, signed "Ricarde of Hollywood," 16 1/4" l. .... **$275-$325**

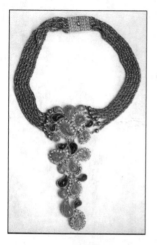

Rare Dior Necklace

Necklace, gold-plated, six chains w/large four-part pink art glass stones drop, curved teardrop shapes, amber teardrop shapes, clear rhinestone trim, signed "Chr. Dior Germany," ca. 1970, 15" l w/5 1/2" l. drop, rare (ILLUS.) .... **$1,000-$1,300**

Necklace, pearl & bead, multi-strand, pearls alternating w/red, blue & green glass beads, gold spacers, 3 1/2" beads drop, signed "deLillo," 18" l. .... **$150-$175**

Necklace, pearl, double strand baroque pearls, ornate filigree drop w/center red marquise stone flower, signed "Miriam Haskell," adjusts to 15" l. .... **$225-$250**

*Pearl, Crystal & Rhinestone
Necklace*

Necklace, pearl, triple strand
baroque pearls in shades of grey,
ornate silvertone floral center, signed "Miriam Haskell," adjusts
to 15" l .... **$185-$225**

Necklace, rhinestone, crystal & pearl, single strand of pearls
alternating w/purple crystal beads suspending a 5" l. triangular
pendant set w/purple cabochons & centered by two large red
oval rhinestones framed by clear rhinestones, three hanging
baroque pearl drops, signed "deLillo," 20" l.
(ILLUS.) .... **$700-$800**

Necklace, rhinestone, "Fruit Salad" design w/red, blue & green
stones in fruit motifs, pavé-set clear stone links, signed "Trifari,"
16" l. .... **$425-$450**

Pins

Carved Bakelite Pin

Pin, Bakelite, carved beige wood seahorse on brown wood,
3 1/8" .... **$100-$125**

Pin, Bakelite, carved palm fronds & coconuts resembling acorns,
dark green, ca. 1930s, 3 1/4" l. (ILLUS.) **$175**

Pin, Bakelite, very densely carved black raised flowers & leaves
set in diamond shape, gold-plated twisted metal frame,
2 3/8" .... **$175-$200**

Pin, brass, bearded man wearing turban, signed "Joseph
Hollywood," 2" .... **$185-$225**

Pin, brass, ornate dimensional openwork, large center cabochon
purple stone, flowers w/purple stone center, ca. 1885,
2" w. .... **$75-$100**

Pin, celluloid, figure of World War II sailor w/rope, marbleized
beige, 2 3/4" .... **$35-$50**

Pin, ceramic on sterling, white cameo on deep blue jasper background, wide ornate silver filigree frame, signed "Wedgwood
Made in England," w/original tag, in original gift box,
1 1/4" d. .... **$165-$1850**

*Enameled
Bow Pin*

*Tiger and Leopard
Pins*

Pin, enamel, bow design in white enamel trimmed in gold, Trifari (ILLUS.) .... **$65-$85**

Pin, enamel & rhinestone, model of a black-enameled leopard w/pavé-set rhinestone trim, Carolee Limited Edition, 1992, 3 1/4" l. (ILLUS. w/tiger) .... **$100-$125**

Pin, gold on sterling, Retro spray flower, leaves, unfoiled open set pink & light blue stones, old Boucher mark, 2 1/4" **$250**

Ornate Gold-plated Pin

Pin, gold on sterling, two large Retro-style flowers, large
turquoise rhinestone pavé-set centers, clear rhinestone trim,
signed "Pennino," 2 7/8 x 2 3/8" **$395**

Pin, gold-plated, antiqued, large red center stone framed by grey
stones, red & grey accent stones & scrolled & leaf-form border,
multichains fringe, signed "Sandor," 4" (ILLUS.) .... **$65-$85**

Diamond-shaped Pin with Crystals

Pin, gold-plated, centered by bust of lady wearing winged helmet, top set w/green, blue, red & violet oval stones, large ornate drop w/figure of Mercury in center, signed "Sathennic Arts," 3 1/2" .... **$125-$150**

Pin, gold-plated & crystals, diamond-shaped openwork form w/rows of crystal Aurora Borealis finish hanging drops that move w/wearer, signed "Vendome," 2 1/2" (ILLUS.) .... **$75-$100**

Pin, gold-plated dimensional design Christmas tree, red, green & blue stones, clear baguette "candles," signed "Original by Robert," 2" .... **$85-$110**

Gold-plated Stickpin & Holder Pin

Pin, gold-plated, five "stickpin" designs in ornate holder, pearls & colored rhinestone accents, unsigned designer quality (ILLUS.) .... **$60-$85**

Pin, gold-plated, large three-dimensional flower w/green rhinestone center & clear rhinestone trim, unsigned designer quality, 2 3/4 x 4" .... **$150-$175**

Figural Scottie Pin

Ornate Gold-plated Pin

Pin, gold-plated, model of Scottie dog, 1 3/4" w. (ILLUS.) .... **$35-$50**

Pin, gold-plated, ornate scrolled top w/large pear-shaped blue stone accented w/pearls & blue rhinestones, suspending five chains w/blue art glass beads & pearls, ending in center star-burst medallion set w/blue art glass bead surrounded by small pearls, signed "Coro," 2 1/4" w., 5" h. (ILLUS.) .... **$125-$150**

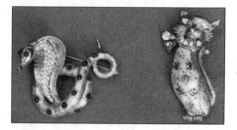

Figural Cat & Cobra Pin

Pin, gold-plated, Retro-style, pink tone floral spray w/green rhinestone trim, ca. 1946, 3 1/2" .... **$45-$65**

Pin, gold-plated sterling silver, flower spray design w/large emerald-cut red glass stone, coiled leaves, signed "Jolle," ca. 1943, 2 1/4" w., 4" h. .... **$165-$195**

Pin, gold-plated sterling silver, star motif w/center blue cabochon stone, small star accents, signed "Nettie Rosenstein," 2" .... **$225-$250**

Pin, goldtone & glass, model of a standing modernistic cat w/white glass & "coralene" style design body, rhinestone collar & eyes, signed "Francoise" (ILLUS. right) .... **$95-$120**

Pin, goldtone & rhinestone, model of a hooded cobra, pavé-set w/rhinestone & cabochon multicolored stones on the body & eyes .... **$85-$115**

Pin, leather, model of cowboy-style hat in light brown w/hanging gold-plated guitar w/strings, matching leather back, ca. 1943, 2 x 2 1/2" .... **$65-$85**

Rhinestone Bow Pin

Rhinestone
Pins

Pin, rhinestone, bow motif completely set w/large pink & clear oval stones, clear square stone trim, signed "Coro," 2 3/4" w. (ILLUS.) .... **$85-$110**

Pin, rhinestone, cabochon-set large oval glass stones in purple, faux agates, faux pink, red & purple gemstones, signed "Robert Original," 2 1/2 x 3" (ILLUS. left) .... **$165-$185**

Floral Rhinestone Pin

Pin, rhinestone, large flower spray design set w/pink tear-drop-shaped & emerald-cut rhinestones, large round pink stone in flower center surrounded by scalloped border set w/clear stones, stems set w/clear stones, leaves accented w/pink square-cut stones, signed "Staret," 3 x 5" (ILLUS.) .... **$500-$525**

Multicolored Rhinestone Pin

Snowflake-shaped Pin

Pin, rhinestone, oval gold filigree metal set w/large topaz surrounded by green, red, blue & purple oval & marquise stones, 2 7/8" (ILLUS.) .... **$125-$150**

Pin, rhinestone & pearl, gold-plated snowflake design, large center baroque pearl w/three-dimensional layered pearl drops & clear pear-shaped & round rhinestones, signed "DeMario NY," 3" d. (ILLUS.) .... **$300-$325**

Large Bow Design Pin

Pin, rhinestone, three-dimensional gunmetal finish bow design w/very large foiled & unfoiled multi-shaped rhinestones in shades of blue, purple, green, pink & citrine, signed "Lawrence Vrba," 4 x 4 1/2" (ILLUS.) .... **$600-$700**

Pin, rhinestones, grape purple border of leaves around marquise-cut & custom made leaf-shaped dark purple & pale blue stones, Aurora Borealis rhinestone centers, 2 3/4" l. .... **$75-$95**

Pin, sterling silver, model of an open-winged bird feeding on a berry, signed "By G. Roupoli" & "Black, Starr & Gorham," 2 1/4" .... **$175-$200**

Pin, sterling silver, Rococo flower & leaf design set w/four large crystals, Cini .... **$325-$350**

Figural Pin with Turquoise

Marcasite Christmas Tree Pin

Pin, sterling silver, scallop shell design w/flying bird inside, large real pearl, ca. 1910, 1 x 1 1/2" .... **$125-$150**

Pin, sterling silver, two seated cats w/green cabochon stone eyes, one cat in matte gold-plated finish, signed "Gorham," 2 3/8" .... **$125-$150**

Pin, white metal, face of native w/hanging turquoise ball earrings, ivory plastic horn headdress w/turquoise trim, signed "Alexander Konda," 3 1/4" h. (ILLUS.) .... **$150-$175**

Pin, white metal, model of a Christmas tree, scalloped branches set w/marcasites & red stones, signature illegible, 2 1/8" (ILLUS.) .... **$55-$75**

Circle Pin with Multicolored Stones

Pin, white metal, ornate open-work metal circle design, 1 3/8" d. raised faux topaz center, cabochon oval multicolored "agate" border, signed "Miracle," 3 1/4" d. (ILLUS.).......... **$195-$225**

Pin, white metal & rhinestone, modeled as an orchid w/curved petals & leaves set w/grey & clear rhinestones, Reinad, 4" h. .... **$250-$275**

Pin/pendant, sterling silver, design w/two horses facing each other over large oval black cabochon stone, 1 3/4 x 2" .... **$100-$125**

Pin/pendant, sterling silver, handmade abstract design w/polished grey shell center, signed "A. Idan." 2 1/4" .... **$100-$125**

Pins, enamel, h.p. figures of a girl & a boy publicizing movie "The 5000 Fingers of Dr. T," Columbia Pictures, set of two .... **$125-$150**

Rings

Ring, gold-filled, large emerald-cut purple stone, 1"... **$75-$100**

Ring, gold-plated & rhinestone, high dome style, latticework design w/amber rhinestones in each section, signed "Trifari" .... **$30-$45**

Ring, sterling silver, cabochon amethyst & marcasites, 1" w. .... **$75-$100**

Ring, sterling silver, cigar band style w/large ruby red center cabochon stone, two wide citrine color cabochons, applied curved designs on dark background, 1" w. .... **$40-$55**

Sets

Art Deco Style Bracelet & Clip

Bracelet & clip, rhinestone, art deco style, the wide bracelet center set w/blue & clear rhinestones, together w/matching shield-shaped clip, gold metal mount, McClelland, the set (ILLUS.) .... **$575-$600**

Bracelet & earrings, metal, ornate gold metalwork links, center link set w/faux amethyst, matching pair of 1 1/2" l. drop earrings w/center-set faux amethyst, the set .... **$75-$95**

Clip & necklace, gold-plated & rhinestone, Retro style diamond-shaped motif necklace set w/green diamond-shaped rhinestones on snakechain, matching pair of 2 3/4" clip-on earrings, signed "Trifari," the necklace 15" l., the set .... **$175-$200**

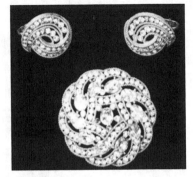

*Rhinestone Pin &
Earrings Set*

Earrings & pin, metal & rhinestone, the pin in ornate gold metal openwork lacy circle design, together w/matching pair of 1" d. clip-on earrings, signed "Trifari," pin 1 3/4" d., the set (ILLUS.) .... **$70-$95**

Necklace, bracelet & drop earrings: rhinestone, hand-set royal blue rhinestones w/clear rhinestone trim, necklace w/central large stones & drops, the bracelet w/double row of stones & a center design, matching clip-on earrings, signed "Eisenberg," earrings 1 3/4" l., necklace adjusts to 16", the set .... **$565-$600**

Necklace, bracelet & pin, gold-plated & rhinestone, matching set w/raised center floral motif set w/multicolored rhinestones, unsigned designer quality, necklace 15" l., bracelet 1 1/4" w., pin 2" d., the set .... **$375-$400**

*Necklace & Earrings
with Green Stones*

Necklace & earrings,
gold-plated chain com-
posed of circular ropetwist & rectangular textured links, some
set w/green rhinestones, five drops set w/large teardrop-shaped
green art glass & amber & green rhinestone accents, ropetwist
frame, the center drop further decorated w/three ropetwist links
set w/small green stones, together w/matching pair of 2 3/4" l.
drop earrings, necklace adjusts to 17" l., the set
(ILLUS.).. **$250-$300**
Necklace, earrings & brooch, rhinestone, the necklace composed
of Aurora Borealis beads suspending a round pendant w/center-
set large rhinestone surrounded by smaller stones, the 1 1/2"
brooch & 3/4" d. earrings match the drop, necklace 20" l., the
set **$300**

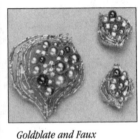

Goldplate and Faux Pearls Set

Rhinestone Necklace and Pin

Necklace & pin, rhinestone, faux cabochon sapphire links w/hand-set clear rhinestone borders, the necklace w/a single row of the sapphires & the pin w/five drops, signed "Kramer," necklace adjusts to 15", pin 3" h., the set (ILLUS.) .... **$425-$450**

Pin & earrings, goldplated metal, a design of openwork branches, the center w/a design of blue & grey pearls w/rhinestone trim, signed "Gasty Paris," manufactured by Grosse, dated "1969," earrings 1" w., pin 2" d., the set (ILLUS.) .... **$100-$125**

Estate Jewelry

Estate jewelry refers to any piece preowned, but in this book it refers to jewelry from the 1960s to the present.

Bar Pins

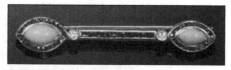

Turquoise & Sapphire Bar Pin

Bar pin, diamond & platinum, designed as three open sections of scrolling design set throughout w/158 small round diamonds, total approx. 4 cts., approx. 10.2 dwt. **$4,312**

Bar pin, turquoise, sapphire & diamond, centered by a row of square-cut sapphires flanked by two small round brilliant-cut diamonds w/navette-shaped cabochon-cut turquoise surrounded by calibré-cut sapphires at each end, one sapphire missing, mounted in 18k white gold (ILLUS.) **$1,150**

Bracelets

Cuff Bangle-style Gold Bracelet

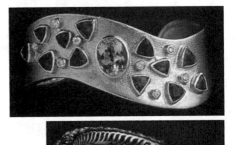

Jeweled Bracelet

Bracelet, bangle-type, gold (14k yellow), beryl, garnet & diamond, cuff style centered w/an oval-shaped green beryl, approx. 12.50 x 10.00 x 7.70 mm. & enhanced by triangular-shaped rhodolite garnets accented by full-cut diamonds, approx. 5 1/2" (ILLUS.) **$690**

Bracelet, bangle-type, gold (14k yellow) & gemstone, hinged tubular reticulated form set w/clusters of colored gemstones, including ruby, sapphire, emerald, turquoise, carnelian & pearl, India, 33.4 dwt. (ILLUS.) **$863**

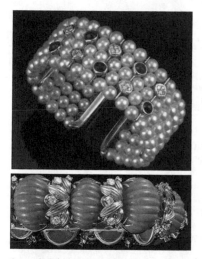

Pearl & Gem-set Cuff Bracelet

Coral & Diamond Bracelet

Bracelet, bangle-type, pearl, ruby, sapphire, emerald & diamond, cuff-style, flexible design w/five rows of cultured pearls measuring approx. 5.50 mm. each, separated by spacers set w/cabochon rubies, sapphires, emeralds & cluster of round brilliant-cut diamonds, 18k yellow gold mount (ILLUS.) **$1,840**

Bracelet, coral & diamond, flexible, designed w/ten fluted, oval-shaped, cabochon-cut corals, each separated by a section of four ribbed gold petals & five round brilliant-cut diamonds, total approx. weight for the 50 diamonds, 3.75 cts., mounted in 18k yellow gold, approx. 7 1/2" l. (ILLUS. of part) **$5,750**

*Diamond &
Gold Toggle
Bracelet*

*Ornate
Diamond
Design
Bracelet*

Bracelet, crystal, consisting of four round reverse-painted crystals
of birds, a hummingbird, a robin, a cardinal & a woodpecker,
14k yellow gold mount, the crystals alternating w/chain links
centering figural gold designs, a tree, a flower & a birdhouse,
American hallmark, fitted box marked "Hancocks & Co."
(ILLUS.) **$3,105**

Bracelet, cultured pearl, ruby & diamond, a triple strand w/60
pearls measuring 6 to 6.5 mm. alternating w/two 14k yellow gold
spacer bars set w/ten round faceted rubies weighing about .70
carats joined by a 14k yellow & white gold tongue-in-groove box
clasp set w/12 round faceted rubies weighing about 1.50 carats
surrounded by 12 round brilliant-cut diamonds weighing about
.20 carats, 1" w., 7" l. **$2,530**

Bracelet, diamond, a central swirled design w/an off-center large
round brilliant-cut diamond surrounded by a mixture of smaller
round brilliant- & baguette-cut & pear-shaped diamonds attached
to a flexible strap composed of round brilliant-cut, baguette-cut
& pear-shaped diamonds having a total weight of approx. 16 cts.,
baguette-cut diamond clasp, mounted in platinum, 6 1/2" l.
(ILLUS.) **$10,350**

Diamond & White Gold Bracelet

Diamond & Platinum Bracelet

Bracelet, diamond, flexible, the center set w/a marquise-shaped, brilliant-cut diamond weighing approx. 0.40 ct., flanked by straight baguette- and round brilliant-cut diamonds, w/a double row of round single-cut diamonds decorating the bracelet & catch ends, having approx. 3.60 cts. total weight, mounted in 14k white gold, w/maker's mark, approx. 7" l. (ILLUS.) **$2,760**

Bracelet, diamond & gold, a wide hinged cuff design of reeded 18k yellow gold w/Greek key motif in bead-set round diamonds mounted in white gold, approx. total diamond wt. 2.00 cts., 55.60 dwt, signed "Tiffany".. **$2,875**

Bracelet, diamond & platinum, flexibly-set w/17 circular-cut diamonds in open circles alternating w/diamond-set openwork geometric links, 6 3/4" l. (ILLUS.) **$1,610**

Unusual Diamond Bracelet

Diamond & Sapphire Bracelet

Bracelet, diamond, repeated sectional, wide, open & intertwining links set w/round brilliant-cut diamonds having an approx. total weight of 7 cts. & further decorated w/pairs of square-cut diamonds, the 28 diamonds having an approx. total weight of 10 cts., mounted in platinum, signed "Koch," 7 1/2" l. (ILLUS.) **$11,500**

Bracelet, diamond, ruby & gold, bangle-type, 14k yellow gold mount, the top portion set w/15 round brilliant-cut diamonds weighing about 2.25 carats alternating w/28 round faceted rubies weighing about .85 carats **$2,300**

Bracelet, diamond, sapphire & platinum, designed w/22 pear-shaped & ten round brilliant-cut diamonds, approx. total weight 13.4 cts., alternating w/ten sugarloaf sapphires, 7" l. (ILLUS. of part) **$14,950**

*Emerald,
Pearl &
Diamond
Bracelet*

Bracelet, emerald, pearl & diamond, centered by an oval cabochon emerald weighing approx. 19.67 cts., framed by pearls &
diamonds, suspended within a bracelet designed w/four strands
of cultured pearls measuring 6 1/2 to 7 mm. w/diamond set terminals & plunger clasp, approx. total wt. 1.26 cts., platinum
mount, 7 1/2" l. (ILLUS.) **$4,600**
Bracelet, gold (14k white & yellow) & aquamarine, centered by
an oval aquamarine, approx. 20.35 x 14.37 x 9.21 mm., within a
platinum filigree & diamond applied plaque, fancy link white
gold bracelet w/yellow gold foxtail border **$805**

*Gold Cuff
Bracelet
with Lions*

Bracelet, gold (14k yellow), crystal & enamel, designed w/four reverse-painted crystals depicting dogs set on an oval link bracelet w/black & light green enamel decoration (crack to one crystal, minor enamel loss) **$1,265**

Bracelet, gold (18k) cuff-type, facing lions in repoussé, signed "Webb" (ILLUS.) **$4,370**

Bracelet, gold (18k) & sapphire, wide, hinged rectangular plaques set w/66 mixed-cut sapphires, approx. total wt. 43.0 cts., separated by chased abstract gold branches, 7 1/4" l. **$3,105**

*Textured
Gold
Bracelet*

Bracelet, gold (18k), textured woven links, signed "Buccellati," 7 3/4" l. (ILLUS.) **$2,875**
Bracelet, gold (18k white) & diamond, flexible design of round links set w/221 round brilliant-cut diamonds, weighing approx. 1.50 cts., 7" l. **$1,100**

Tiffany Coral & Diamond Bracelet

Gold & Diamond Bracelet

Bracelet, gold (18k yellow), coral & diamond, a semi-rigid design constructed from seven fluted coral-set sections, each separated by a heavy gold wire-designed flower set w/a round brilliant-cut diamond having a total weight of approx. 1.15 cts., signed "Tiffany & Co.," 7" l. (ILLUS.) **$5,060**

Bracelet, gold (18k yellow), designed in an alternating pattern of open rectangular & modified knot links, one link inscribed, hall-marked & signed "Cartier, Inc.," Swiss, 55.9 dwt., 7 1/2" l. **$3,220**

Bracelet, gold (18k yellow) & diamond, 3/4" wide band w/twist-ed gold wire design, set throughout w/256 small round dia-monds, total approx. 13.50 cts., signed "Tiffany," approx. 53 dwt. (ILLUS.) **$19,550**

*Unusual Diamond &
Gold Bracelet*

*Enamel &
Diamond
Bracelet*

Bracelet, gold (18k yellow) & diamond, wide hinged cuff-style
decorated along center-line w/a detachable, flexible platinum
bracelet decorated w/marquise-, baguette- & round brilliant-cut
diamonds set in a ribbon motif, total approx. diamond weight
9.30 cts., cuff signed, platinum bracelet numbered, each ap-
prox. 6 1/2" l. (ILLUS.) **$7,475**

Bracelet, gold (18k yellow), enamel & diamond, a flexible, fluid,
reptilian design decorated w/blue & green enameling & two rows
of equispaced round brilliant-cut diamonds w/total approx.
weight of 3 cts., approx. 7" l. (ILLUS.) **$2,875**

*Pearl & Diamond
Bracelet*

*Sapphire &
Diamond
Bracelet*

Bracelet, pearl & diamond, four strands of pearls measuring
approx. 7.70 mm., separated by spacers set w/four round brilliant-cut diamonds, diamond-set domed shell motif clasp centered by a row of baguette-cut diamonds & bordered by baguette-cut diamonds, approx. total wt. 7.00 cts., platinum clasp,
14k white gold spacers (ILLUS. of part) **$6,900**

Bracelet, sapphire & diamond, a flexible design set w/seven
emerald-cut blue sapphires alternating w/seven emerald-cut yellow sapphires, having a total weight of approx. 103 cts., accented
between each sapphire w/a small round brilliant-cut diamond
flanked by two tapered baguette diamonds, mounted in platinum,
numbered & signed "Oscar Heyman," 7" l. (ILLUS.) .. **$23,000**

Brooches

Fish Brooch

Brooch, amethyst & diamond, designed as a cluster of grapes set w/oval, faceted amethysts accented w/round brilliant-cut diamonds, the leaves pavé-set w/round single-cut diamonds, having a total weight of approx. 33 cts. for the amethyst & approx. 2.50 cts. for the diamonds, mounted in 18k yellow gold & 14k white gold **$2,530**

Brooch, aquamarine, ruby & diamond, a three-dimensional blow fish w/an oval-shaped, cabochon-cut aquamarine mouth, round faceted ruby eyes, set w/various hues of fancy champagne-colored diamond scales, diamond accents in the gills & mouth, mounted in 18k yellow gold, aquamarine weighs approx. 12 cts., the 111 diamonds approx. 6.50 cts. total weight, signed, numbered & w/hallmark, Vantichelen (ILLUS.) **$3,220**

Diamond Bow Brooch

*Fancy Colored Diamond
Floral Brooch*

Brooch, diamond, bow design pavé-set w/round brilliant-cut diamonds & bordered by baguette diamonds, 360 diamonds approx. 4.20 cts., 18k white gold mount (ILLUS.) **$3,450**

Brooch, diamond, floral spray design set w/round brilliant-cut diamonds, stems set w/straight baguette-cut diamonds, approx. total weight 4.75 cts., mounted in platinum **$2,530**

Brooch, diamond, floral spray design w/seven round colored diamonds ranging in color from fancy yellow to brown yellow to light grey, completed by a rectangular-cut fancy yellow diamond, approx. total wt. 7.68 cts., pavé-set diamond leaf, 14k white gold mount (ILLUS.) **$10,350**

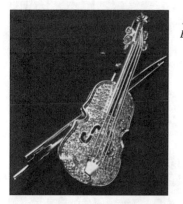

Diamond & Ruby Violin Brooch

Brooch, diamond & pearl, bumblebee design, the platinum upper body & wings pavé-set w/81 round brilliant-cut diamonds, weighing approx. 1.40 cts., the lower body set w/one baroque Tahitian black pearl measuring 12.7 mm., 1 1/2" w., 1" l. **$1,725**

Brooch, diamond, ruby & 14k yellow & white gold, designed as a violin, the body pavé-set w/50 round faceted diamonds weighing approx. .50 cts., the neck of the violin set w/11 square-cut rubies weighing approx. .40 cts. (ILLUS.) **$805**

Brooch, diamond & sapphire, abstract design of two slender crescent shapes, one platinum set w/27 round diamonds, total approx. 1.23 cts. & the other 18k yellow gold set w/24 calibré-cut sapphires, total approx. 2.58 cts., signed "Tiffany & Co. 13879" **$4,600**

*Emerald & Diamond
Frog Brooch*

Brooch, diamond & sapphire, circle design set w/20 round brilliant-cut diamonds weighing approx. .80 cts., alternating w/16 square-cut blue sapphires weighing approx. 1.60 cts., platinum mount.................. **$1,265**

Brooch, emerald & diamond, modeled as a leaping frog, the body set w/an oval-shaped carved emerald, pavé-set round single-cut diamonds in the legs & head w/round cabochon-cut emerald eyes, mounted in 18k white & yellow gold, w/hallmarks (ILLUS.) **$4,140**

Brooch, enamel, a three-dimensional butterfly design w/moveable wings that open & close, decorated w/lavender, yellow, green,

Unusual Cartier Butterfly Brooch

Cartier Gold & Diamond Flower Brooch

black, orange & white enameling in a geometric pattern on both sides, round brilliant-cut diamond eyes & ribbed 18k yellow gold body, numbered & signed "Cartier" (ILLUS.) **$3,450**

Brooch, gold (14k yellow), diamond & ruby, designed as a spray of daisies centered by box-set rubies & tied w/a diamond-set ribbon, signed "Tiffany & Co." **$1,380**

Brooch, gold (18k), textured knot design w/four ropetwist tassel terminals, signed "Tiffany & Co.," Italy **$2,760**

Brooch, gold (18k yellow) & diamond, flower design, the center articulated petals set w/round diamonds, platinum collet settings, approx. total diamond wt. .70 cts., signed "Cartier Paris, No. 00584 or 06584" (ILLUS.) **$5,750**

*Gold & Enamel
Clown Brooch*

Brooch, gold (18k yellow) & enamel, designed as an enameled yellow gold clown sitting in a textured white gold crescent moon w/diamond accents (ILLUS.) **$4,600**

Brooch, gold (18k yellow) & ruby, modeled as a hummingbird, the textured bird perched on a flowering branch, the flowerhead centered by a cluster of five round rubies, diamond accent, 9.10 dwt. **$633**

*Stylized Leaf
Design Brooch*

Brooch, gold (18k yellow), sapphire & diamond, stylized leaf on
a branch accented w/round-cut sapphires, approx. 0.95 cts. &
round-cut diamonds, approx. 0.50 cts. (ILLUS.) **$863**
Brooch, gold (18k yellow), two swans w/necks crossed, textured
wings & body, emerald eyes (one missing), 15.1 dwt. **$805**
Brooch, gold, modeled as a bison, textured 18k yellow gold
w/red stone eyes & round brilliant-cut diamond accents, signed
"Cartier, No. 20577," 13.0 dwt. **$863**
Brooch, gold & silver, spray of three textured yellow bicolored
gold leaves & pods surmounted by silver wire thistles, signed "M.
Buccellati" **$2,588**

Hematite, Dyed Jasper & Pearl Brooch

Brooch, hematite, jasper, pearl & 18k yellow gold, center set w/a large dyed jasper tablet surrounded by various shaped hematite & cultured pearls set in ribbed cone-shapes, additionally enhanced w/seven small round diamonds, approx. .30 cts. (ILLUS.) **$2,185**

Opal Birds Brooch

Cultured Pearl & Diamond Brooch

Brooch, opal, ruby, diamond & 18k yellow gold, designed as three birds in flight, featuring full-cut diamonds enhanced by tri-angular-shaped opal wings, accented by calibré-cut rubies (ILLUS.) **$1,035**

Brooch, pearl & diamond, flower design, the petals & leaves com-posed of baroque pearls centered by a grey pearl surrounded by five prong-set round brilliant-cut diamonds, the stem set w/nine tapered baguette-cut diamonds, platinum mount **$20,700**

Brooch, pearl, platinum & diamond, centered by a cultured pearl measuring approx. 18.30 mm., further designed w/44 round brilliant-cut diamonds & 14 straight baguettes, approx. total wt. 4.88 cts., terminal set w/cut-corner triangle-cut diamonds, approx. total weight 2.03 cts., signed "Winston" for Harry Winston, original leather pouch (ILLUS.) **$20,700**

*Ruby &
Diamond
Brooch*

Brooch, reverse-painted crystal, depicting a standing boxer dog within an oval 14k gold frame, signed "W.F. Marcus" **$920**

Brooch, ruby & diamond, designed as two tapered rows of bead-set round brilliant-cut diamonds intertwined w/curved gold wires termi-nating in three rows of prong-set round, faceted rubies, mounted in platinum & 18k yellow gold, Güblin, numbered w/hallmarks (ILLUS.) **$1,380**

Brooch, ruby, emerald, diamond & 18k gold, designed as a cluster of strawberries w/cabochon rubies & emeralds on curved stems w/diamond-set caps, pierced & textured diamond-set

*Ruby & Emerald
Berry Brooch*

leaves, approx. total wt. 2.01 cts., French assay marks, 28.2 dwt., together w/Raymond Yard box (ILLUS.) **$3,738**
Brooch, ruby & gold, horse chestnut design, the articulated outer shell opening to reveal a prong-set diamond & ruby center, 18k yellow gold mount, signed "Tiffany & Co." **$2,645**
Brooch, sapphire, diamond & bicolor gold, designed as three textured yellow gold birds perched on a brushed rose gold branch, bodies & eyes set w/blue sapphires, emerald plumes, pavé-set & marquise-cut diamond accents, 18k gold **$2,990**

Sapphire, Emerald & Diamond Brooch

Brooch, sapphire, emerald & diamond, a spray design featuring pear-shaped sapphires, approx. 5.00 cts., pear-shaped emeralds, approx. 2.00 cts. & pear-, marquise-, oval- & baguette-cut diamonds, approx. 10.50 cts., platinum mounting (ILLUS.) **$15,525**

Cameos

Shell Cameo Brooch

Cameo brooch, carved shell, depicting winged female figures leading a group of prancing horses within a horizontal oval 14k yellow gold frame, applied wiretwist detail (ILLUS.) **$748**

Cameo brooch, sardonyx, depicting the bust of a male in profile within an 18k yellow gold laurel & berry motif frame, signed "M. & Co." for Marcus & Co. **$1,725**

Stone Cameo Ring

Cameo earrings, carved shell & jet, designed as a jet ball suspending pendant tear-drop-shaped inset w/shell cameos w/woman's profile, pr. (minor wear to cameos) **$259**

Cameo earrings, carved shell & tortoiseshell, oval tops suspending an openwork scrolled tortoiseshell frame centered by an oval cameo, pr. **$316**

Cameo pendant/brooch, agate, depicting Diana, goddess of the hunt, within an 18k yellow gold scroll motif frame set w/ten seed pearls, retractable bail, cameo signed "E. Girardet," together w/box (hairline to agate, minor lead solder to back of frame) **$1,265**

Cameo ring, rectangular shape set w/a deeply carved & detailed carnelian cameo of a soldier's profile, mounted in 14k yellow gold (ILLUS.) **$403**

Cuff Links

*Cat's Eye
Chrysoberyl
Cuff Links*

Cuff links, chrysoberyl & 14k yellow gold, each centering an oval-shaped cabochon-cut cat's eye chrysoberyl, having a total weight of approx. 3.30 cts., set in oval-shaped domed disks engraved w/a florentine finish, pr. (ILLUS.) **$2,415**

Cuff links, citrine & diamond, pyramidal-shaped design, faceted citrine, the top of which is studded w/a small round brilliant-cut diamond, attached to a flexible chain & rigid bar back, mounted in 18k yellow gold, pr. **$1,035**

Cuff links, emerald, double ball form, pavé bead-set w/faceted emeralds, rose gold mount, pr. **$748**

Gold & Enamel Cuff Links

Cuff links, enamel & 18k yellow gold, blue & white enamel stripes surrounding an oval blue enamel center, minor chips & scratches to enamel, signed "Webb," pr. (ILLUS.) **$2,185**

Cuff links, enamel, coral & pearl & 18k yellow gold, figure of a man w/pearl head & coral body, black enameled jacket & pants riding a broomstick-handle horse, pr. **$920**

Cuff links, gold (14k yellow) & star sapphire, designed w/a collet-set oval star sapphire, one measuring approx. 9.89 x 7.99 mm., the other 9.35 x 8.71 mm., yellow gold T-bar, pr. .. **$403**

Cuff links, gold (18k) & diamond, depicting a demon's face, old mine-cut diamond-set mouth, hallmark for MR, pr. **$920**

Cuff links, gold (18k), enamel & diamond, designed as black spades centered w/a collet-set rose-cut diamond, pr. **$460**

Cuff links, gold (18k yellow), double-sided links designed as an owl perched on a bar of calibré-cut rubies & decorated w/rose-cut diamond eyes, pr. **$2,070**

Gold Cuff Links with Enamel Stripes

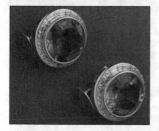

Citrine & Gold Cuff Links

Cuff links, gold (18k yellow) & enamel, double-sided octagonal shape, decorated w/a border of blue enamel, pr. **$460**

Cuff links, gold (18k yellow) & enamel, oval-shaped design enhanced by alternating stripes of blue & reddish brown enamel, each signed "Tiffany & Co.," pr. (ILLUS.) **$403**

Dress set, citrine & 14k yellow gold, pair of cuff links, each featuring one round-cut citrine measuring approx. 16.80 x 16.80 x 11.30 mm., together w/three matching shirt studs, each centering one round-cut citrine measuring approx. 7.50 x 7.50 x 5.50 mm., the set (ILLUS. of cuff links) **$460**

Earrings

*Coral & Turquoise
Earrings*

Earrings, amethyst & mabe pearl, designed w/interchangeable centers & framed w/circular- & graduating baguette-cut diamonds, 14k white gold mount, clip-on, pr. **$2,185**

Earrings, coral, diamond & turquoise, centering a large round fluted coral cabochon surrounded by 12 round brilliant-cut diamonds, approx. 1.50 cts., w/a border of 12 oval-shaped cabochon-cut turquoises, mounted in 18k yellow & white gold, clip-on, pr. (ILLUS.) **$2,760**

Coral & Emerald Earrings

Earrings, coral, emerald & diamond, centering an oval-shaped cabochon-cut emerald surrounded by two round brilliant-cut diamonds & bordered by ten oval-shaped cabochon-cut corals, each separated by a heavy gold wire w/a twisted wire scalloped border, 18k yellow & white gold mount, approx. 4.50 cts of emerald & 2.50 cts. diamonds, clip-on, pr. (ILLUS.) **$2,760**

Earrings, diamond & 18 k. gold, pavé-set diamond stylized bean shape, signed "Elsa Peretti" for Tiffany & Co., pr. **$3,220**

Earrings, diamond, a long scrolling floral design decorated w/marquise-, baguette, emerald-, pear- and round brilliant-cut diamonds w/a total weight of 17 cts. total, mounted in platinum, pr. **$5,750**

Earrings, diamond, circular-cut stud-type, each weighing approx. 0.85 cts., mounted in gold, pr. **$4,600**

*Elegant Diamond
Earrings*

Earrings, diamond, designed as pavé-set natural pink diamond
hoops highlighted by an emerald-cut diamond, 18k yellow gold
mount, signed "Cartier No. 51630," French hallmarks, boxed,
pink diamonds accompanied by Gem Testing Laboratory of Great
Britain certificate, pr. **$12,650**

Earrings, diamond & emerald, the top in a spray of round-, mar-
quise- & pear-shaped diamonds, further enhanced by round- &
pear-shaped emeralds, flexibly supporting a smaller spray of diamonds & a pear-shaped emerald drop, approx. total diamond
weight 2.58 cts., platinum & 18k yellow gold mount,
pr. (ILLUS.) **$3,450**

Diamond & Gold Earrings

Earrings, diamond & gold, (18k yellow & white gold), a diamond-set floral design w/ribbed petals suspending a detachable spray of ribbed gold leaves & diamonds, total weight of approx. 3.42 cts., pr. (ILLUS.) **$2,990**

Earrings, diamond & platinum, each prong-set w/one round brilliant-cut diamond, suspending four marquise-cut diamonds & five round brilliant-cut diamonds, approx. total wt. 4.30 cts., & ending in two round brilliant-cut diamonds, approx. wt. 2.40 & 2.68 cts., 14k white gold findings, pr. (chip to one large stone) **$14,950**

Earrings, diamond & platinum, hoop style, channel-set w/baguette-cut diamonds, approx. total wt. 2.28 cts., hallmark, pr. **$2,530**

Emerald & Diamond Earrings

Earrings, diamond, ruby & 18k yellow gold, oval half-hoop design alternating round-cut rubies & diamonds, approx. 2.20 cts. diamond wt., approx. 6.75 cts. ruby wt., pr. **$4,600**

Earrings, diamond, snowflake design set w/round brilliant-cut diamonds, approx. 1.40 cts., set in platinum & gold findings, pr. **$1,380**

Earrings, emerald & diamond, each centering a pear-shaped, faceted emerald surrounded by pavé-set round brilliant-cut diamonds, two small emerald accents at top, mounted in 18k yellow gold, approx. 1.30 cts. emeralds & 9.90 ct. diamonds, pr. (ILLUS.) **$2,760**

Gold Leaf Design Earrings

Earrings, gold (14k yellow) & ruby, designed w/a wiretwist gold knot suspending a reeded pear-shaped ruby drop within a wiretwist gold frame, signed "Cartier," pr. **$2,530**

Earrings, gold (18k), round slightly domed, textured & engraved w/foliate designs, clip-type, signed "Buccellati," pr. **$1,495**

Earrings, gold (18k yellow) & diamond, carved ribbed leaf center-set w/seven round brilliant-cut diamonds in a floral design w/diamond accents along leaf edge, diamond total approx. 1.70 cts., clip-on, pr. (ILLUS.) **$2,070**

Earrings, gold (18k yellow) & diamond, doorknocker design w/a fluted & hammered finish, each arched top set w/19 round diamonds, total approx. .50 ct. each, signed "Webb," approx. 33.3 dwt., pr. **$3,220**

Earrings, gold (18k yellow), diamond & emerald, designed as hoops, alternately set w/bands of small round diamonds & emeralds, the 48 diamonds totalling approx. 1.47 cts., the 60 emeralds total approx. 2.33 cts., signed "SDG Cartier 30326," approx. 13.2 dwt., pr. **$4,025**

Starburst Earrings

Earrings, gold, pearl & diamond, starburst design, one centered by a cultured white pearl measuring approx. 10.27 mm., the other by a cultured black pearl measuring approx. 10.15 mm., surrounded by prong-set round diamonds mounted in 18k white gold, clip backs w/retractable posts, pr. (ILLUS.) **$6,325**

Earrings, morganite & pearl, centered by a round faceted morganite surrounded by seed pearls, 18k gold mount, pr.. **$2,185**

Earrings, opal & diamond, centered by a heart-shaped opal, measuring approx. 13.10 x 11.49 x 3.95 mm. surrounded by single-cut diamonds, 14k white gold mount, clip-on, pr.. **$1,265**

Earrings, pearl & diamond, each set w/a South Sea pearl, one measuring approx. 14.40 mm., the other 14.90 mm., surmounted by a baguette diamond bow, 14k. yellow gold mount, pr.. **$2,300**

*Diamond &
Pearl Earrings*

Earrings, pearl & gem, centered by an oval amethyst, surrounded
by an alternating pattern of oval amethyst, aquamarine, citrine,
peridot & pearls, 14k yellow gold mounts, pr. **$1,035**
Earrings, pearl & platinum, the tops composed of 15 fancy-cut
diamonds suspending a South Sea cultured baroque pearl
w/pavé-set diamond caps, pearls measure approx. 12.3 mm.,
approx. diamond wt. 15.00 cts., pr. (ILLUS.) **$21,850**

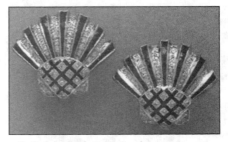

Shell-shaped Ruby & Diamond Earrings

Earrings, ruby, diamond & 18k yellow gold, designed as shells & alternately set throughout w/bands of small round diamonds & calibré-cut rubies, approx. 16.8 dwt., pr. (ILLUS.) **$2,300**

Earrings, ruby & diamond, a triple-tiered, oval-shaped outline w/an oval cabochon-cut ruby in the center top, surrounded by 36 round brilliant-cut diamonds having a total weight of approx. 5 cts. for rubies & approx. 3.75 cts. for the diamonds, mounted in 18k yellow gold, signed, pr. **$2,300**

Earrings, ruby & diamond, centered by an oval ruby weighing approx. 4.00 cts. & edged w/two rows of single-cut diamonds, approx. total 2.00 cts., millegrain accents, 18k white gold mount, pr. **$4,715**

*Sapphire &
Diamond
Earrings*

Earrings, sapphire & diamond, a rectangular heavy ribbed gold design top & a circular design at the base which is set w/five round faceted sapphires weighing a total of approx. 6 cts. & four round brilliant-cut diamonds w/a total weight of approx. 0.60 ct., mounted in 18k yellow gold, signed "Webb," pr. (ILLUS.) **$5,750**

Earrings, sapphire & diamond, each set w/an oval faceted sapphire cradled by four round brilliant-cut & three marquise-cut diamonds w/a total weight of 1.60 cts., total weight of sapphires 7 cts., mounted in 18k white gold, pr. **$5,750**

*Prong-set
Sapphire &
Diamond
Earrings*

Earrings, sapphire & diamond, prong-set oval blue sapphires &
bead- & prong-set round diamonds, approx. total diamond wt.
3.19 cts., sapphire wt. 17.88 cts., 18k white gold mount & bicol-
or findings, pr. (ILLUS.) **$4,888**
Earrings, sterling silver, 14k yellow gold & sapphire, "The Nile"
design of sterling silver wings w/14k yellow gold feathered terminals set w/a round cabochon sapphire, signed "Erte No.

"The Nile"
Earrings by Erte

226/250," accompanied by a Circle Fine Art Corp. certificate of authenticity, pr. (ILLUS.) **$690**
Earrings, tourmaline, agate & gold, a carved pale green tourmaline top surmounting an oval cabochon agate dyed blue-green, applied gold bead accents, 22k yellow gold mount, signed "Luna," pr. **$1,093**

*Turquoise &
Sapphire Earrings*

Earrings, turquoise, sapphire & diamond, centering an oval-shaped, cabochon-cut sapphire, approx. 4.60 cts., surrounded by ten round brilliant-cut diamonds, approx. 2.50 cts., bordered by ten oval-shaped cabochon-cut tuquoises, each separated by a heavy gold wire, twisted wire scalloped border in 18k yellow & white gold, clip-on, pr. (ILLUS.) **$2,875**

Necklaces/Pendants

Amethyst, Pearl & Gold Necklace

Necklace, amethyst, 14k yellow gold & pearl, collet-set oval amethyst links, centered by two amethyst link drops, seed pearl accents (ILLUS.) **$1,495**

Necklace, amethyst, the platinum baton link chain set a intervals w/ten natural pearls, suspending a large pear-shaped amethyst topped by a diamond-set bail, the diamonds totalling approx. .55 ct. **$1,610**

Necklace, cultured pearl, tourmaline & diamond, the single strand w/74 pearls measuring 8 to 8 1/2 mm suspending an 18k white gold floral pendant set w/a large oval purplish red tourmaline surrounded by 40 round melée diamonds weighing about .60 carats joined by an 18k white gold fishhook clasp, 26" l. **$1,265**

Necklace, diamond & 18k gold, diamond-set chevron, approx. total weight 2.82 cts., suspended from a baton link chain, signed "Webb," in blue silk envelope **$2,530**

Amethyst & Diamond Necklace

Necklace, diamond & amethyst, shield-shaped pendant centered by a modified heart-shaped cabochon amethyst measuring approx. 33.99 cts. framed within an openwork floral pattern accented w/29 collet-set circular-cut diamonds weighing approx. 1.50 cts. & 13 circular-cut amethysts, minor chip to back of cabochon amethyst, one amethyst missing, silver-topped 14k yellow gold mount, suspended from a 14k yellow gold chain of amethyst flowerheads spaced by figure-eight links (ILLUS.) **$3,105**

Necklace, diamond & 18k white gold, choker-type Florentine finish button-shaped bezel link mount set w/88 round brilliant-cut diamonds weighing approx. 3 cts., 16" l. **$3,680**

Necklace, diamond, centered by a bezel-set pear-shaped diamond, approx. 1.50 cts., completed by a 14k yellow gold snake chain, 15" l. **$2,300**

Necklace, diamond, emerald, ruby & sapphire, bib-style 18k yellow gold chain set w/12 round brilliant-cut diamonds w/total weight of approx. 3.60, 13 round faceted sapphires weighing approx. 4.50 cts., nine round faceted rubies, approx. 3.25 cts. & ten round faceted emeralds weighing approx. 2.50 cts., chain approx. 39.5 cm., 15 1/2" l. **$5,750**

Tiffany Diamond Riviere Necklace

Necklace, diamond & platinum, a repeated design of lozenge-shaped sections that alternate w/small navette-shaped sections, each decorated w/round brilliant- and single-cut diamonds w/a weight of 6 cts., mounted in platinum, 14" l. **$4,370**

Necklace, diamond & platinum, set w/59 baguettes in a crossover design, suspending 31 circular & 30 marquise-cut diamonds, joined by 56 baguette-cut diamond links, completed by a barrel clasp, approx. total weight 32.6 cts., 16" l. **$31,050**

Necklace, diamond Riviere, 80 graduated prong-set round brilliant-cut diamonds ranging in size from approx. 1.59 to 0.16 cts., approx. total wt. 33.50 cts., mounted in platinum, signed "Tiffany & Co.," ca. 1960s, in original fitted Tiffany box, 15 1/2" l. (ILLUS.) **$91,600**

Necklace, diamond Riviere, set w/81 graduated round brilliant-cut diamonds ranging in size from 0.16 to 1.54 cts., total wt. 30.0 cts., platinum mount, accompanied by seven GIA certificates **$51,750**

Necklace, diamond, suspending a stylized ribbon motif set w/round & baguette-cut diamonds, terminating in a free-hanging

Diamond Ribbon Design Necklace

drop set w/a marquise-shaped, brilliant-cut diamond weighing approx. 0.36 ct., surrounded by & topped w/round diamonds, mounted in platinum & attached to an open link, platinum chain, approximately 17" l. (ILLUS.) **$3,680**

Necklace, emerald beads, triple strand of graduated oval emerald beads ranging from 2.70 to 8.10 mm., diamond-set 14k white gold clasp w/faceted emerald accent, 21" l. **$1,093**

Necklace, emerald & diamond, set w/257 prong-set round diamonds suspending five drops set w/pear-shaped emeralds, approx. total wt. 6.00 cts., surrounded by two rows of prong-set round diamonds, foliate marquise-cut diamond caps, approx. total wt. 16.50 cts., platinum mount, 14" l. **$14,950**

Necklace, glass & metal, silver & gold-plated scrolling leaf design chain set w/foiled blue glass stones **$1,035**

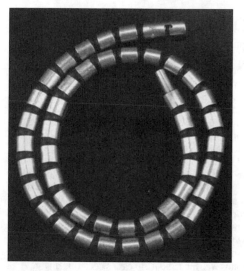

*Gold &
Lapis
Necklace*

Necklace, gold (14k yellow), choker-type, wide gold snake chain band w/a groove to the center, approx. 64.9 dwt., 14 to 16" l. **$2,760**

Necklace, gold (18k) & lapis, tubular gold links spaced by lapis rondelles, hallmark, 15 3/4" l. (ILLUS.) **$1,955**

Necklace, gold (14k yellow) & diamond, a four section tube style necklace, the lower curved sections set w/graduated round dia-

monds & suspending a bezel-set light brown shield-shaped diamond, approx. 11.70 cts., surrounded by graduated round brilliant-cut diamonds, approx. 3.65 cts. **$12,075**

Necklace, gold (14k yellow), diamond & ruby, choker-type, 3/8"
wide snake band set to the front w/a scrolling device adorned
w/ten small round diamonds, total approx. 1.50 cts. & calibré-
cut rubies, approx. 57.4 dwt. **$2,300**

Necklace, gold (18k yellow), centered by a ram's head w/emer-
ald eyes suspended by two finely woven mesh chains w/ram's
horn & repoussé spacers, signed "Lalaounis," 67.9 dwt., 16" l.
(solder marks evident near clasp) **$2,185**

Necklace, gold, 18k yellow gold wide double-band braided choker-type w/tiny links, 15 1/2" l., 1" w. **$2,645**

Necklace, gold, cultured pearl, ruby & diamond, a single strand
of 40 pearls measuring 7 1/2 to 8 mm. centering a 14k yellow
gold openwork looped floral pendant w/two large ruby half-
beads & 28 round faceted rubies weighing about 9 carats, the
border set w/96 round faceted melée diamonds weighing about
1.45 carats suspending a bellflower pendant set w/26 round
melée diamonds weighing about .40 carats centering a large
ruby half-bead weighing about 3 carats joined by a 14k yellow
gold tongue-in-groove clasp set w/five round faceted rubies
weighing about .50 carats, 15" l. **$2,300**

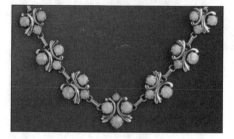

*Opal & Gold
Necklace*

Necklace, gold & pearl, a vine design set w/baroque pearls, detailed gold leaves & textured gold buds topped w/baroque pearls, 16" l. **$1,725**

Necklace, gold, ropetwist design, the textured 18k yellow gold rope links intertwined w/an 18k white gold double trace link chain, Italian hallmarks, 70.5 dwt., 19 1/2" l. **$1,495**

Necklace, gold, sapphire & diamond, a 14k yellow gold herring-bone chain suspending a blue sapphire & diamond pendant set w/three dark blue sapphires weighing about 2 carats, alternating w/32 round brilliant-cut diamonds weighing about 1 carat, chain can be made longer, 20" l. **$920**

Necklace, opal & 14k yellow gold, featuring round-shaped opal cabochons measuring from approx. 7.00 x 7.00 x 2.50 to 4.00 x 4.00 x 2.00 mm., fancy links, 16 3/4" l. (ILLUS. of part) **$1,840**

*Fine Black Opal &
Diamond Necklace*

Necklace, opal & diamond, the textured chain suspending an oval
cabochon-cut black opal that weighs approx. 8.63 cts. & exhibits
a fine color pattern of predominantly red, blue, green, orange &
yellow "fire," surrounded by 28 marquise-shaped brilliant-cut
diamonds w/a total weight of approx. 2 cts., the central portion
of the chain set w/round, brilliant- and baguette-cut diamonds
w/a total approx. weight of 1.60 cts., mounted in 18k white gold
& platinum, 16" l. (ILLUS.) **$13,800**
Necklace, pearl, 36 South Sea black pearls ranging in size from
9.60 to 13.50 mm., the silver & gold round clasp set w/a ruby &
diamond **$9,200**

*Cultured Pearl &
Amethyst Necklace*

Necklace, pearl, a double strand of cultured pearls, ranging from approx. 8.70 to 9.40 mm., w/a 14k gold knot-style clasp w/pavé bead-set diamond accents, 16" l. **$3,565**

Necklace, pearl, a strand of graduated black Tahitian pearls measuring 10.00 to 14.00 mm., completed by an 18k yellow gold clasp set w/tapered baguette-cut diamonds, 19 1/2" l. **$16,100**

Necklace, pearl, a torsade comprising 14 twisted strands of cultured pearls measuring approx. 2.75 mm. each, joined by a jeweled buckle clasp, pavé-set w/round diamonds, edged w/channel-set square-cut rubies, emeralds & sapphires, mounted in 18k yellow gold, 15" l. **$4,600**

Necklace, pearl & amethyst, a double strand of 113 cultured pearls terminating in an 18k yellow gold clasp centering an oval faceted amethyst within an interwoven white & green enamel frame accented w/eight round brilliant-cut diamonds, Italian maker's mark (ILLUS.) **$4,600**

Multi-strand Peridot & Sapphire Necklace

Necklace, pearl, single strand of 37 graduated cultured natural colored black South Sea pearls measuring 9.2 to 14.5 mm. joined by a 14k white gold barrel form tongue-in-groove clasp set w/four round brilliant-cut diamonds, 19" l. **$9,200**

Necklace, pearl, single strand of 85 cultured pearls approx. 9 to 9.5 mm. in diameter, 33 1/4" l. **$4,600**

Necklace, pearl, single strand of graduated black South Sea cultured pearls ranging in size from 11.00 to 14.70 mm., 18k. white gold pavé-set diamond ball clasp, approx. 1.00 cts., 18" l. **$14,950**

Necklace, peridot, 14 strand torsade of faceted beads completed by an 18k gold reverse-hook clasp, 18-19 1/4" l. **$3,220**

Necklace, peridot & sapphire, composed of 30 strands of small peridot & sapphire beads w/an 18k white & yellow gold leaf design clasp, 16" l. (ILLUS.) **$1,955**

Cartier Ruby & Diamond Necklace

Necklace, ruby, diamond & platinum, comprising 80 graduated baguette-cut diamonds spaced by 83 circular-cut rubies, French hallmarks, signed "Cartier Paris No. 05037," 15 1/2" l. (ILLUS. of part).................... **$27,600**

Ruby & Diamond Necklace

Necklace, ruby & diamond, the 9k yellow gold braided design w/ten oval diamond & ruby set links, a center floral design centered by a diamond surrounded by round faceted rubies & suspending a floral pendant set w/diamonds & rubies & surrounded by a diamond-set frame, oval & round faceted rubies approx. 6.80 cts., round brilliant-cut diamonds approx. 3.50 cts., 16" l. (ILLUS.).. **$1,265**

Necklace, sterling silver & topaz, collar-type, comprising four tapered & jointed sterling silver links centered by a large rectangular smoky topaz, ca. 1970s.. **$633**

Turquoise & Pearl Bib Necklace

Necklace, turquoise & 18k gold, bezel-set oval turquoise joined by fine chain links, 45" l. **$1,265**

Necklace, turquoise & pearl, bib-style open net design consisting of multiple gold quatrefoils each set w/a round turquoise, suspending a fringe of 22 freshwater pearls, mounted in 18k yellow gold, 15 1/2" (ILLUS.) **$1,725**

Necklaces, diamond, choker-type, each w/two rows of elongated octagonal links accented w/368 pavé-set diamonds, total wt. approx. 17.32 cts., w/fittings to be worn as one necklace, 18k yellow gold mount, 104 dwt., pr. **$17,250**

Antique Coin & Gold Pendant

Pendant, carved tourmaline, oval form, depicting the profile of a classical female within a 14k gold frame, decorated w/wiretwist accents (missing pin stem) **$518**

Pendant, Chinese amethyst, carved as a bird perched on a branch w/fruit, amethyst bead terminal, seed pearl accents, completed by a purple macramé cord **$115**

Pendant, diamond solitaire, heart-shaped diamond approx. 1.00 ct. in a platinum bezel suspended from a fine platinum trace line chain, 17" l. **$3,565**

Pendant, gold (18k yellow), tourmaline & pearl, round form centered by an antique coin, the frame inscribed "Elizabeth - First - 1533 - 1603" & set w/four tourmalines & a small round diamond & suspending a tear-drop-shaped cultured pearl, approx. 17.1 dwt. (ILLUS.) **$1,150**

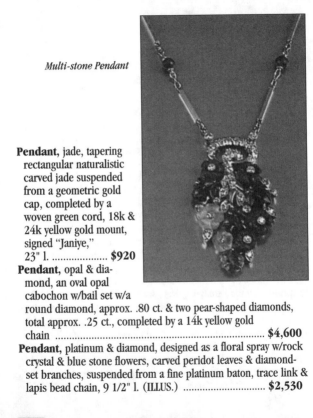

Multi-stone Pendant

Pendant, jade, tapering rectangular naturalistic carved jade suspended from a geometric gold cap, completed by a woven green cord, 18k & 24k yellow gold mount, signed "Janiye," 23" l. **$920**

Pendant, opal & diamond, an oval opal cabochon w/bail set w/a round diamond, approx. .80 ct. & two pear-shaped diamonds, total approx. .25 ct., completed by a 14k yellow gold chain **$4,600**

Pendant, platinum & diamond, designed as a floral spray w/rock crystal & blue stone flowers, carved peridot leaves & diamond-set branches, suspended from a fine platinum baton, trace link & lapis bead chain, 9 1/2" l. (ILLUS.) **$2,530**

Tiffany Fish Pendant

Pendant, sapphire & diamond, modeled as a long-tailed fish, the body decorated w/26 round faceted sapphires & five round faceted demantoid garnets, the mouth, head & tail decorated w/round single-cut diamonds & the eyes accented w/two cabochon-cut rubies, mounted in 18k yellow gold, signed "Tiffany, Schlumberger" (ILLUS.) **$5,175**

Pendant, topaz & diamond, an elongated, rectangular-shaped topaz weighing approx. 11 cts., the top accented w/round brilliant-cut & marquise-shaped diamonds w/a total weight of approx. 0.40 cts., mounted in 18k white gold **$1,610**

Pendant & chain, gold, molded crystal & amethyst, the handcrafted tested 14k yellow gold floral headdress set w/seven round faceted amethysts weighing about .50 carats, the headdress enclosing a molded crystal face of a young girl, w/a goldfilled curb-link chain, signed "Walter Bauscher," pendant 1 1/2 x 2 1/4" **$575**

*Diamond & Cultured Pearl
Pendant/brooch*

Pendant/brooch, diamond, pearl & 14k yellow gold, the modified triangular-shaped brooch designed w/ribbon & star motifs,
center set w/a cultured pearl, surrounded by 160 round diamonds, approx. 5.50 cts., & suspending a cultured pearl drop
(ILLUS.) **$5,750**

Pendant/brooch, diamond, ruby & sapphire, designed as an
eagle in flight, 18k yellow & white gold mount, the body pavé-set
w/round brilliant-cut diamonds, approx. 1.90 cts., wings bordered w/54 round faceted rubies, approx. 1 ct. & 37 round faceted blue sapphires, approx. .75 cts., 2 1/2" w. **$1,380**

Pins

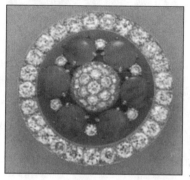

Diamond & Jade Circle Pin

Pin, diamond & 14k white gold, Caduceus design, set w/an old European-cut diamond approx. 0.92 cts., further set w/26 bead-set diamonds, approx. total wt. 0.50 cts. & eight bead-set rubies **$1,610**

Pin, diamond, circular design set w/29 round brilliant-cut diamonds weighing approx. 3.2 cts., mounted in platinum **$2,300**

Pin, diamond, jade & platinum, a circle design set w/25 round full-cut diamonds, total approx. 6.25 cts., hallmarked M & Co., together w/an insert pin designed w/six jade cabochons alternately set w/six small round diamonds surrounding a dome pavé-set w/41 small round diamonds, total approx. 2 cts. (ILLUS.) **$8,625**

Pin, emerald & diamond, a circle set w/21 round emeralds & three sprays of pear- & marquise-shaped diamonds set in platinum, approx. total diamond wt. 1.83 cts., 18k yellow gold

Jeweled Bow Pin

mount, signed "SB, No 39854 5" (large chip to one emerald) **$2,070**

Pin, peridot & gold, circle form w/faceted oval peridots alternating w/14k yellow gold leaves, gold bead accents, signed "Tiffany & Co." **$1,093**

Pin, platinum & diamond, scroll design set w/round diamonds, approx. 3.71 cts., in a feather motif, signed "Mauboussin, Paris," French hallmarks (two diamonds missing) **$2,530**

Pin, ruby, diamond & garnet, modeled as a ladybug, body & articulated wings set w/rubies & diamonds, cabochon tsavorite garnet accent, ruby eyes, 18k gold mount **$1,610**

Pin, ruby, diamond & gold, designed as a knotted bow & suspending an ovoid drop set w/numerous pink rubies, the knot accented w/diamond melée, minor lead solder evident, Alemany & Co. (ILLUS.) **$6,325**

Pin, sapphire & 14k gold, a flower design w/blue sapphire petals centered by a pearl, yellow & blue sapphire & diamond accents, 14k gold mount, signed "Tiffany & Co." **$1,840**

Rings

*Aquamarine &
Diamond Ring*

Ring, aquamarine & diamond, an emerald-cut aquamarine, approx. 3.04 cts. in a border of round brilliant & tapered baguette-cut diamonds, approx. 0.97 ct., 18k white gold mount (ILLUS.) **$1,150**

Ring, cat's-eye chrysoberyl & diamond, men's, the chrysoberyl weighing approx. 8.00 cts., gypsy-set in a platinum mount, flanked by two trapezoidal-shaped diamonds weighing approx. 0.75 cts. each **$8,050**

Ring, chalcedony, tapering band style centered by an oval lavender chalcedony, flanked by two gold medallions within a wiretwist border, gold bead accents, 14k bicolor gold mount, hallmark for Elizabeth Gage **$1,265**

Ring, chrysoberyl, diamond & 18k yellow gold, centering a round cabochon-cut cat's eye chrysoberyl, weighing approx. 15.5 cts., flanked by two tapered baguette-cut diamonds............ **$16,100**

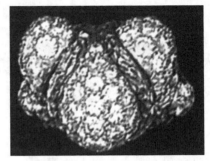

Triple Dome Diamond Ring

Ring, coral & diamond, centered by an oval angel skin coral measuring approx. 11.40 x 8.80 mm., surrounded by round brilliant-cut prong-set diamonds, approx. total wt. 0.50 cts., platinum mount, signed "Trio" **$748**

Ring, diamond & 18k yellow gold, pavé-set diamond triple dome style, approx. 6.00 cts., the three sections separated by textured gold bands (ILLUS.) **$3,450**

Ring, diamond, a round brilliant-cut diamond, approx. 9.30 cts., held in a heavy box attached to an 18k yellow gold flexible curb link chain shank **$15,525**

Ring, diamond, a round brilliant-cut diamond solitaire weighing approx. 3 cts., mounted in platinum **$14,950**

Ring, diamond, an emerald-cut diamond weighing 3.53 cts., mounted in 18k yellow gold, w/Italian hallmark & maker's mark, w/GIA report **$23,000**

Pear-shaped Diamond Ring

Ring, diamond, centering a pear-shaped brilliant-cut diamond weighing 5.92 cts., flanked by six baguette-cut diamonds, mounted in platinum, accompanied by GIA report (ILLUS.) .. **$36,800**

Ring, diamond, centering a round brilliant-cut diamond weighing approx. 0.90 ct. w/six round single-cut diamonds in the shoulders, mounted in 14k white gold, accompanied by a cradle ring decorated w/14 round brilliant-cut diamonds set in floral leaf designs, weight approx. 0.60 cts., mounted in 14k white gold **$6,900**

Ring, diamond, eternity band set w/graduated marquise-cut diamonds, approx. 7.00 cts., 14k white gold mount **$5,175**

Ring, diamond, "Etoile" style, centered by a circular-cut intense yellow diamond weighing 1.02 cts., framed by ten pear-shaped colorless diamonds w/total weight of 1.44 cts., platinum mount, signed "Tiffany & Co.," boxed **$13,800**

Ring, diamond & gold, dinner-type, 22k yellow gold wide mount, the top portion set w/a pavé of 67 graduated round brilliant-cut diamonds weighing about 2.90 carats, Cartier, size 5 1/4.. **$3,680**

Ring, diamond & gold, solitaire, the 18k white gold four-prong A-Box mount set w/one round brilliant-cut diamond weighing about 1.03 carats flanked by two round brilliant-cut diamonds weighing about .28 carats, size 5 1/4 .... **$4,140**

Ring, diamond & gold, the 14k yellow & white gold six-prong Tiffany mount set w/one round brilliant-cut diamond weighing exactly 2.39 carats, size 4 1/2 .... **$6,900**

Ring, diamond & gold, twin-style dinner-type, the 14k white gold bypass-designed mount set w/two round brilliant-cut diamonds weighing about .95 & 1 carat flanked by ten baguette diamonds weighing about .30 carats, size 6 .... **$4,600**

Ring, diamond & platinum, a center pear-shaped diamond enhanced w/two tapered baguettes, approx. 7.20 cts. (ILLUS. on next page) **$13,800**

Ring, diamond & platinum, the platinum four-prong Tiffany mount set w/one round brilliant-cut diamond weighing about 2.85 carats flanked by two tapered baguette diamonds weighing about .50 carats, size 9 .... **$19,500**

Ring, diamond & ruby, an oval prong-set Burma ruby approx. 1.00 cts., flanked by six circular-cut diamonds, approx. total wt. 0.50 cts., 18k yellow gold ribbed mount **$1,150**

Pear-shaped Diamond Ring

Ring, diamond & sapphire, three-stone design centered by a prong-set emerald-cut diamond weighing approx. 3.50 cts., flanked by two prong-set emerald-cut sapphires measuring approx. 7.38 x 6.40 x 4.58 mm & 7.50 x 6.52 x 4.55 mm., platinum mount, hallmark **$13,800**

Ring, diamond solitaire, centered by a marquise-cut diamond, approx. 4.20 cts., baguette-set platinum mount, signed "Yard," accompanied by GIA certificate **$49,450**

Ring, diamond solitaire, centered by a pear-shaped diamond, weighing 2.71 cts., flanked by baguette-cut diamonds, platinum mount, accompanied by GIA certificate **$21,850**

*Emerald &
Diamond
Dinner Ring*

Ring, diamond solitaire, centered by a round brilliant-cut diamond, approx. 5.5 cts., flanked by tapered baguettes, platinum mount.. **$25,300**

Ring, diamond solitaire, centered by an emerald-cut diamond, approx. 11.00 cts., flanked by tapered baguettes, platinum mount.. **$41,400**

Ring, emerald & diamond, dinner-type, set w/a marquise emerald weighing approx. .75 cts., surrounded by 19 square & baguette diamonds weighing approx. .85 cts. & five round brilliant-cut diamonds weighing approx. .15 cts., 18k yellow gold mount (ILLUS.) **$460**

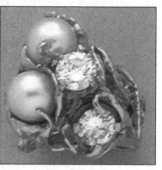

Diamond & Pearl Ring

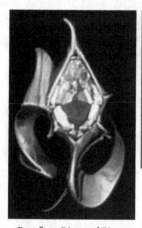

Free-form Diamond Ring

Ring, gold (14k yellow) & diamond, a free-form design mounted w/a kite-shaped diamond, approx. 1.25 cts. (ILLUS.).... **$1,093**
Ring, gold (14k yellow), diamond & pearl, the grapevine style mounting centered by two round brilliant-cut diamonds, total approx. 2 cts. & two cultured pearls, approx. 10.7 dwt. (ILLUS.) **$5,462**
Ring, gold (18k yellow) & citrine, centered by an emerald-cut cit-rine within a domed, textured gold mount, gold wire accents, signed "Schlumberger" for Tiffany & Co. **$1,725**

Gold, Diamond & Pearl Ring

Ring, gold (18k yellow) & diamond, bombé design set w/alternating rows of round brilliant-cut diamonds, approx. 2.16 cts. & twisted gold wire... **$1,150**

Ring, gold (18k yellow) & diamond, comprising six rows of ropetwist bands, accented by three white gold bead-set diamond curved X's, signed "Tiffany, Schlumberger"................... **$2,990**

Ring, gold (18k yellow), diamond & pearl, the wide tapered band edged w/gold beads & pavé-set w/58 round full-cut diamonds, total approx. 1.25 cts., set across the top w/three cultured pearls contained in beaded collars, signed "Chanel" & numbered, approx. 12.5 dwt. (ILLUS.).. **$2,530**

Ring, gold (18k yellow) & silver, gentlemen's, centered by a Roman Republic silver denarius depicting the Roman god Janus, ca. 119 B.C., 14.5 dwt. (ILLUS. on next page) **$719**

*Gentlemen's Ring
w/Roman Denarius*

Jade & Diamond Dinner Ring

Ring, jade & diamond, 18k white gold openwork mount center set w/a rectangular cabochon apple green jade stone measuring 12.4 x 5.5 mm., flanked by 42 round brilliant-cut diamonds, ap-prox. .50 cts. (ILLUS.) **$316**

Ring, jadeite jade & diamond, a jade measuring 18.5 x 13.0 x 6.9 mm. framed by 18 circular-cut diamonds, approx. total wt. 2.70 cts., platinum mount (testing indicates the jadeite jade has not been enhanced) **$9,775**

*Natural Pearl & Diamond
Ring*

Ring, moonstone & cat's-eye, designed w/two oval prong-set
moonstones outlined by 25 cat's-eye chrysoberyl, pierced gallery,
18k gold mount **$1,093**

Ring, opal & diamond, centered by an oval black opal doublet
surrounded by round tapered baguette-cut diamonds, 18k yellow
gold mount **$1,380**

Ring, opal & diamond, centered by an oval black opal, measuring
approx. 14.40 x 9.80 x 3.10 mm., surrounded by prong-set
round brilliant-cut diamonds, approx. total wt. 1.00 cts., 18k yellow gold mount... **$2,300**

Ring, pearl & diamond, a stylized, lozenge-shaped open crown
framed w/round diamonds, centering three natural pearls measuring from approx. 7.8 mm. to 6.5 mm., flanked by two small
natural pearls, approx. 3.7 mm., mounted in 18k white gold,
accompanied by SSEF report stating all the pearls are natural
(ILLUS.) **$2,415**

*Peridot &
Diamond Ring*

Ring, peridot & diamond, centered by an oval peridot measuring
approx. 12.61 x 10.61 x 7.25 mm., flanked by six round diamonds, 14k white gold mount **$374**
Ring, peridot & diamond, designed w/a marquise-cut peridot,
measuring approx. 20.68 x 9.29 x 7.00 mm., set at an angle in a
diamond foliate-style mount, approx. total diamond wt. .96 cts.,
ruby accents, 18k yellow gold mount, French hallmark
(ILLUS.) **$920**
Ring, platinum, sapphire & diamond, centered by a cushion-cut
sapphire, approx. 8.59 x 8.22 x 7.50 mm., surrounded by eight
round brilliant-cut diamonds, approx. 2.65 cts., signed
"Boucheron, Paris, No. 49147" (slight abrasions to
sapphire) **$14,950**

*Ruby &
Diamond Ring*

Ring, ruby, diamond & 14k white gold, centered by an oval-
shaped ruby measuring approx. 8.90 x 6.55 x 3.65 mm, encir-
cled by full-cut diamonds **$1,610**

Ring, ruby, diamond & 18k yellow gold, checkerboard design featuring three rows of horizontally set rubies, approx. 4.50 cts.,
further accented w/small round brilliant-cut diamonds, approx.
0.25 cts. **$1,610**

Ring, ruby & diamond, center oval faceted ruby, weighing approx.
5 cts., flanked by two round brilliant-cut diamonds w/total
weight of approx. 1.35 cts., mounted in 18k yellow gold, Italian
hallmark (ILLUS.) **$17,250**

Ring, sapphire & 14k gold, set w/two clip-cornered triangular-cut
sapphires, measuring approximately. 15.48 x 14.25 x 8.13 mm.
& 15.71 x 14.17 x 9.17 mm., white gold mount
(ILLUS. on next page) **$863**

Sapphire & Gold Ring

Yellow Sapphire & Diamond Ring

Ring, sapphire & diamond, a center oval-shaped, faceted yellow sapphire weighing approx. 5.70 cts., flanked by six round brilliant-cut diamonds w/an approx. total weight of 0.50 ct., mounted in 18k white gold (ILLUS.) **$3,450**

Ring, sapphire & diamond, center set w/an old mine-cut diamond, approx. 2.10 cts., further enhanced by four corner prong-set sapphires measuring approx. 3.30 x 4.50 mm., 14k yellow gold mount (chips to girdle of diamond, chips to sapphires) **$8,050**

Unusual Yellow Sapphire & Diamond Ring

Ring, sapphire & diamond, centered by a cushion-cut sapphire approx. 10.08 x 8.98 x 7.12 mm., surrounded by marquise- & circular-cut diamonds, approx. total 1.40 cts., stamped "S, C & L" for Shreve, Crump & Low, accompanied by AGTA colored stone certificate **$41,400**

Ring, sapphire & diamond, centering a pear-shaped, faceted yellow sapphire weighing approx. 16.70 cts. w/four heavy prongs, each set w/square princess-cut diamonds, the ring having a heart-shaped outline when viewed from the side profile, decorated w/two rows of square princess-cut diamonds in the shoulder portions & round brilliant-cut diamonds on the sides, having a total weight of approx. 7 cts., mounted in platinum & 18k yellow gold, Italian hallmark, Spoleto Gioielli (ILLUS.) **$14,950**

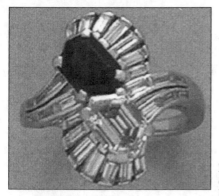

Sapphire & Diamond Bypass Ring

Ring, sapphire & diamond, centrally set w/an oval-shaped cabochon-cut sapphire weighing approx. 11 cts., surrounded by round single-cut diamonds & accented on each side w/a round brilliant- & baguette-cut diamond, mounted in platinum **$4,830**

Ring, sapphire & diamond, collet-set oval yellow sapphire within a diamond-set openwork band w/engraved foliate decoration, 18k white & yellow gold mount, signed "M. Buccelatti" **$3,910**

Ring, sapphire, diamond & platinum, bypass style, diagonally set w/one trapezoid-shaped diamonds, approx. 1 ct. & a similarly shaped sapphire, approx. 1 ct. & enhanced w/26 baguette-cut diamonds, total approx. .75 cts. (ILLUS.) **$4,600**

Ring, sapphire, joined bands, one centered by an emerald-cut yellow sapphire, the other w/an emerald-cut blue sapphire, each measuring approx. 6.10 x 9.70 x 4.80 mm. flanked by tapered baguettes, 18k yellow gold mount.................................... **$4,600**

Ring, sapphire, man's, cabochon sapphire measuring approx. 11.8 x 9.5 x 6.5, flanked by two baguette-cut diamonds, textured 14k white gold mount.. **$3,450**

Ring, star sapphire & diamond, a center oval cabochon-cut star sapphire weighing approx. 20 cts., flanked by two square-cut & two tapered baguette-cut diamonds w/a total approx. weight of 1.10 cts., mounted in platinum...................................... **$4,370**

Ring, tanzanite & 14k gold, centered by an oval faceted tanzanite, measuring approx. 17.62 x 12.76 x 11.72 mm. within a foliate gold mount, round brilliant-cut diamond accents.......... **$3,220**

Ring, tanzanite, set w/an oval-shaped faceted tanzanite weighing approx. 3.63 cts. & flanked by two round brilliant-cut diamonds having a total weight of approx. 0.20 ct., mounted in a wide bombé mounting of 18k white gold **$2,990**

Ring, topaz & diamond, centered w/a rectangular-shaped, faceted topaz weighing approx. 9.50 cts., the sides accented w/round & small emerald-cut diamonds w/an approx. total weight of 0.60 ct., mounted in 18k white gold **$1,725**

Ring, turquoise & diamond, centered by a prong-set sugarloaf turquoise, approx. 19.5 x 15.68 mm., surrounded by 18 round brilliant-cut diamonds, approx. total wt. 2.16 cts., mounted in 18k yellow gold, signed "David Webb" **$1,610**

Ring, turquoise, ruby & diamond, centered by a pear-shaped turquoise highlighted by round brilliant-cut diamonds & round rubies, 18k yellow gold scroll mount, signed "David Webb" **$1,725**

Sets

*Garnet &
Citrine
Bracelet &
Earrings*

Bracelet & earrings, gold (18k yellow), garnet & citrine, the
hinged bangle bracelet w/a matte finish & set across the top
w/rectangular-cut citrines & garnets, together w/matching pair of
demi-hoop clip-on earrings, total approx. 69.3 dwt., the set
(ILLUS.) **$1,725**
Bracelet, necklace & ring, coral & diamond, the double strand
coral bead necklace w/a center circle set w/diamonds suspending a detachable coral heart pendant decorated w/diamonds, the
bracelet w/three oval-shaped cabochon-cut coral surrounded by
diamonds on an 18k white gold link chain, the oval coral ring
accented w/diamonds, all designed in 18k white gold & set

Coral & Diamond Suite

w/round brilliant-cut, single-cut & marquise-shaped diamonds
w/approx. total weight of 4 cts., necklace 15" l., the set
(ILLUS.) **$6,325**

*Diamond &
Enamel Bracelet*

*Floral Design Bracelet,
Ring & Earrings*

Bracelet & ring, gold (14k yellow), diamond & enamel, the rigid
bracelet a circular domed spoke design, each spoke decorated
w/dark blue enameling w/a round brilliant-cut diamond set
between each spoke & in the top & center w/blue enameled
sides, each decorated w/a centerline of five round brilliant-cut
diamonds, ring w/matching design, bracelet 6", the set (ILLUS of
bracelet) **$2,300**

Bracelet, ring & earrings, gold (18k yellow), the bracelet a
rigid, hinged bangle w/floral textured openwork design, together
w/matching ring & semi-hoop earrings, bracelet 7", signed
"Buccellati," maker's mark, the set (ILLUS.) **$2,530**

Gold "Pick-up-Sticks" Brooch & Earrings

Brooch & earrings, gold (18k yellow), sapphire & diamond, "Pick-up-Sticks" design, the brooch composed of crisscrossed gold rods w/beaded ends containing eight faceted sapphires & four round diamonds, approx. .32 cts., together w/matching pair of earrings, the set (ILLUS.) **$1,035**

Georgina Gold & Diamond Brooch & Earrings

Brooch & earrings, gold (14k yellow), a domed floral design brooch of thick gold wire, together w/pair of matching earclips, signed "Tiffany & Co.," hallmark, total wt. 24.2 dwt. **$1,035**

Brooch & earrings, gold (18k yellow), the brooch in a contemporary "bird's nest" design pierced w/a crossed pair of 14k white gold "twigs," together w/pair of similar contemporary design earrings, each piece decorated w/a round brilliant-cut diamond, approx. diamond total weight of 0.75 ct., Georgina, the set (ILLUS.) **$1,035**

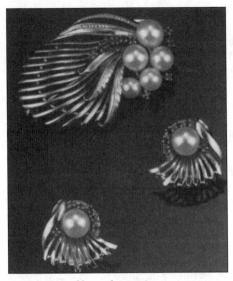

Pearl & Emerald Brooch & Earrings

Brooch & earrings, pearl & emerald, the 14k yellow gold
brooch designed as a stylized fern set w/five cultured pearls &
emeralds, matching clip earrings, hallmark, the set
(ILLUS.) **$345**

Leaf Brooch & Earrings

Brooch & earrings, ruby & 18k yellow gold, the brooch designed as a textured leaf entwined by a smooth gold vine enhanced w/ruby "berries," together w/similar clip earrings, hallmark, the set (ILLUS.) **$518**

Brooch & earrings, ruby & diamond, a floral spray brooch set en tremblant w/108 rubies & 36 bead set & bezel-set diamonds, 18k white gold mount, matching pair of clip earrings, the set **$4,888**

Diamond Dress Set

Dress set, diamond, a
pair of gentlemen's double-sided cuff links designed as buttons,
each pavé-set w/round brilliant-cut diamonds, together w/four
matching shirt studs, an approx. total weight of 5 cts., mounted
in platinum, the set (ILLUS.) **$8,050**

Dress set, gold (14k) & moonstone, a pair of oval cabochon
moonstone cuff links, together w/similar round moonstone
studs, hallmark for Larter & Sons, the set **$1,265**

Dress set, gold (14k yellow) & hematite, the cuff links designed
w/hematite beads set in gold claw mountings, together w/three
matching studs, 18k yellow gold mounts, 14k gold findings, the
set **$1,495**

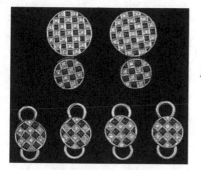

*Onyx & Diamond
Dress Set*

Dress set, gold (14k yellow) & sapphire, a pair of rectangular-shaped brushed gold plaques centered by a row of calibré-cut sapphires, cabochon sapphire terminals on T-bar, signed "Tiffany & Co., No. S449," together w/a set of three matching shirt studs, No. 941, the set **$2,875**

Dress set, gold (18k white), onyx & diamond, pair of cuff links of circular design featuring square-cut onyx & round brilliant-cut diamonds in checkboard pattern, together w/four matching studs, approx. 0.70 cts. (ILLUS.) **$2,300**

Earrings & ring, aquamarine, each piece centering an oval-shaped, cabochon-cut cat's eye aquarmarine in an 18k yellow gold ribbed frame w/satin finish, maker's mark & signed "Bach," approx. total weight of the three stones .45 cts., the set **$3,680**

Aquamarine Earrings & Ring

Earrings & ring, aquamarine, each piece centering an oval-shaped, cabochon-cut cat's eye aquarmarine in an 18k yellow gold ribbed frame w/satin finish, maker's mark & signed "Bach," approx. total weight of the three stones .45 cts., the set (ILLUS.) **$3,680**

Necklace & bracelet, pearl, the necklace composed of a triple strand w/approx. 163 natural colored light golden yellow fresh-water cultured pearls measuring 8 to 8 1/2 mm., together w/a matching triple strand bracelet w/69 pearls, each joined by matching 14k yellow gold button form tongue-in-groove clasps, necklace 17" l., bracelet 7 1/2" l., the set...................... **$1,035**

Gold Necklace & Earrings

Necklace, brooch & earrings, gold (yellow) & diamond, contemporary leaf fringe necklace, a leaf spray brooch w/round brilliant-cut diamond accents, approx. 1.30 cts., together w/matching pair of leaf earrings, each set w/three round brilliant-cut diamonds, approx. total wt. .30 cts., necklace 15 1/2" l., the set.. **$2,070**

Necklace & earrings, gold (18k yellow), a leaf design w/very finely textured finish, separated by small gold nugget-like designs w/matching earrings, signed w/Italian hallmarks, M. Buccellati, necklace approx. 15 3/4" l., the set (ILLUS.) **$4,600**

Lapis Lazuli & Diamond Set

Necklace, pendant & bracelet, lapis lazuli & diamond, the
necklace designed w/circular links of lapis lazuli alternating
w/navette-shaped, twisted gold links that each contain a row of
five round, brilliant-cut diamonds, the bracelet of similar design,
the large oval-shaped pendant-drop decorated w/an oval-shaped,
pierced lapis lazuli surrounded by two twisted gold wires, w/a
circle of 12 round brilliant-cut diamonds at the top, all mounted
in 18k yellow & white gold, approx. total weight of diamonds
2.50 cts., necklace 26" l., bracelet 7 1/2" l., the set (ILLUS. of
part) **$1,150**

*Mabe Pearl & Diamond
Pendant*

Pendant & earrings, pearl & diamond, the pendant set w/a pear-shaped mabe pearl measuring approx. 21.52 x 13.98 mm., framed in bead-set round brilliant-cut diamonds, together w/a matching pair of clip earrings, each w/a chevron of round brilliant-cut diamonds at the top, approx. total diamond wt. of set 1.65, 14k yellow gold mounts, the set (ILLUS. of pendant) **$1,495**

Watches

Bracelet Watch

Bracelet watch, No. 41597, Model 18KW or 1859, 11 jewels, key wind & set from back, P.S. Bartlett .... **$600-$1,100**

Bracelet watch, gold (14k yellow), wide gold geometric design belt & tassel bracelet w/14k yellow gold case w/hinged lid, high-relief floral motif highlighted w/black enamel, silver matte finish rectangular dial w/black enamel Arabic & yellow goldtone circular hour chapters, ca. 1950, P. Buhre, Swiss, 6 1/2" l. **$345**

Bracelet watch, gold (18k pink), ruby & diamond, rigid bracelet w/concealed dial, two overhanging triple grips holding watch, alternating w/diamond-set decoration, four-body, solid, polished guilloché bombé cover set w/diamonds & surrounded by rubies, matte silver dial w/applied gold indexes & Arabic numerals, "Bâton" gold hands, dial, case & movement signed, Vacheron & Constantin, Genève, ca. 1952 (ILLUS.) **$2,070**

*Platinum &
Diamond-set
Dress Watch*

Dress watch, platinum & diamond, keyless, three-piece w/satiné
back & diamond-set band & bow, the bezel w/baguette diamond
indexes, silver satiné dial w/minute ring on border of bezel,
white gold "feuilles" hands, signed on dial, case & movement,
Patek Philippe & Cie, Genève, ca. 1944 (ILLUS.) **$7,245**

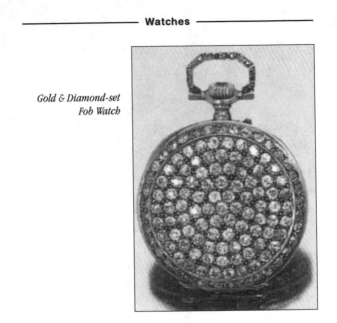

*Gold & Diamond-set
Fob Watch*

Fob watch, gold (18k yellow) diamond-set keyless, four-body
"Louis XVI," pavé-set overall w/old-cut diamonds, hinged gold
cuvette, white enamel dial w/Roman numerals & blue outer
Arabic minute ring, gold "Louis XV" hands, ca. 1880, Swiss
(ILLUS.) **$2,622**

Gold & Enamel Fob Watch

Fob watch, gold (18k yellow) & enamel, four-body, massive, "bassine," engine-turned in a vermicelli pattern, the back decorated w/a flower in high relief against a green, yellow & scarlet flinqué enameled ground, hinged gold cuvette w/engine-turned border, white enamel dial w/Roman numerals & outer Arabic minute ring, blued steel hands, ca. 1900, Swiss (ILLUS.) **$759**

Gold & Garnet
Fob Watch & Clip

Fob watch w/clip, gold (18k yellow), four body keyless "bassine," polished, the back set w/a large garnet cabochon within a stylized chased foliage frame, hinged gold cuvette, matching gold & garnet clip, white enamel w/Arabic numerals & sunk subsidiary seconds, gold hands, 15 jewel, dial & movement signed "Longines," made for L. Peslier à Avalon, Swiss, ca. 1890 (ILLUS.) **$1,380**

Unique Lapel Watch

Lapel watch, designed as a violin, two-piece, polished, frosted
silver dial w/applied gold indexes, gold "feuilles" hands, signed
on dial, case & movement, Rolex, ca. 1950s
(ILLUS.) **$4,140**

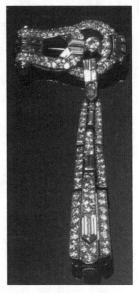

Art Deco Lapel Watch

Lapel watch, diamond & emerald, art deco style, the top
designed as a stylized buckle set w/round cabochon-cut & calibré-cut emeralds on one end, the diamond side supporting a
long tapering segmented ribbon set w/one hexagonal- & one bul-
let-shaped diamond, round, baguette- & trapezoid-cut diamonds, mounted in platinum, the watch on reverse side
w/Vacheron Constantin movement, 18 jewel, rhodium-plated,

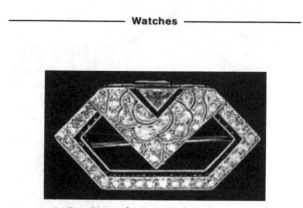

Art Deco Diamond & Onyx Lapel Watch

designed by Verger, France, ca. 1928, French hallmarks, maker's mark & signed (ILLUS. on previous page) **$19,550**

Lapel watch, diamond & onyx, art deco style, a hexagonal design set w/a row of round single-cut diamonds w/a small row of French-cut black onyx, the top w/a V-shaped design set w/a triangular-shaped diamond within a frame of French-cut black onyx (one onyx missing) w/round, single-cut diamonds decorating the V that pivots to reveal a small square watch w/white dial w/black Arabic numerals & gunmetal blue hands, frame numbered & signed "Golay Fils & Stahl," mounted in platinum (ILLUS.) **$8,050**

Antique Enamel & Diamond Watch

Lapel watch, enamel & diamond, enameled portrait surrounded by rose-cut diamond scrollwork & green guilloché enamel, verso depicting a lute & doves, 18k yellow gold case, white porcelain dial w/black Arabic numerals, dust cover inscribed "Grand Prix/Paris/1889," suspended from a fleur-de-lis pin set w/old European-cut diamonds, seed pearl accents, 18k yellow gold mount, one small diamond missing, minor enamel loss, boxed (ILLUS.) **$2,875**

Art Nouveau Lapel Watch

Lapel watch, enamel & gold, art nouveau style, engraved 18k yellow gold case decorated w/purple guilloché enamel & highlighted by a central gold star w/rose diamond accents, suspended from a lapel pin designed as a diamond bicycle wheel flanked by guilloché enamel wings & a spray of diamond stars, white porcelain dial w/black Arabic numerals & subsidiary seconds dial w/gold numerals, scroll hands, tiny scratches to case, in original fitted box labeled "Patek Philippe & Co., Geneve, Grand Prix a Paris 1889, Membre du Jury-Paris 1900" (ILLUS.) **$4,485**

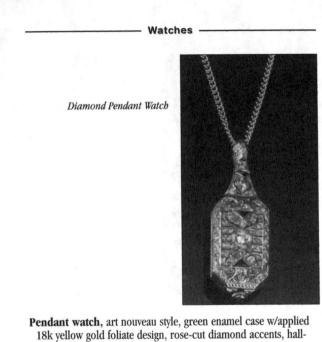

Diamond Pendant Watch

Pendant watch, art nouveau style, green enamel case w/applied 18k yellow gold foliate design, rose-cut diamond accents, hallmark, white porcelain dial, royal blue Arabic numerals, LeCoultre & Cie **$978**

Pendant watch, diamond, art deco style, pierced & engraved rectangular case set throughout w/round diamonds, triangular blue stone accents, suspended from a sterling silver curb link chain, cream colored dial w/black Arabic numerals, L. & S.L. Nerny, 20" l. (ILLUS.) **$1,265**

Art Deco Pendant Watch

Pendant watch, diamond & sapphire, art deco style, diamond & sapphire encrusted case centered by a bezel-set marquise diamond, bail set w/a pear-shaped & round diamond, mounted in platinum w/millegrain accents, platinum bar link & seed pearl chain, No. 30735, Tiffany & Co., 19" l. (ILLUS.) **$5,463**

Gold & Enamel Pendant Watch

Pendant watch, gold (18k yellow) & enamel, keyless, three-body, entirely decorated w/a powder blue flingué enamel, the back w/painted white enameled flowers on the border & applied w/a rose-cut diamond set basket of flowers, suspended from a ribbon & bowl design set w/rose-cut diamonds, hinged gold cuvette engraved w/name of owner, frosted engine-turned silver dial w/Arabic numerals, gold Breguet hands, signed on dial, case & movement, Vacheron & Constantin, Genèe, ca. 1915 (ILLUS.) **$2,070**

*Smith Patterson
Pendant Watch*

Pendant watch, hunting case, art noveau style, Smith Patterson
Co., goldtone dial w/black Roman numerals, initialed case,
chased & engraved griffin brooch, hallmarked for Bippart,
Griscom & Osborn, 14k yellow gold (ILLUS.) **$443**

Pocket Watch with Horse Portraits

Pocket watch, enamel & 18k yellow gold, keyless "Reglage de Precision," four body, "demi-bassine" front cover w/finely painted portraits of two horses over translucent blue enamel w/"basket pattern" engine-turning, within a round white opaque & translucent dark blue frame, back cover w/painted horseshoe intertwined w/laurel leaves over the same background & frame as the front, gold hinged cuvette, bow & crown chased w/scrollings, matte-gilded Arabic numerals, "Cathedrale hands," dial & case signed "Borel Fils & Cie, Neuchâtel," Borel's trademark on movement, made for H. Shtulevich, Elisabethgrad, ca. 1910 (ILLUS.) **$5,750**

*Lady's Gold
Pocket Watch*

Pocket watch,
gold (14k tricolor)
hunting case, Elgin,
3/4 plate nickel
movement, white
enameled dial
w/Roman numer-
als, subsidiary sec-
onds dial, gold
cuvette, tricolor gold case centered by a monogrammed medallion on one side & a floral bouquet on the other, ca. 1885, dial &
movement signed "Elgin," case marked "P.K. & Co." **$374**
Pocket watch, gold (14k yellow) & enamel, hunting case, lady's,
engraved case No. 15500 w/black enamel tracery, polychrome
enamel decoration of a man & a woman dancing in the moon-
light, the verso w/blue enamel decoration, white porcelain dial
w/black Roman numerals (ILLUS.) **$489**

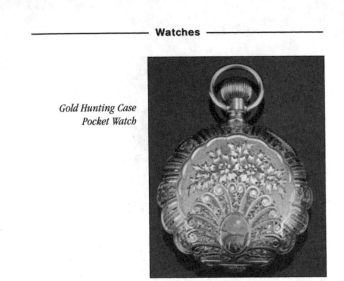

*Gold Hunting Case
Pocket Watch*

Pocket watch, gold (14k yellow), hunting case, white porcelain
dial w/black Roman numerals, Hampden, movement No.
596090, loose crystal, engraved gold case w/scalloped edge, No.
65487 (ILLUS.) **$460**

Pocket watch, gold (18k), hunting case, American Watch Co.,
3/4 plate nickel movement marked "Appleton Tracy & Co., Nr.
702529," white enameled dial w/Roman numerals, subsidiary
seconds dial, gold cuvette, case engraved w/floral scrolls
trimmed w/black enamel, ca. 1873, case, dial & movement
signed **$345**

*Antique Gold Hunter
Case Pocket Watch*

Pocket watch, gold (18k) hunting case, American Watch Co., full plate gilt movement marked "Appleton, Tracy & Co., Nr. 778941," white enameled dial w/Roman numerals, subsidiary seconds dial, gold cuvette, engine-turned case w/floral engraving, ca. 1875, movement & dial signed, case signed "B & T" **$575**

Pocket watch, gold (18k yellow) chased hunting case, polychrome goldtone foliate dial, fussee movement no. 1367 marked "Dublin," coppertone Roman numerals, key missing, mid-19th c. (ILLUS.) **$1,265**

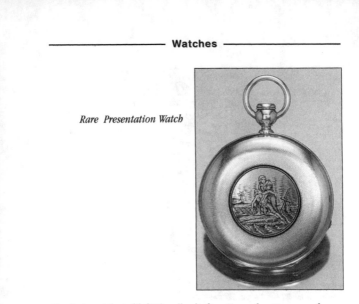

Rare Presentation Watch

Pocket watch, gold (18k yellow), fine & rare hunting case, four-body, massive, "bassineet filets," engine-turned w/reeded band, the cover centered w/a black champlevé enameled scene depicting a life rescue at sea, the back w/the emblem of the United States of America, dedication engraved inside cover, "presented by Ulysses S. Grant (1869-1877), President of America, to Capt. J. Petterson for the rescue of the crew of the AM. BARK PLEIADES - 1870," white enamel dial w/Roman numerals & sunk subsidiary seconds, blued steel "spade" hands, signed on dial & back plate, American Watch Co., Waltham, Massachusetts, ca. 1870 (ILLUS.) **$11,040**

*Gold & Enamel
Pocket Watch*

Pocket watch, gold &
enamel hunting case, 18k
yellow gold case inlaid w/cobalt blue enamel on both sides &
further enhanced by rose-cut diamonds & gold foliate detail,
chips to enamel, Racine Perrot, No. 37207, key wind, white
porcelain dial w/black Roman numerals (ILLUS.) **$690**

Pocket watch, hunting case, men's, American Waltham, 14k gold
case, 17 jewels adjustable, shield engraving on the case, works
marked by P.S. Barlett, Waltham, Massachusetts, ca. 1906 .. **$952**

Pocket watch, hunting case, men's, American Waltham Co., P.S.
Bartlett, white enameled dial & small second, blued steel hands,
Roman numerals, movement #1331680, patent pinion, 14k yellow gold case w/engine-turned design & monogrammed
crest.. **$743**

*Gruen Pocket Watch
& Chain*

Pocket watch, hunting case, men's, Elgin National Watch Co., 14k mixed-color gold ornately engraved case w/floral yellow, green & rose gold engraving surrounded a repoussé engraving of a deer in rose gold, the reverse engraved w/a center shield of rose gold surrounded by floral designs in yellow, white, green & rose gold bordered w/scalloped edge front & back, 17 jewels, ca. 1924........................... **$3,360**

Pocket watch, hunting case, men's, Gruen, No. 96516, white dial w/black Arabic numerals, subsidiary seconds dial, chased & engraved case depicting a griffin, includes 48" l. trace link chain accented w/eight small cultured pearls & swivel hook, 14k yellow gold (ILLUS.) **$575**

*Jurgensen
Pocket Watch*

Pocket watch, hunting case, men's, Illinois Watch Company Bunn model, Springfield, Illinois, 18k yellow gold engraved case, 21 ruby jewels, adjusted teperature, five positions, Isochronison, double rolled, working, ca. 1910 .... **$532**

Pocket watch, hunting case, man's, Jurgensen (J. Alfred), No. 785, white procelain dial, subsidiary dial for seconds, fancy hands, highly jeweled movement, patent 1865, Copenhagen, 18k gold (ILLUS.) **$3,000**

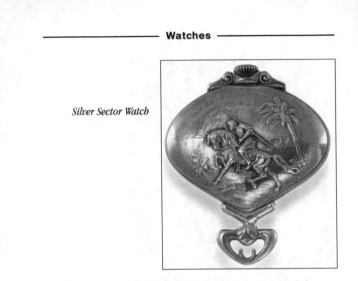

Silver Sector Watch

Pocket watch, open face, gold (18k yellow) case enameled w/butterflies & flowers edged in cobalt blue enamel, red guil-loché & seed pearl accents open face, white porcelain dial, Roman numerals, blue steeled hands, unusual skeletonized pol-ished steel movement signed "Bovet, London," bow set w/pearls, enamel watch key, English hallmarks on back cover (surface scratches to case, some enamel damage to edge, hairline to dust cover) **$3,910**

Pocket watch, silver, keyless "Sector Watch," four body, fan-form, back w/low relief decoration depicting an Arab on horse-back, camels, palm tree & sunset in background, hinged silver cuvette, matte silver w/hour Arabic sector, blue steel hands, back

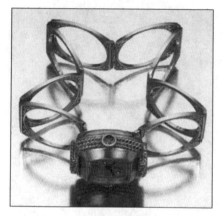

*Unusual
Ring/Wrist Watch*

signed "Holy Frèes" & movement signed "Record Watch Co.," ca.
1920 (ILLUS. on previous page) **$2,185**
Ring/wristwatch, gold (14k yellow), tonneau shape decorated in
a twisted rope pattern w/sapphire set winding crown, one shoulder containing the clasp, the shank unfolding for the length of
the bracelet, pink gold tonneau shape dial w/black Arabic
numerals, blued steel "bâton" hands, signed on dial, case &
movement, Uti, Paris, ca. 1960s (ILLUS.) **$8,280**
Wristwatch, 15 jewels, repeater, repeats on gong, repeater
wound by bolt above hand, stainless steel, ca. 1930,
Driva.. **$3,500-$4,500**

Doxa 17 Jewel Wristwatch

Illinois Direct Read Wristwatch

Wristwatch, 17 jewels, chronological, cal. 1220, gold-filled, ca. 1940, Doxa (ILLUS.) .... **$175-$275**
Wristwatch, 17 jewels, direct read, chrome case & band, ca. 1925, Illinois (ILLUS.) .... **$225-$325**
Wristwatch, Babe Ruth, Babe on dial, leather strap, ca. 1948, U.S. Time (no box, fair condition) .... **$225-$300**

Men's Cartier Wrist Watch

Wristwatch, datejust, quick set, oyster stainless steel band, 30 jewel, ca. 1970s, Rolex .... **$900-$1,100**

Wristwatch, lady's, Uti movement, round goldtone dial w/ruby indicators, one-half framed in graduating calibré-cut channel-set rubies, snake link bracelet, French hallmarks, 18k yellow gold, Lehman (dial slightly discolored) **$1,495**

Wristwatch, man's, No. 46600J, engraved dial w/black tracery enamel, black leather strap, yellow gold clasp, Italian hallmarks, 18k yellow gold, Gianmaria Buccellati **$6,900**

Wristwatch, man's, rectangular convex white dial w/black Roman numerals, rounded gold bezel, black leather strap, 18k yellow gold, Cartier (ILLUS.) **$1,380**

*Swiss Bangle-
type Braacelet
Watch*

*Unusual Diamond
Wrist Watch*

Wristwatch, bangle-type, gold (18k yellow) & diamond, keyless "Boule de Genève" type, diamond-set design decorated at the top w/diamond-set applied gold triangular segments, glazed back cover w/view of movement, dark blue enamel w/white Arabic numerals, gold hands, Swiss, ca. 1895 (ILLUS.) **$3,910**

Wristwatch, diamond & leather, the bracelet depicting a snake w/a wrap-around leather "snakeskin" textured band, pavé-set w/round diamonds in the head & tail w/ruby accents in the eyes & tip of tail, the oval-shaped dial pavé-set w/round single-cut diamonds mounted in 18k yellow gold, numbered & signed "Chopard," 6" l. (ILLUS.) **$5,750**

Art Deco Diamond Wristwatch

Wristwatch, diamond & platinum, art deco lady's model, rectangular case framed by round single-cut diamonds accented by triangular- and marquise-cut diamonds, the bracelet decorated w/round, single- and baguette-cut diamonds, total diamond weight of 4.30 cts., mounted in platinum, Pastor Watch Co., 7" l. **$5,750**

Wristwatch, diamond & platinum, art deco style w/a repeated, rectangular, geometric link design, each centering an emerald-cut diamond flanked by round, single-cut diamonds, the links bridged by a pair of baguette-cut diamonds, having a total weight of approx. 20 cts., the rectangular watch w/white face, black Arabic numerals, mounted in platinum, signed on dial, Vacheron & Constantin, approx. 7" l. (ILLUS.) **$27,600**

Wristwatch, diamond & platinum, the silver circular dial surrounded by diamonds & flanked by two circular links set w/diamonds, completed by diamond-set line-type band, signed "Cartier" **$3,680**

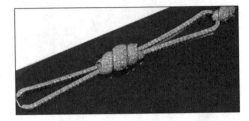

*Diamond
Wristwatch*

Wristwatch, diamond, the cover having a bombé design w/three
sections of pavé-set round, brilliant-cut diamonds w/a double
row bracelet of round brilliant-cut diamonds & a smaller, bombé designed diamond-set catch w/approx. total weight of 13. cts.
for all 222 diamonds, mounted in platinum, measuring approx.
17.3 cm., 6 3/4" l., watch w/Swiss 17 jewel, unadjusted,
monometallic balance anti-shock movement, signed & numbered, 1960s, Van Cleef & Arpels, New York, New York
(ILLUS.) **$17,825**

Wristwatch, diamond, the rectangular-shaped watch is decorated
on the top w/round single- & baguette-cut diamonds w/round
brilliant-, single- & baguette-cut diamonds lining the bracelet, all
having a total weight of approx. 8 cts., mounted in platinum, 6
1/2" l. **$6,325**

Wristwatch, gentlemen's 9k white & yellow gold, rectangular,
two-body, massive, polished, yellow gold case, white gold fillet
on stepped sides, white gold stripes in relief on bezel, flat top
crystal, two-tone silver dial w/painted Arabic numerals, auxiliary
seconds dial, dial, case & movement signed, Rolex, Prince
Railway, 1930s **$6,555**

Rare Gentlemen's Wristwatch

Wristwatch, gentlemen's rare early tonneau-shaped, two-body, solid polished, hinged bezel, gold screw bars, champagne dial w/radium-coated radial Arabic numerals, "Skeleton" radium-coated hands, velvet strap w/18k yellow gold Patek Philippe buckle, dial, case & movement signed, Patek Phillippe & Cie, Genève, ca. 1915 (ILLUS.) **$31,740**

Jaeger Revero Wristwatch

Wristwatch, gentlemen's, rectangular, stainless steel "Staybrite" & 18k yellow gold, four-body, solid, polished, reeded bezel, dust-protecting cap, matte silver dial w/painted gold Arabic numerals, painted black Arabic numerals on a satiné silver ring dial for minutes, "Epée" yellow gold hands, ca. 1940s, dial, case & movement signed, Jaeger, Reverso (ILLUS.) **$6,210**
Wristwatch, gold (14k), 17 jewels, double teardrop lugs, ca. 1945, Driva .... **$125-$200**

Lady's Gold & Diamond Wristwatch

Wristwatch, gold (14k white) & diamond, the straight lattice-work band set w/96 round diamonds, total approx. .96 cts., centering an oval case w/conforming white dial w/black Roman numerals & surrounded by 24 round diamonds, total approx. 1.20 cts., signed "Baume & Mercier Geneve" (ILLUS.) **$4,025**

Wristwatch, gold (14k yellow), Retro-style, Florentine finish triangular case, joined by a twin strand 14k yellow gold rope bracelet w/hinged locking clasp, rectangular white enamel dial w/raised circular & triangular goldtone hour chapters, Acme Watch Co., ca. 1940, 7" l. **$345**

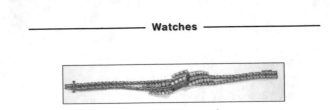

Cartier Diamond & Gold Wristwatch

Wristwatch, gold (18k yellow) & diamond, the curved link gold bracelet centrally lined w/two rows of round brilliant-cut diamonds having a total weight of approx. 3.50 cts., the back winding watch contains a Swiss 17 jewel, unadjusted, 2 1/2 ligne size movement by Blancpain Rayville S.A., "Cartier" signed on dial, 7" l. (ILLUS.) **$5,750**

Wristwatch, gold (18k yellow) & malachite, the deployment band centering a circular case, the conforming malachite dial w/date aperture, the dial signed "Rolex Oyster Perpetual Datejust" **$2,990**

Wristwatch, gold & diamond, silvertone rectangular dial w/black abstract indicators, covered w/a buckle design set w/17 round-cut & four baguette-cut diamonds, integral textured 18k white gold band, approx. tdw. 1.58 cts., Piaget, 7" l. **$2,530**

Wristwatch, reeded round cover centered by a star sapphire w/baguette-cut diamonds, surrounded by single-cut diamonds, reeded round bracelet links, each centered by a round star sapphire & two baguette-cut diamonds, 14k white gold mount, Lucien Piccard, ca. 1950 .... **$575**

Glossary

A

Algrette: Jewels mounted in a shape resembling feathers or a feather motif.

A-jour Setting: An open work setting in which the bottom portion of the stone can be seen. Also a setting in which the metal has open work.

Albert Chain: A watch chain for a man or a woman with a bar at one end and a swivel to hold a watch at the other.

Alma Chain: A chain with broad ribbed links

B

Baguette: A stone cut in the shape of a narrow rectangle.

Banded Agate: Agate that has bands of lighter and darker colors. It can be onyx (black/white), cornelian (orangish red/white), or sardonyx (brown/white).

Bangle: A rigid bracelet often tubular and hinged.

Basse-taille: An enameling technique in which a translucent enameling is applied to an engraved metal surface.

Baton: A stone cut in the shape of a long narrow rectangle.

Beauty Pins: Pins popular from the mid-1800s until after the turn of the century. Usually under two inches long with rounded ends.

Belcher Mounting: A claw-type ring mounting on which there were many variations. Popular from the 1870s through the 1920s.

Benoition Chain: A chain worn suspended from the top of the head that encircled the head and dropped down onto the bosom.

Bezel: A metal rim that holds the stone in a ring, a cameo in its mounting, or a crystal on a watch.

Black Amber: A misnomer for jet.

Bloomed Gold: A textured finish on gold that is created by immersing in acid to give it a matte pitted effect.

Bog Oak: Wood preserved in the bogs of Ireland and used to make jewelry during the Victorian era.

Bohemian Garnet: A dark red pyrope garnet.

Brilliant Cut: A cut that returns the greatest amount of white light to the eye. It usually has 57 or 58 facets. Usually used for diamonds or other transparent stones.

Briolettes: A teardrop-shaped cut covered with facets.

Brooch: An ornamental piece of jewelry that has a pin back for affixing it to clothing or hats. Usually larger in scale than the ones referred to as "pins."

Brooch-watch: A watch with a brooch affixed so it is worn as one would wear a brooch.

Bulla: A round ornamental motif found in ancient jewelry.

C

Cabochon: A stone cut in round or oval shape in which the top is convex shaped (not faceted).

Cairngorm: Yellow brown to smoky yellow quartz named after the mountain range in which it is found in Scotland.

Calibre Cut: Small stones cut in the shape of squares, rectangles, or oblongs used to embellish jewelry.

Cameo: A layered stone in which a design is engraved on the top layer and the remainder is carved away to reveal the next layer, leaving the design in relief. Also done in shell, coral, and lava.

Cameo Habille: A type of cameo in which the carved head is adorned with a necklace, earrings, or head ornament set with small stones.

Cannetille: A type of metal decoration named after the type of embroidery made with fine twisted gold or silver thread. It is done using thin wires to make a filigree pattern. Used frequently in England in 1840.

Carat: A unit of weight for gemstones. Since 1913 one metric carat is one-fifth of a gram or 200 milligrams.

Carbuncle: Today used to refer to a garnet cut in cabochon. In the middle ages it referred to any cabochon-cut red stone.

Cartouche: An ornamental tablet used in decoration or to be engraved, usually symmetrical.

Celluloid: One of the first plastics. A compound of camphor and gun cotton. Highly flammable.

Champlive: An enameling technique in which enamel is put into areas engraved or carved into the metal.

Channel Setting: A type of setting in which stones of the same size are held in place by a continuous strip of metal at the top and bottom, literally creating a channel for the stones.

Chasing: The technique of embellishing metal by hand using hammers and punches to make indentations, thus raising the design.

Chatelaine: A metal clasp or hook worn at the waist from which hang a variety of useful items suspended by chains.

Chaton: The central or main ornament of a ring.

Cipher: A monogram of letters intertwined.

Claw Setting: A style of ring setting in which the stone is held by a series of vertically projecting prongs.

Clip: A piece of jewelry resembling a brooch but instead of having a pin stem to fasten into clothing, it has a hinged clip that hooks over and into the fabric. Very popular from the 1920s-1940s. Sometimes made as a brooch that incorporated a double clip. It could be worn as a brooch or disassembled and used as a pair of clips.

Cloisonne: An enameling technique in which the enamel is placed into little preformed compartments or cells built on to the metal.

Collet Setting: A ring setting in which the stone is held by a circular band of metal.

Coronet Setting: A round claw setting in crown-like design.

Cravat Pin: The same as a tie pin.

Creole Earrings: A hoop style in which the metal is thicker and wider at the bottom than at the top.

Croix a la Jeanette: A piece in the form of a heart from which a cross is suspended. A form of French peasant jewelry. Circa 1835.

Crossover: A style of ring, bracelet or brooch in which the stoneset decorative portions overlap and lie alongside each other.

Crown Setting: An open setting resembling a crown.

Cultured Pearl: A type of pearl induced and stimulated by man to grow inside a mollusk.

Curb Chain: A chain in which the oval flattened links are twisted so that they lie flat.

Cushion Cut: A square or rectangular shape with rounded corners. Also called "antique cut."

Cut Steel Jewelry: Jewelry made of steel studs which are faceted. Popular from the 1760s until the late 19th century.

Cymric: A trade name used by Liberty & Co. for articles sold by them which were designed and manufactured by English firms. The name was adopted in 1899.

D

Designer: A person who designs jewelry. Occasionally they were also makers of jewelry.

Damascene: The art of encrusting metals with other metals.

Demi-parure: A matching set of jewelry consisting of only a few pieces such as a necklace with matching earrings or a bracelet with matching brooch.

Demi-hunter: A watch with a lid over the face in which there is a circular hole in the middle to expose the hands of the watch.

Dog Collar: A type of necklace consisting of rows of beads or a wide band worn snugly around the neck.

Doublet: An assembled stone consisting of two materials, usually garnet and glass.

E

Edwardian Jewelry: Jewelry made during the reign of Edward VII, 1901-1910, that does not fall into the art nouveau or Arts and Crafts movement category.

Electro-plating: The process of covering metal with a coating of another metal by using electrical current.

Electrum: A pale yellow alloy made by mixing 20% gold and 80% silver.

Enamel: A glass-like material used in powder or flux form and fired onto metal.

Engine-turning: Decoration with engraved lines produced on a special lathe.

Engraving: A technique by which a design is put into a metal surface using incised lines.

Eternity Ring: A ring with stones set all the way around. Symbolizing the "never-ending" circle of eternity.

F

Fede Ring: An engagement ring which features two hands "clasped in troth."

Ferronniere: A chain that encircles the forehead as portrayed in Leonardo da Vince's "La Bel Torronnier." A 16th century adornment; it was revived during the Victorian era.

Filigree: Ornamental designs made by using plain twisted or plaited wire.

Fob: A decorative ornament suspended by a chain usually worn with a watch.

Foil: A thick layer or coating used on the back of stones to improve their color and brilliance.

French Jet: It is neither French nor jet, instead this term usually refers to black glass.

G

Gate: A channel in a mold through which the molten metal flows during the white metal spin-casting process. Also refers to that part of the cast piece that is wasted.

Gilloche: Engraved decoration of geometric design achieved by engine turning. Usually used as a base for translucent enamel.

Girandole: Brooch or earring style in which three pendant stones hang from a large central stone.

Gunmetal: An alloy of 90% copper and 10% tin that was very popular in the 1890s.

Gutta-percha: A hard rubber material made from the sap of a Malayan tree. Discovered in the 1840s, it was used for making jewelry, statuary, and even furniture.

Gypsy Setting: A type of setting in which the stone is set down flush in the mounting.

H

Hairwork Jewelry: Jewelry made using hair worked on a table or jewelry that incorporates hair and was worked on a palette.

Hallmark: A group of markings used on silver or gold in England since 1300 to designate the fineness of the metal, the town in which it was assayed, and the name of the maker.

Holbeinesque: A style of jewelry popular in England in the 1870s. Its inspiration was from the design of Hans Holbein the Younger.

Hunting Case: A watch that has a lid covering the face. A case spring is activated by pushing on the crown causing the lid to pop open.

I

Incise: A line cut or engraved in a material.

Intaglio: A design cut below the surface of stone. The opposite of a cameo.

Intarsia: The use of stones to make a picture by cutting them out and inlaying them flushed into a background stone.

J

Jabot Pin: A type of stick pin worn on the front of ladies' blouses.

Jet: A very lightweight black or brownish black material that is a variety of the coal family.

K

Karat: Pure gold is 24 karats. The karat of gold alloy is determined by the percentage of pure gold. For instance 18K gold is 750 parts pure gold and 250 parts other metal or 18 parts pure gold and 6 parts other metal.

L

Lava Jewelry: Jewelry made of the lava from Mt. Vesuvius. Usually carved into cameos or intaglios and sold as souvenirs of the "grand tour."

Laveliere: A light scaled necklace usually consisting of a pendant or pendants suspended from a chain. In the 1890-1910 era it usually had a baroque pearl appendage. The word is probably derived from the Duchess de la Valliere, a mistress of Louis XIV.

Line Bracelet: A flexible bracelet composed of stones of one size or graduating in size, set in a single line.

Luckenbooth Brooches: So called because they were sold in street stalls (Luckenbooths) near St. Giles Kirk in Edinburg. The motif usually consisted of one or two hearts occasionally surrounded by a crown. When the motif included the initial "M," the brooch was referred to as a Queen Mary Brooch.

M

Macle: A flat-bottomed diamond crystal.

Mandrel: A replica made of wax or white metal used as a core onto which metal is deposited during the electroplating process.

Marcasite: A misnomer that is now the commonly accepted trade name for pyrite. Popular from the 18th century onwards.

Marquise: A boat-shaped cut used for diamonds and other gem stones. Also called a "navette" shape.

Memento Mori: "Remember you must die." Grim motifs such as coffins, skeletons, etc. Worn as a reminder of one's mortality.

Millegrain: A setting in which the metal holding the stone is composed of tiny grains or beads.

Mizpah Ring: A popular ring of the 19th century consisting of a band with the word Mizpah engraved across the top. "May the Lord watch between me and thee while we are absent from the other."

Mosaic: A piece of jewelry in which the pattern is formed by the inlaying of various colored stones or glass. Two types of mosaic work are Roman and Florentine.

Mourning Jewelry: Jewelry worn "in memory of" by friends and relatives of the deceased. Often sums of money were set aside in one's will to have pieces made to be distributed to mourners attending the funeral.

Muff Chain: A long chain worn around the neck and passed through the muff to keep it secure.

N

Necklace Lengths: Choker-15 inches, Princess-18 inches, Matinee-22 inches, Opera-30 inches, Rope-60 inches long.

Nickel Silver: A combination of copper, nickel, zinc, and sometimes small amounts of tin, lead, or other metals.

Niello: A decorative technique in which the metal is scooped out (in the same manner as champlive) and the recessed area is filled with a mixture of metallic blue black finish. The technique dates back to the Bronze Age.

O

Old Mine Cut: An old style of cutting a diamond in which the girdle outline is squarish, the crown is high and the table is small. It has 32 crown facets plus a table, and 24 pavilion facets plus a culet.

P

Paste Jewelry: Jewelry that is set with imitation glass gems. Very popular in the 18th century, it provides us with many good examples of the jewelry from that time period.

Parure: A complete matching set of jewelry usually consisting of a necklace, earrings, brooch, and bracelet.

Pate de Verre: An ancient process in which glass is ground to powder, colored, placed in a mold, and fired. It was revived in the 19th century and used to make many pieces of art nouveau jewelry.

Pave Setting: A style of setting in which the stones are set as close together as possible, presenting a cobblestone effect.

Pebble Jewelry: Scottish jewelry (usually silver) set with stones native to Scotland. Very popular during the Victorian era.

Pendeloque: A faceted drop-shaped stone (similar to a brio-lette) that has a table.

Pietra-dura: (Hard Stone). Flat slices of chalcedony, agate, jasper, and lapis lazuli used in Florentine mosaic jewelry.

Pinchbeck: An alloy of copper and zinc invented by Christopher Pinchbeck in the 1720s that looked like gold. It was used for making jewelry, watches, and accessories. This term is very misused today. Some dealers refer to any piece that is not gold as "pinchbeck."

Pique: A technique of decorating tortoiseshell by inlaying it with pieces of gold and silver. Popular from the mid-17th century until Edwardian time.

Platinum: A rare heavy, silvery white metallic element that is alloyed with other metals and used to make fine pieces of jewelry.

Plique-a-jour: An enameling technique that produces a "stained glass effect" because the enamel is held in a metal frame without any backing. An ancient technique, it was revived and used extensively by art nouveau designers.

Poincon: A French term for the mark on French silver similar to the English hallmark.

Posy Ring: A finger ring with an engraved motto (often rhymed) on the inner side.

R

Regard Ring: A finger ring set with six stones of which the first letter is each spell REGARD. The stones most commonly used were: Ruby, Emerald, Garnet, Amethyst, Ruby and Diamond.

Repousse Work: A decorative technique of raising a pattern on metal by beating, punching, or hammering from the reverse side. Often called embossing.

Rhinestone: Originally rock crystal found along the banks of the Rhine river. Today, a misnomer for colorless glass used in costume jewelry.

Rhodium: A white metallic element that is part of the platinum group. Because of its hard reflective finish it is often used as a plating for jewelry.

Riviere: A style of necklace containing individually set stones of the same size or graduating in size that are set in a row without any other ornamentation.

Rose Cut: A cutting style in which there are 24 triangular facets meeting at the top with a point. The base is always flat. Diamonds cut this way are usually cut from macles.

Ruolz: A gilded or silvered metal named after the inventor of the process who was a French chemist.

S

Sautoir: A long neck chain that extended beyond a woman's waist. Usually terminating in a pendant or tassel.

Signet Bangle: A hinged tubular bracelet with a central plaque for engraving. Very popular in the 1890-1910 time period.

Signet Ring: A ring with a central plaque on which one's initials were engraved. Sometimes a seal or crest was used.

Scarf Pin: A straight pin approximately 2-1/2 inches long with a decorative head. It was used between 1880-1915 to hold the ties in place. It is the same as a tie pin.

Seed Pearl: A small pearl weighing less than 1/4 grain.

Shank: The circle of metal that attaches to the head of a ring and encircles the finger.

Sprue: A rod attached to the base of a mold model to provide a channel in the mold through which the wax can flow. This sprue also becomes a part of the wax and consequently a part of the casting.

Star Setting: A popular setting in the 1890s in which the stone is placed in an engraved star and secured by a small grain of metal at the base of each point.

Stomacher: A large triangular piece of jewelry worn on the bodice and extending below the waistline. An 18th century style that was revived during the Edwardian period.

Swivel: A fitting used to attach a watch to a chain. It has an elongated spring opening for attaching the watch. The swivel allows the watch to hang properly.

Synthetic: A manmade material with the same physical, chemical, and optical properties as the natural. Not to be confused with imitation.

T

Taillé d Epergne: An enameling technique in which engraved depressions are filled with opaque enamel.

Tiffany Setting: A round six-prong mounting with a flare from the base to the top.

Trademark: The mark registered with the U.S. Patent Office that identifies a wholesaler or retailer.

V

Vermeil: Gilded silver. Sterling silver with a gold plating.

White Gold: An alloy of gold, nickel, and zinc developed in 1912 to imitate the popular platinum.

White Metal: A base metal of tin, lead, bismuth, antimony, and cadmium used in the manufacturing of costume jewelry. The tin content can vary from 17 to 92 percent. It can be electroplated to any color desired.

Is It Priceless or Worthless?

Antiques Detectives present

How to be a
Jewelry Detective

"Elementary" clues to solving
the mysteries of jewelry

by C. Jeanenne Bell, G.G.
"The Jewelry Detective"

**How to be a
Jewelry Detective**
by C. Jeanenne Bell, G.G.
Now you can tell for yourself.
One of the nation's leading
jewelry authorities, C.
Jeanenne Bell, puts her 30
years of expertise to work for
you, providing the clues that
separate the old from the
new, the gold from the gold-
plated, the diamonds from the
rhinestones and the junk from
the jewels.

Softcover • 5½x8½
166 pages
160 b&w photos
32-page color section
Item# JLRTC • $18.95

To order call **800-258-0929**
Offer ACB3

kp **krause publications**
P.O. Box 5009-ACB3
Iola WI 54945-5009
www.krausebooks.com

Shipping & Handling: $4.00 first book,
$2.25 each additional. Non-US addresses
$20.95 first book, $5.95 each additional.

Sales Tax: CA, IA, IL, KS, NJ, PA, SD, TN, WI
residents please add appropriate sales tax.